P9-DIG-192

DATE DUE

DEMCO, INC. 38-2931

ALSO BY THE AMERICAN HEART ASSOCIATION

American Heart Association Cookbook, 5th Edition
American Heart Association Low-Fat, Low-Cholesterol Cookbook
American Heart Association Low-Salt Cookbook
American Heart Association Quick and Easy Cookbook
American Heart Association Kids' Cookbook
American Heart Association Brand Name Fat and Cholesterol Counter
American Heart Association Family Guide to Stroke

ALSO BY THE AMERICAN CANCER SOCIETY

American Cancer Society Cookbook

Living Well, Staying Well

RC
268
.A47
1996

American Heart
Association SM
Fighting Heart Disease
and Stroke

Living Well, Staying Well

Big Health Rewards from Small Lifestyle Changes

American Heart Association and
American Cancer Society

TIMES ⓣ BOOKS

RANDOM HOUSE

MAR 1 2 1996

Copyright © 1996 by American Heart Association and American Cancer Society

All rights reserved under International and Pan-American Copyright Conventions. Published in the United States by Times Books, a division of Random House, Inc., New York, and simultaneously in Canada by Random House of Canada Limited, Toronto.

Library of Congress Cataloging-in-Publication Data
American Heart Association/American Cancer Society
Living well, staying well : big health rewards from small lifestyle changes—1st ed.
p.   cm.
Includes index.
ISBN 0-8129-2477-0
1. Cancer—Prevention.   2. Heart—Diseases—Prevention.
I. American Heart Association.   II. American Cancer Society.
RC268.A47   1996
616.1′205—dc20   95-4743

Manufactured in the United States of America
9 8 7 6 5 4 3 2
First Edition

Book design by Deborah Kerner

Acknowledgments

Many people worked together to make this joint American Heart Association–American Cancer Society effort a reality.

The American Heart Association expresses its gratitude to volunteers W. Virgil Brown, M.D.; Albert Oberman, M.D.; and Judith K. Ockene, Ph.D., for countless hours of sharing both their expertise and their enthusiasm for the project. AHA staff members contributing to this book included Dudley H. Hafner, executive vice president; M. Cass Wheeler, deputy executive vice president; Rodman D. Starke, M.D., senior vice president, Office of Scientific Affairs; Mary Winston, Ed.D., senior science consultant; Sam Inman, former vice president, corporate relations; Consumer Publications Department staff members Peter Landesman, consumer publications consultant; Jane Ruehl, senior editor; and Janice Roth Moss, editor; and lead word processor Debra Bond and former word processor Gerre Gilford.

The American Cancer Society wishes to thank Michael F. Heron, national vice president, public affairs; James Lowman, M.D., M.P.H., scientific program director; Roberta Moss, M.P.H., director, program development and applications; and Michael Thun, M.D., director, analytic epidemiology, for their guidance in helping determine the scope of the book and suggesting many people who provided useful information on a wide range of topics. Both Lynne Camoosa and Amy Stone of the Scientific Communications staff also provided valuable assistance.

Both organizations gratefully acknowledge the superb job done by Susan Ince, who took mountains of information and transformed it into the text you are reading. To accomplish this, she gleaned material from countless written resources, as well as from American Cancer Society and American Heart Association volunteers and staff.

We also wish to thank the many people who shared their personal stories to help you make small lifestyle changes that really can help you live well and stay well.

Preface

FOR MORE THAN HALF A CENTURY, THE AMERICAN HEART ASSOCIATION and the American Cancer Society have worked to confront the diseases that are responsible for a huge proportion of the deaths in the United States. The American Heart Association strives to reduce disability and death from cardiovascular diseases and stroke. The American Cancer Society is dedicated to preventing cancer, saving lives, and diminishing suffering from cancer. With committed volunteers in communities across the nation, we pursue our separate missions through active programs of research, education, advocacy, and public service. Although this is our first joint book, we have been partners in a number of other projects for a long time.

Over many years of research, compelling scientific evidence has mounted indicating that lifestyle factors—all the daily decisions you make about what to eat, how active to be, and whether to smoke—have a major impact on the incidence of both cancer and cardiovascular disease. To a large extent, the protective factors overlap: The same strategies help protect against both heart disease and cancer. That presented our organizations with a lifesaving opportunity—to translate what we have learned about lifestyle into a simple tool you can use to help prevent these diseases.

At a time when all of us are bombarded with seemingly contradictory news related to lifestyle and health, a primary message of this book is particularly reassuring. You *don't* have to trade protection against one disease for protection against another. The major recommendations discussed here help prevent both heart disease and cancer. In fact, the recommendations are the ingredients in an overall healthful lifestyle that will also help prevent osteoporosis, lung disease, and obesity.

Living Well, Staying Well is far more than a compilation of our separate health recommendations and educational materials. In each lifestyle area, it takes you from scientific evidence to self-assessment to a variety of possible pathways toward a more healthful life.

As the book was being prepared, more than one hundred people generously shared their experiences in making lifestyle changes. In lengthy interviews, they described the successes they had achieved and the difficulties they had encountered, so that you can benefit from what they learned along the way. Their comments, reflecting the wide variety of attitudes and approaches that can all lead you to a more healthful lifestyle, are interspersed throughout the book.

We hope you will make this book and its strategies your own, integrating them in a way that suits your temperament and your likes and dislikes. You can read as little or as much as you want about the science behind the recommendations. You can choose whatever starting point you want in making changes. Perhaps it will be the area that seems the most urgent, or maybe it will be the most doable or the most challenging.

If enough people adopt the principles of behavior explained in the following pages, that could have a major impact on the amount of suffering and premature deaths resulting from cancer or heart disease. We hope you and those you care about will use this book to reap the benefits of preventive health care and to improve your overall quality of life.

Sidney C. Smith, Jr., M.D.   Raymond E. Lenhard, Jr., M.D.
President, American Heart   President, American Cancer
    Association   Society

Contents

Living Well,
Staying Well

CHAPTER 1

The Power of Prevention

IF YOU ARE LIKE MOST OTHER PEOPLE, YOU WANT TO LIVE A LONG TIME.
Even more important, you want to spend as much of your life as possible in vibrant good health—comfortable in your mind and body and having the energy, curiosity, and strength to enjoy each day to the fullest. This book can help you do that.

By making a few positive changes in your lifestyle, you can feel and look better today and increase the chance that you will avoid the two most common obstacles to a long and healthy life, *heart disease* and *cancer.*

These two diseases are the top killers in the United States. Every year, more than 1.5 million people have a heart attack and about 500,000 have a *stroke;* more than 600,000 die of heart disease and stroke. In 1994, more than 1.2 million people were diagnosed with cancer, and more than 500,000 died. If rates stay the same, well over half the people living today will eventually confront heart disease, cancer, or both.

Will you be one? Why do some of us stay healthy while others become ill? Is there anything you can do to avoid these diseases?

The answers to such questions aren't clear-cut. However, research has found many factors that greatly influence our risk of developing cancer and heart disease. They involve lifestyle—all the choices we make each day about how to spend our time, what to eat and drink, and whether to smoke. Each lifestyle choice may not seem significant by itself. Taken together, though, more healthful choices offer each of us something quite amazing: the power to help prevent disease.

Not all the answers are in, but the evidence on lifestyle is so impressive that the American Heart Association and the American Cancer Society want to put that power in your hands NOW.

The Need for Prevention

With advances in science, the practice of medicine has expanded dramatically. The emphasis has shifted from primarily treating disease in its later stages to detecting it earlier or learning to prevent it entirely.

For decades, cancer experts have emphasized the importance of detecting cancer early, when treatment is most effective. Some of the most impressive reductions in cancer deaths have come through early detection. In cervical cancer, for example, in the past forty years the death rate has plummeted 75 percent in the United States because women conscientiously have Pap smears to detect *precancerous* cells before they spread.

Medical professionals also have gotten some well-deserved recognition for their role in reducing heart disease deaths in people with a history of heart disease. Physicians have learned how to break up *blood clots* quickly, bypass clogged arteries to bring nourishment to the heart, and use medications to reduce the risk of a second heart attack.

The result of all that research and medical action is that people are more likely to survive heart disease than ever before. After years of going up, death rates from heart attack started a gradual decline in the mid-1960s, falling by more than half between 1963 and 1991.

Ordinary people practicing prevention deserve much of the credit for the turnaround in the death toll. The scope of the change is simply too striking for any medical treatment to be entirely responsible.

Defining a healthful lifestyle was the product of years of medical and public health research. In large numbers, people are beginning to follow the tenets of such a lifestyle, and their habits are paying off in fewer premature deaths. To minimize the risk of heart disease and cancer, it's best to develop healthful habits at a young age, before trouble begins. Don't wait for early detection of problems or for known *risk factors* to develop (see pages 9–10 and 12–13).

Why not wait for signs of risk? Because, for many people, they come too late to help. In fact, of every three people who die of a heart attack, one of them was unaware of *any* risk before the fatal event. The day before the attack each of those people could have truthfully said, "I don't have a heart problem."

WARNING SIGNS FOR HEART ATTACK AND STROKE

Heart Attack
- Uncomfortable pressure, fullness, squeezing, or pain in the center of the chest that lasts more than a few minutes or leaves and returns;
- Pain spreading to the shoulders, neck, or arms;
- Chest discomfort with lightheadedness, fainting, sweating, nausea, or shortness of breath.

You may not have all these symptoms with a heart attack. Don't take needless chances, though. If some of them start to occur, get help right away.

Stroke
- Sudden weakness or numbness of the face, arm, or leg on one side of the body;
- Sudden dimness or loss of vision, particularly in one eye;
- Loss of speech, or trouble talking or understanding speech;
- Sudden, severe headaches with no apparent cause;
- Unexplained dizziness, unsteadiness, or sudden falls, especially along with any of the previous symptoms.

We now know, however, that the stage is set for cancer or heart disease over many years, in a series of changes. A healthful lifestyle and prevention-oriented medical care often can halt or reverse these changes.

Although earlier is better, it is never too late to get real benefits from lifestyle changes. This is true even if you are in poor health or have been diagnosed with heart disease or cancer. To understand what changes you might need to make and why, you need to know how the heart works and what causes cancer.

HEART DISEASE AND LIFESTYLE BASICS

Every part of the body needs oxygen and nutrients in order to live. The circulatory system is responsible for delivering them.

The *circulatory system* is a 60,000-mile-long network of elastic tubes through which blood flows. It includes the heart, the lungs, and blood vessels of various sizes. Oxygen-filled blood travels to all the tissues and organs of the body through *arteries*, small arteries called *arterioles*, and minute blood vessels called *capillaries*. Blood returns to the heart through *veins* and *venules* (small veins).

As blood circulates, it picks up waste products from the body's cells. These waste products are removed as they're filtered through the kidneys, liver, and lungs.

The heart is a four-chambered muscular pump a little larger than your fist. Each day, it empties and refills approximately 100,000 times—pumping in a sequence of highly organized contractions of its chambers.

Blood, carrying the waste product carbon dioxide, first enters the right atrium of the heart. While the heart is relaxed, the blood flows through the tricuspid valve into the right ventricle. An electrical signal starts the heartbeat, and the atrium contracts. This contraction "tops off" the filling of the ventricle. Shortly after the atrium contracts, the right ventricle contracts. As this occurs, the tricuspid valve closes and the blood is pumped into the lungs. There it picks up oxygen and releases carbon dioxide.

The bright red, oxygen-filled blood returns to the left atrium of the heart. While the heart is relaxed, blood flows through the mitral valve into the left ventricle. As the atria contract, the left ventricle becomes

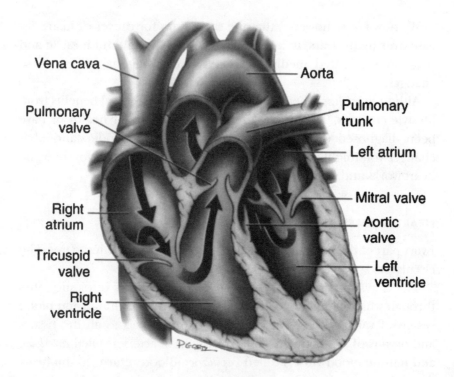

Vena cava — Aorta

Pulmonary valve — Pulmonary trunk

Left atrium

Right atrium — Mitral valve

Tricuspid valve — Aortic valve

Right ventricle — Left ventricle

full. The ventricle contracts with a vigorous squeeze, the mitral valve closes, and the blood is propelled into the arteries.

When oxygen-rich blood leaves the heart, its first priority is to nourish the heart muscle itself. The first arteries that branch off the *aorta,* or main artery, are *coronary arteries.* They deliver blood to the heart. A *heart attack,* also called a *myocardial infarction,* occurs when the blood supply to the heart muscle is cut off. *Angina,* or *angina pectoris,* is the pain that results when the heart muscle doesn't get all the oxygen it needs.

Most heart disease is caused when the coronary arteries become partially clogged. That condition is known as *coronary heart disease,* sometimes called *coronary artery disease.* When the coronary arteries are healthy, their inside linings are clean, smooth, and slick. The artery walls are flexible and readily expand to let more blood through when the heart needs to work harder to meet physical *stress.*

When anything disturbs the flow through the coronary arteries to the heart muscle, conditions are right for a heart attack. Sometimes a diseased coronary artery constricts in a spasm, causing temporary loss of blood supply and pain. Spasms seldom last long enough to cause a heart attack. The more usual cause of poor flow is *atherosclerosis,* a slow process that can damage and obstruct arteries. Fortunately, atherosclerosis is amenable to lifestyle changes.

What Is Atherosclerosis and How Does It Develop?

The very word *atherosclerosis* sounds like bad news: *athero* means "gruel" or "paste," and *sclerosis* means "hardness." It's characterized by deposits of fatty substances, *cholesterol* (a fatlike substance made by the body and eaten in animal products), cellular waste products, calcium, and fibrin (a clotting material in the blood) in the inner lining of an artery. The resulting buildup is called *plaque.*

The development of atherosclerosis is a complex process. Precisely how it begins or what causes it isn't known, but several theories have been proposed.

In the most prominent theory, atherosclerosis is thought to begin because the inner, protective lining of the artery (called the *endothelium*) becomes injured. Three of the possible causes of damage to the lining are (1) elevated levels of cholesterol and *triglyceride* (a fat that comes from food or is made in the body from other energy sources, such as carbohydrates) in the blood; (2) high blood pressure; and (3) cigarette smoke.

Once the cells in the artery wall are damaged, they may separate from the wall, exposing collagen, smooth muscle, and other tissues underneath. Initially, *platelets* stick to the collagen. This process gradually leads to the formation of plaque. Over time, atherosclerosis increases, reducing the diameter of the artery. Eventually, a blood clot may form at the site of the damage, blocking the artery and stopping the flow of blood.

	WHERE PLAQUE HURTS		
Location	**What They Feed**	**Symptoms of Blockage**	**Ultimate Danger**
Coronary arteries	Heart	Chest pain because not enough blood is reaching parts of the heart muscle	Heart attack, death of heart muscle tissue from lack of oxygen
Carotid arteries	Brain	Sudden, unexplained dizziness, especially in conjunction with other symptoms; weakness; or loss of speech (a transient ischemic attack, or ministroke)	Stroke with paralysis of one side of the body from too little oxygen reaching the brain cells
Femoral arteries	Legs	Peripheral vascular disease, causing cramping pain and fatigue in the calves *when walking*	Gangrene, need for amputation
Renal arteries	Kidneys	Difficult-to-treat high blood pressure	Kidney failure

One of the more recent theories suggests that fats, cholesterol, and other substances in the blood can become trapped within the artery wall. When this happens and they accumulate, they become "modified" by a process called *oxidation*. The end results are the formation of cells in the endothelium where atherosclerotic lesions form and the development of a fatty streak.

When the arteries of three-year-olds are examined, most already have faint streaks of fat at the points where atherosclerosis is likely to occur. Significant levels of atherosclerosis do not occur in everyone, however. It usually takes decades for atherosclerosis to become problematic. That leaves plenty of time for you to take action to prevent a heart attack.

A heart attack usually occurs in one of two ways. In one, atherosclerotic lesions continually narrow a vessel over a period of years or even decades. Sometimes, however, the condition can turn into unstable angina or a heart attack in minutes. In the second, an artery that is closed off even 40 to 60 percent may suddenly develop a break at the shoulder of a lesion. Bleeding results, and if the *thrombus,* or blood clot, is large enough, it may totally block the artery. When that happens, a heart attack may occur. The possibility that a piece of calcified plaque would become loose and totally block an artery is rare.

Risk Factors and Contributing Factors

The American Heart Association has identified several risk factors for coronary heart disease. Many of them can be changed, but some of them cannot. The more risk factors you have, the greater the chance that you will develop heart disease. The more risk factors you eliminate or control, the lower the chance will be. The major risk factors and contributors to heart disease are:

- *Age.* Each year, more than half of all heart attack victims are age sixty-five or older.
- *Cigarette/tobacco use.* Smoking doubles the risk of heart attack. Smoking damages artery linings and makes them like a magnet that attracts plaque.
- *Cholesterol.* As the level of cholesterol in the blood goes up, so does the risk of heart attack. Low-density lipoproteins (LDLs) are the major cholesterol carrier in the blood. If you have high levels of LDL cholesterol, often called bad cholesterol, you're at increased risk of heart disease. In contrast, high levels of high-density lipoproteins (HDLs), often called good cholesterol, seem to protect against heart attack.
- *Diabetes. Diabetes* seriously raises your risk of developing cardiovascular disease. More than 80 percent of people with diabetes die of some form of heart or blood vessel disease.
- *Heredity.* If your parents had heart disease before the age of fifty-five, you are more likely to develop it than are people whose parents were not affected.
- *High blood pressure. High blood pressure,* also called *hypertension,* adds to the heart's workload and strains the arteries. That raises the risk of stroke, heart attack, kidney failure, and atherosclerosis.
- *Inactivity.* Lack of physical exercise is a risk factor for coronary heart disease.

◆ *Being male.* Men have a greater risk of heart attack than premeno-pausal women, and men have attacks earlier in life.

◆ *Obesity.* Excess body fat, or *obesity,* contributes to the development of other risk factors, such as high cholesterol, diabetes, and high blood pressure.

CANCER AND LIFESTYLE BASICS

Cancer is not a single disease. Rather, it's a catchall name for more than one hundred diseases that have something in common. No matter what type of cancer is involved, abnormal cells develop and their growth spins out of control.

All your organs, bones, muscles, skin, blood, and other fluids are made up of cells—microscopic building blocks that share a common design but are specialized to perform distinct functions. Inside each of your cells is a copy of your *DNA*. It furnishes genetic information that controls what kind of cell is formed (blood cell? muscle? skin?), how big it is, how long it lives, and how often it duplicates so that a body organ will be just the right size and in good repair.

When a cell becomes cancerous, its DNA is altered in such a way that the cell can no longer regulate itself or reproduce normally. Genetic signals that say "grow" or "don't grow" go awry, so a cell does not stop duplicating itself when it should. The cell may develop a peculiar shape or keep churning out copies of itself when none are needed.

Groups of cells that divide too much and form in masses within organs are called *tumors,* or *neoplasms* (which simply means "new growth"). Tumors can be either *benign* or *malignant.*

Benign tumors may interfere with body functions and require surgical removal. However, in most cases they are not life threatening, because they do not spread to other parts of the body.

Malignant, or cancerous, tumors can destroy healthy *tissue.* They intrude on its territory, rob normal cells of nutrients, and produce harmful chemicals. Unlike cells in benign tumors, stray *cancer cells* from malignant tumors can break away from the original tumor and travel through the bloodstream or *lymphatic system* to form new tumors in distant organs in the body. This process is called *metastasis.* Tumors in the new location are called *metastases,* or *secondary tumors.*

When cancer cells are growing in their original site, cancer is said to be localized. If detected at this stage, it often can be cured. If not checked, however, most cancers will spread. When metastases occur in distant organs, treatments are less successful. That's why early detection and proper treatments are essential. If the spread of cancer cells cannot be halted, the cancer can result in death.

What causes cancer? All cancer cells have defects in their DNA. But that does *not* mean that all—or even most—cancer is hereditary. About 60 percent of cancer is clearly related to environmental or lifestyle factors—what we eat, whether we smoke, the air we breathe, and the chemicals we're exposed to. Researchers strive to add to our knowledge of how environmental insults can damage DNA. They also try to find why some people are more likely than others to get certain types of cancer.

One area of improved understanding is the identification of *oncogenes*. These are stretches of DNA that help transform a normal cell into a cancer cell when they are activated. *Viruses* and carcinogenic chemicals and substances may "turn on" these oncogenes.

By studying oncogenes, over the years researchers have developed a two-step model of how a normal cell might change into a cancer cell. In this model, an *initiator,* such as cigarette smoking or exposure to X rays, starts damage to a cell. That damage can lead to cancer. Cells already damaged by initiators can be further harmed by *promoters*. Promoters are not cancer-causing themselves but encourage the growth of tumors once the process is started. For example, it has been shown that when combined with cigarette smoking, drinking alcohol promotes the development of cancer of the mouth and throat. Thus, smoking is the initiator and alcohol is the promoter—and the two combined are a serious cancer threat. Researchers also are trying to identify chemicals that act as antipromoters to counteract the impact of cancer promoters or block initiators before they do their damage.

Carcinogens are substances that have been shown either to initiate or to promote cancer in humans. Researchers have identified these substances through studies with animals and in human research. In the human studies, they've looked at the differences in cancer incidence between groups of people.

The two-step model of cancer brings with it good news for prevention and treatment: The development of cancer is not a split-second zap that turns a good cell irretrievably bad. The process is complex and usually occurs in stages over ten years or more. Therefore, the more we learn about prevention, the more time we have to change.

CANCER'S SEVEN WARNING SIGNS

The seven warning signs of cancer, listed below, are important to know, but in recent years the American Cancer Society hasn't stressed them quite as much. Because we have learned so much about the lengthy cancer process, we hope most cancers and their precursor conditions can be detected *before* the warning signs occur.

1. Change in bowel or bladder habits;
2. A sore that does not heal;
3. Unusual bleeding or discharge;
4. Thickening or lump in breast or elsewhere;
5. Indigestion or difficulty in swallowing;
6. Obvious change in wart or mole;
7. Nagging cough or hoarseness.

If you have any of these symptoms, see your physician.

The lifestyle factors that follow can influence many types of cancer.

♦ *Cigarette/tobacco use.* Smoking accounts for about 30 percent of all cancer deaths and is responsible for about 87 percent of lung cancers. The use of chewing tobacco, pipes, and cigars also raises the risk of certain types of cancer. It is estimated that in 1994, about 165,000 people died of cancer as a result of using tobacco.

♦ *Sunlight.* Exposure to ultraviolet radiation from the sun is a major factor in the development of *melanoma,* a deadly skin cancer. Almost all *squamous cell skin cancers* (slower-growing cancers) and *basal cell skin cancers* are sun related. If people protected themselves from the sun's rays, about 90 percent of the 700,000 skin cancers diagnosed in 1994 could have been prevented.

♦ *Heavy alcohol use.* Cancers of the mouth, throat, esophagus, and liver occur more frequently in heavy drinkers. This is particularly true when the drinker also uses tobacco. Excessive alcohol use was responsible for about 17,000 cancer deaths in 1994.

♦ *Nutrition.* Diet plays a significant role in the development of several types of cancer.

♦ *Obesity.* People who are 40 percent or more overweight increase their risk of colon, breast, prostate, gallbladder, ovarian, and uterine cancers.

- *Occupational hazards.* Exposure to several industrial agents increases the risk of various cancers. These agents include asbestos, chromate, nickel, and vinyl chloride.
- *Radiation.* Excessive exposure to radiation raises cancer risk.
- *Estrogen use.* Taking estrogen to control menopausal symptoms can increase the risk of endometrial cancer. To lessen this risk, most doctors also prescribe progesterone.

RISKY BUSINESS

Life is a game of odds. Increasingly, recommendations for important life decisions are based on research data. That data is provided in the form of statistics that give the odds for facing health problems. These statistics may guide our purchase of insurance, determine our need for certain medical tests, or cause us to change our habits.

Preventing disease also is a matter of understanding and playing the odds. Are your health concerns in line with statistical reality? Ask yourself whether you're more worried about driving, smoking cigarettes, flying in an airplane, skydiving, or getting killed by a shark. Here's how the odds stack up for the average man of thirty-five:

- Chance of dying in a single airline trip—1 in 815,000
- Chance of dying in a single skydiving jump—1 in 96,296
- Chance of being killed in a car accident before his sixty-fifth birthday—1 in 143
- Chance that smoking will kill him by the age of sixty-five—1 in 5

Judging strictly by the statistics, your chance of surviving a shark attack is actually *better* than your chance of surviving a heart attack or some cancers. Worldwide, only seven to ten people die each year from shark attacks. The good news is that, all in all, changing lifestyle habits to prevent cancer and heart disease can be a very healthy bet.

For some risk factors, heart disease and cancer specialists have graphic knowledge of how lifestyle can damage or protect the body. For others, advice is based overwhelmingly on odds information from *epidemiology*, the science that analyzes how often diseases occur and who is most likely to get them.

A classic example of the preventive power of epidemiology occurred before germs and bacteria were discovered. At the time, cholera was killing people in Europe. An alert physician named John Snow noticed that the people in his town who were getting sick were the ones who drew their water from a certain pump. He didn't wait to nail down the cause. Instead, he had the handle removed from the tap, saving the lives of many people.

Although our knowledge about cancer and heart disease is now far more detailed, epidemiology still often leads the way. Regarding smoking, for example, comparing the disease and death counts between smokers and nonsmokers gave a clear indication of danger. That comparison was followed by increasing evidence on how the various constituents in tobacco smoke cause harm. We don't completely understand why some lifestyle choices are associated with illness. However, we try to heed the risk information that epidemiology supplies. For example, if a thirty-five-year-old male smoker knows that there is a 1-in-5 chance that smoking will kill him by age sixty-five, he might be very motivated to kick the habit.

THE HIGH-RISK BLUES

You are stuck with some risks for life. You can't change your parents, age, sex, or race.

If you have been labeled at high risk for cancer, heart disease, or some other condition, you don't need to feel doomed. Risk figures cannot say what will happen to you or to anyone else. All they mean is that statistically tracking thousands and thousands of people has shown the connection with a given risk factor.

For example, car insurance companies often charge higher premiums for drivers under age twenty-five. That does *not* mean that you won't have an accident if you're older or that you necessarily are a careless driver if you are younger.

In some cases, knowing your risk can save your life or serve as a wake-up call to protect your health. For example, each year about forty people die from bee stings. That's a tiny portion of all bee-sting victims and not something to worry about—unless you are allergic to bees. If you are sensitive to bees, your body is primed to overreact and send you into shock when you're stung. You have thus entered the high-risk group for bee-sting deaths. Even so, your fate still is not sealed. The chance that you, as a sensitized person, will go into shock when stung is about 60 percent, not 100 percent. And because you know you're at special risk, you can choose to take action to make your life safer. You might decide to take the desensitization shots your doctor suggests or carry a first-aid kit to counter the effects of a sting. Knowing your risk puts you in more control than the person who doesn't know that the next sting could be deadly.

"Everybody on my father's side died of heart disease. On my mother's side are aunts who died of cancer in their twenties, forties, and sixties. I figure I might as well smoke if I want and eat what I want and enjoy myself for as long as I'm here."

"My husband doesn't exercise much, but he doesn't have to. He comes from a very long-lived family."

Both these people are wrong. Your genes can put you in a high-risk group for certain diseases, but those genes only rarely seal your fate. Unless you are an identical twin, you are a unique genetic creation. You share no more than half your genes with even your closest relatives. If you have a genetic predisposition to cancer or heart disease, what does that mean? Well, it doesn't mean you're sure to get either one. In almost all such cases, certain lifestyle factors would have to come into play before the diseases occur.

Some people have a gene that causes them to become seriously ill if they eat fava beans. That's not a death sentence—just an emphatic eating tip! In a less extreme way, most genes are the same. Let's say you have inherited a tendency to metabolize cholesterol poorly—something that affects about 1 in 100 people. Through the use of cholesterol-lowering medications and a low-fat, low-cholesterol eating plan, you often can reduce your blood cholesterol to a level about as low as that of someone with "better" genes and a less healthful lifestyle.

If you had a parent who died of cancer, a heart attack, or another illness at a relatively young age, don't feel that you are destined to repeat his or her medical history. If you are predisposed to lung cancer, don't smoke. If you are predisposed to develop adult-onset diabetes, don't become overweight. If your body doesn't metabolize cholesterol well, limit saturated fat and dietary cholesterol in what you eat. If you are fair-skinned and sunburn prone, stay out of the sun as much as possible; wear protective clothing, including a hat; and use sunscreen.

Keep in mind that many diseases that occur in families are caused by more than inherited genes. You share more than some of your parents' genes. Chances are, you have shared hundreds or thousands of meals with them. You may have grown to share their priorities in life (work first, exercise last?) or their pleasures (cigars? tennis? apple pie?). As you learn more about the relationship between lifestyle and cancer and heart disease, you have the power to undo any unhealthful learned behaviors. And just as genetics does not seal your health future, neither does any single lifestyle factor. Many factors play a role in the genesis of cancer and heart disease—and the risk from several factors in combination may be more than the sum of the individual risks. That means that even if it seems impossible to develop a completely healthful lifestyle, it is worthwhile to improve as many factors as you can.

PUTTING RISKS IN PERSPECTIVE

When you read the latest medical news, it is easy to become needlessly alarmed, falsely reassured, or just plain confused by all the different ways of talking about risks.

For example, one study of British doctors has been ongoing since the 1950s and has provided valuable information about the risk of smoking. The findings can be stated many ways.

Absolute risk is the chance something will occur. Early results from the British study revealed that 71 out of every 100,000 smokers die of lung cancer each year.

That number is important, but it doesn't tell smokers whether they are safer, or in more danger, than their nonsmoking friends.

Relative risk compares risk between groups of people. When relative risks are presented, one group is always designated as 1, and the results from the other group are expressed in multiples of that. A relative risk of 2 means that the risk is doubled; a relative risk of 0.5 means that the risk is cut in half.

In the same British study, smokers had a relative risk of about 10, meaning they were ten times more likely to die of lung cancer than were nonsmokers.

Whenever you read about relative risk, look for the absolute risk. That will help you keep the figures in perspective. Even if something triples or quadruples the risk of a very rare cancer or other illness, the absolute risk still is not very high.

Attributable risk helps educators and policymakers look at the big picture—how many cases of a disease can be attributed to a given risk factor. In the British study, those 71 smokers weren't the only ones to die of lung cancer each year. So did 7 in every 100,000 nonsmoking physicians. That told the researchers that 7 of the smokers would have developed lung cancer even without the habit. That means that 64 of the 71 lung cancer deaths in smokers, or about 90 percent, were attributable to smoking.

For an individual, attributable risk doesn't translate into definitive answers about cause and effect. If you are a smoker with lung cancer, the studies can't tell you whether you are one of the 90 percent who got it from smoking or one of the 10 percent who would have developed it anyway.

In policy terms, attributable risk means a lot. In this example it means that 90 percent of lung cancer cases could be eliminated if people stopped smoking. That's why the American Cancer Society and the Surgeons General of the United States give the smoking issue such high priority.

As an experiment in using attributable risk, let's say you read that a disease has a 20 percent risk attributable to wearing striped socks. If everyone in the country stopped wearing striped socks, only 20 percent of the cases would be avoided. That's not too high. Nevertheless, you might very well decide that giving up striped socks is an easy lifestyle change that you are willing to make—no matter how slim a safety margin it brings you. Now say that 20 percent of the cases were attributed to becoming a parent after the age of thirty. The percentage is the same, but many other factors enter into a decision about when to become a parent. The disease-prevention component might legitimately remain a minor factor in your personal choice.

How to Use This Book

Don't feel that you must read this book all at once. And please don't feel that you must finish it before you start making changes toward a healthful lifestyle. The earlier you start making those changes, the better.

Your doctor may have already pinpointed a lifestyle area that could use improvement, or your answers to the "How's Your Lifestyle?" quiz on pages 20–3 may guide you toward a good starting point. If you have already been thinking about changing a part of your life, read the chapter dealing with that area first. Or start with the section that seems the easiest, and let that first accomplishment inspire you in other areas.

Each chapter lays out, in simple terms, the heart disease and cancer connections to the primary focus of that chapter. If you want to see a definitive tally of risks and visualize the mechanics of what is happening in your body, these sections are for you. They may inspire you to take action. They also might show you how to be more encouraging to a loved one striving to make changes. If medical talk is not your cup of tea, skip right to the advice.

Practical advice sections in each chapter give instructions for getting started. They also talk about choices for people of vastly different personalities and physical conditions. Quotes from people who offer their experiences—both cautionary and celebratory—punctuate each chapter. Although their names are not given, these are real people who share your problems.

Keep the book on hand so you can refer to different sections whenever you need an explanation, encouragement, or advice. If your physical condition changes or you find you have fallen short of your goals, reread the pertinent chapters to motivate yourself and get back on track.

WHAT YOU WILL FIND IN THIS BOOK

Advice Backed by Solid Science
If something is recommended in this book, you can be sure plenty of scientific evidence attests to its value.

Donations to the American Heart Association and the American Cancer Society support research and make its results available to the public. A single research project may be innovative and well constructed. It may garner many headlines. Scientists may even consider its lead very promising. But if it is the only one of its kind, the AHA and the ACS will not issue a recommendation based on just that one study.

The two groups ask highly regarded scientific investigators to digest the evidence on a subject and make appropriate recommendations. The suggestions in this book are based on a combination of evidence from laboratory research, epidemiology studies, and careful *clinical trials* that directly assess the benefit of making certain lifestyle changes.

This does not mean that this book offers the final word on any subject. Ongoing research may yield more information that could cause the two groups to refine their advice. If you have questions about up-to-date guidelines on a specific topic, contact the American Heart Association or the American Cancer Society (see page 291).

Lots of Choices

People come with a range of schedules, personalities, motivations, responsibilities, and priorities. Therefore, no one path leads to good health for everyone.

Look at the available choices, and try the ones that feel right to you. If you like keeping track in writing of your health goals and strategies, great. If you don't, put the pen down and put the advice into action. If you like making changes a tiny step at a time, that's fine. If you'd rather make many changes to your lifestyle at once, go ahead. If one approach doesn't work, you will learn from the attempt and have plenty of other choices for a second approach. The important thing is to keep trying.

A Lifespan Perspective

The sooner you begin to enjoy a healthful lifestyle, the more disease-preventive power it has. However, you can benefit from such a lifestyle even if your health is poor. Each chapter of this book tells you ways to take control of lifestyle changes you can make. Each chapter also includes information on raising children in a healthful environment. Tips include exercising together, cooking nutritious meals the whole family will enjoy, and creating a smoke-free home.

WHAT YOU WON'T FIND IN THIS BOOK

Magic Bullets

Remember the mad dash to buy oat bran? The health-conscious people who got up every morning to make sticky oat bran porridge or oat bran muffins? The proliferation of oat bran products, many of which (such as fried oat bran potato chips) were of dubious value?

During the frenzy, the American Heart Association did not come forward to recommend oat bran, despite limited research studies indicating its value. The organization took a less flashy, but ultimately more livable, approach to the latest magic bullet to come along. The AHA explained that oat bran is a perfectly good fiber (see page 119), but it is useful only as part of an overall healthful eating plan and a livable lifestyle.

As much as you might like to believe in the magic bullet, the truth is that it will probably never come. The power you have to try to prevent heart disease and cancer comes instead in a host of small choices that you make every day.

Blame or Guarantees

Cancer and heart disease are common. You may face one or both of them. If you do, no one can know for sure whether a certain aspect of your lifestyle caused your illness. No matter how carefully you live, you won't live forever. You can, however, improve your health and your enjoyment of the time you live.

The American Cancer Society and the American Heart Association care about people—protecting the healthy, treating the sick, and guiding the next generation toward the most healthful life possible. The organizations consider it scientifically foolhardy, as well as meanspirited, to blame people for becoming ill.

So assess your lifestyle habits realistically and start making changes that can improve your health and enjoyment of life. But don't add blame and guilt on top of illness if it occurs.

Pick-Your-Disease Diets

If you follow the latest medical research reports on television and in the newspapers, you can end up feeling that everything you eat or do causes illness. You also may think you must trade off prevention of one disease for prevention of another. Want to avoid osteoporosis? Eat plenty of calcium-rich dairy products. Want to avoid heart disease? Put away those high-fat, high-calorie dairy foods.

The ACS and the AHA are collaborating on this project so you won't feel that you have to set the stage for one disease in order to keep another one at bay. The beauty of the accumulated research is the fit between advice on cancer and advice on heart disease. Attention to the same lifestyle factors protects against both.

To help you pinpoint which aspects of your life are already on a disease-preventive track and which could use improvement, take the following "How's Your Lifestyle?" quiz.

How's Your Lifestyle?

Do these statements describe you? Answer "yes" or "no" for each one.

_____ **1.** Pasta and whole grain breads and cereals are a major part of my nutrition plan.

_____ **2.** I enjoy chewing tobacco or snuff.

_____ **3.** I seldom wear sunglasses.

_____ **4.** I protect myself against sexually transmitted diseases.

_____ **5.** I eat fried foods almost every day.

_____ **6.** I never exert myself enough to sweat or breathe hard.

_____ **7.** No weight-loss eating plan has ever worked for me.

_____ **8.** I like charcoal-grilled foods.

_____ **9.** I have a doctor or other health-care professional I can talk to about my lifestyle, nutrition, and exercise habits.

_____ **10.** I take vitamin supplements to guard against disease.

_____ **11.** I live with, work with, or carpool with a smoker.

_____ **12.** I use only nonfat dairy products.

_____ **13.** I have diabetes.

_____ **14.** My excess weight is carried on my stomach (a "spare tire"), not my hips and thighs.

_____ **15.** I know my blood pressure and cholesterol levels.

_____ **16.** The new food labels confuse me.

_____ **17.** Salt is the seasoning I prefer on almost everything.

_____ **18.** I have to stop and rest awhile when walking up stairs.

_____ **19.** At work, we have good ventilation.

_____ **20.** I eat at least five servings of fruits and vegetables each day.

_____ **21.** I use birth control pills or hormone-replacement therapy.

_____ **22.** I switched to low-tar and low-nicotine cigarettes.

_____ **23.** To get a better tan, I use a sunlamp at home or go to a tanning salon.

_____ **24.** I use butter and regular cheese in cooking and when munching.

_____ **25.** I know how to examine my breasts or testicles, and I do that every month.

_____ **26.** Pickles, ham, and smoked foods are my favorites.

_____ **27.** I exercise only on weekends.

_____ **28.** There are no chemicals or fumes at my workplace.

_____ **29.** I have fish or vegetarian entrées more often than meat.

_____ **30.** I eat until I am stuffed.

_____ **31.** I am confused by news stories about cancer risks.

_____ **32.** I use whole milk or half-and-half with my coffee and cereal.

_____ **33.** I have tried to stop smoking but never succeeded for long.

_____ **34.** If my doctor doesn't suggest screening tests, I feel comfortable asking about them.

_____ **35.** I am more than twenty pounds overweight.

_____ **36.** I am too busy to exercise.

_____ **37.** I frequently get sunburned.

_____ **38.** I smoke cigarettes, cigars, or a pipe.

_____ **39.** I regularly take aspirin to protect my heart.

_____ **40.** I eat meat at least once a day.

_____ **41.** I used to smoke but I quit.

_____ **42.** I don't own a pair of shoes comfortable enough for a long walk.

_____ **43.** My grocery cart is filled with more prepackaged foods than ingredients for make-it-yourself dishes.

_____ **44.** On most days, I drink more than three cocktails, beers, or glasses of wine.

_____ **45.** My blood pressure is normal or under control with medication.

_____ **46.** My home has been checked for radon, and it's okay.

Evaluating Your Answers

If you answered "yes" to 1, 12, 20, or 29, you have a head start in protecting your health through your nutrition plan. See chapter 3 for more ideas.

If you answered "yes" to 2, 11, 22, 33, or 38, see chapter 2 for an exciting array of health benefits that could be yours if you were not exposed to tobacco. That chapter also provides an encouraging variety of support systems ready to help you give up tobacco.

If you answered "yes" to 3, 23, or 37, see chapter 6 for easy ways to lessen your exposure to ultraviolet radiation. Methods for better protecting yourself against skin cancer also are discussed there.

If you answered "no" to 4, see chapter 6. Some sexually transmitted viruses can cause cancer.

If you answered "yes" to 5, 24, 32, or 40, chapter 3 will show you some simple and tasty ways to lower the fat in what you eat.

If you answered "yes" to 6, 18, 27, 36, or 42, you could boost your energy and lower your risk of disease by adding more exercise to your life. Chapter 4 may help you get started.

If you answered "yes" to 7, 14, 30, or 35, chapter 3 may help you achieve and maintain a healthful weight without feeling deprived.

If you answered "no" to 19, 28, or 46, see chapter 6. You may be able to lower your exposure to health-damaging chemicals.

If you answered "yes" to 8, 17, or 26, read chapter 3 to see whether your taste buds are interfering with your desire to protect your health.

If you answered "no" to 9, 15, 25, 34, or 45, chapter 5 will tell you some things you can do to strengthen the disease-preventive partnership between you and your doctors.

If you answered "yes" to 10, 31, or 39, turn to chapter 6 to learn what research has found out about protection.

If you answered "yes" to 13, look for information spread throughout this book. Diabetes increases the risk of heart disease and multiplies the danger of other risk factors. The sections on smoking, proper nutrition, and exercise can help you make needed changes. It is doubly important for you to make these changes.

If you answered "yes" to 16 and 43, you can learn to assess the ingredients in packaged foods. Chapter 3 will help you.

If you answered "yes" to 21, see chapter 6 to make sure you are using these effective medicines in ways that maximize their health benefits and minimize their risks.

If you answered "yes" to 41, congratulations! To see how much healing your body has done, read chapter 2.

If you answered "yes" to 44, see chapter 3 to learn how to enjoy alcohol safely.

You *Can* Give Your Body a Smoke-Free Future

"I stopped smoking at midnight, June 12, 1976. It was the hardest thing I ever did and is still the greatest triumph of my life."

IF YOU ARE A SMOKER, THE SINGLE MOST IMPORTANT THING YOU CAN do to reduce the risk of heart disease and cancer is to become a nonsmoker.

The good news is that you *can* quit smoking, even if you have tried many times before and have always gone back. Smoking is very different from other habits. Many people can use sheer willpower to stop biting their fingernails or eating rich desserts. Willpower alone is seldom enough to conquer tobacco, however. Doctors now have a better understanding of the strong grasp of nicotine addiction and can offer new tools to ease the disturbing physical symptoms of withdrawal.

No matter what your personality or smoking profile, a variety of aids is available to help you. Those aids range from self-help books to live-in programs. Choose one or take advantage of several that suit your temperament and lifestyle.

Every day more than 3,500 people will stop smoking *permanently*. You can join them. The first step is to find a reason to stop smoking that is meaningful to you. After you've made that decision, the next step is to develop a plan. In this chapter, we'll talk about both those aspects of quitting smoking.

What Will Motivate You to Make the Decision?

"When I had almost convinced myself to quit smoking, I went to a doctor in town. He gave me the blow-by-blow details of what it's like to die of lung cancer. Before then, I couldn't listen. That time, it was a powerful incentive."

Smoking is responsible for 30 percent of all cancer deaths and 30 percent of all heart attack deaths. In the United States, one in every five deaths from all possible causes is related to smoking.

The problem is that knowing the health risks doesn't necessarily make it any easier to stop. If you smoke, chances are that you *would* like to quit but aren't sure you can. Probably you've already tried, maybe several times. You may have spent days or even years away from cigarettes before starting to smoke again.

If grim statistics, films of former Marlboro men choking, and pictures of grimy, tar-clogged lungs motivated each of us to stop smoking, there wouldn't be 50 million smokers in the United States. Each smoker needs to find a personal motivation for quitting. What motivates you doesn't necessarily motivate someone else. One of the items below—or something else entirely—may provide the catalyst for you to make a lasting change:

- Living longer;
- Having free hands;
- Feeling better;
- Saving money;
- Looking better;
- Smelling better;
- Being pregnant;
- Setting a healthy example for your children;
- Cleaning the air in your home;
- Getting doctors' orders;
- Working in a smoke-free setting;
- Showing a loved one you care;
- Saving your teeth;
- Breathing more easily;
- Escaping nicotine's hook;
- Disliking tobacco company tactics.

To help you find the incentive that will work, this chapter lays out health-related and other reasons to quit.

Butt Out for Your Health

Let's start with the bad news: what the ingredients in tobacco products do in your body and how that can result in the stark probabilities of disease and death. Then the good news: a calendar of rewards you will gain by becoming a nonsmoker. *They start twenty minutes after your last puff* and are still getting better fifteen years later.

If you've smoked for a long time, a litany of health damage already done may make you feel like lighting up in hopelessness. If it does, flip first to the health benefits section (see page 37). Look at the evidence that shows that you can reverse some health damage once you stop—even if you have been diagnosed with cancer or heart disease. Or move beyond health concerns to the many other reasons to quit smoking (see page 38).

WARNING: YOU WON'T FIND THIS INGREDIENT LIST ON CIGARETTE LABELS

What's in a cigarette? Tobacco, of course, which is a complex plant substance that includes some deadly chemicals. In addition, manufacturers douse tobacco with chemicals designed to make cigarettes light easily, burn at a precise speed, and stay lit when you put them down. The tobacco products that concern the American Cancer Society and the American Heart Association most are nicotine, tar, carbon monoxide, and other toxic gases.

TOXIC SUBSTANCES IN TOBACCO PRODUCTS

Nicotine

Nicotine is a toxic chemical that, in nature, is found only in tobacco. For plants, it's a protective insect killer. For humans, it's a poison that, if taken in large enough amounts, can kill by completely paralyzing the breathing muscles.

If you felt like you turned green when you first tried a cigarette or feel sick now after smoking more than usual, nicotine is probably responsible.

"When nicotine is introduced, like when you don't smoke for two years and then start again, it's not a pleasant experience. But it quickly becomes a habit that has to be fed."

Nicotine is an addictive drug. It is as addictive as the chemically related plant products heroin, cocaine, or crack, according to some government scientists. Nicotine skews brain chemistry, changing the nerve-to-nerve communication in different brain locations. It also spurs the release of a variety of *hormones* and nerve cell messengers. A smoker may experience these changes positively—feeling calmer, more energetic, or both—or negatively—feeling depressed or irritable and nervous. If an addicted person stops taking in nicotine, a predictable medical syndrome of withdrawal symptoms occurs.

Although cancer and heart disease are the most well known and deadly consequences of smoking, the Food and Drug Administration believes that nicotine addiction is the primary disease caused by smoking. The disease of nicotine addiction strikes smokers of any age. Many children become hooked before they are even old enough to buy cigarettes legally.

It is easy to see how people get hooked on nicotine. For one thing, the drug's impact is immediate. After a drag off a cigarette, it takes just seven seconds for nicotine to get into your bloodstream and reach your brain. That's faster than if you had injected the nicotine directly into a vein. Also, the body develops tolerance to nicotine, as it does to other addictive drugs. Within an hour, the same amount of nicotine will not have as strong an effect. If you want to feel the same, you must smoke more. Pack-a-day smokers routinely give themselves close to two hundred nicotine hits a day.

Tobacco companies seem well aware of nicotine's addictive pull. The FDA has accused tobacco manufacturers of packing cigarettes with enough nicotine to produce and sustain addiction even though technology is available that can remove nicotine from tobacco. In 1994 the FDA warned tobacco manufacturers that it may someday claim the right to regulate tobacco products as drugs.

You may feel relaxed from the effects of nicotine. However, every puff is causing physical stress all over your body. Under nicotine's influence the flow of blood and oxygen through the body decreases. Temporarily, blood vessels narrow and blood pressure rises, and your heart may beat as much as an extra thirty-three times each minute.

Tar

Besides nicotine, tobacco smoke contains thousands of other toxic chemicals. Tar is the catchall name for oily, microscopic globs that contain many of these substances. When you breathe in tobacco smoke, the hot tar particles immediately irritate the inside of your mouth and throat. Inhaled into the lungs, they cool into sticky deposits that contain more than 4,000 chemical substances. Forty-three of them cause or promote cancer, and another 401 are known to cause other types of bodily harm.

For example, *aromatic amines* are formed when tobacco doesn't burn completely. They have been associated with bladder cancer. Another group of substances, called the *polynuclear aromatic hydrocarbons,* are carcinogenic by themselves. They are even more likely to cause tumors if they are combined with certain other substances, such as alcohol or asbestos, or if your diet is poor. *Nitrosamines* are cancer-causing chemicals formed during the curing and processing of tobacco. Despite the reduction in other components of tar in recent decades, the amount of nitrosamines in cigarettes has actually increased since the 1950s, when manufacturers introduced blended tobacco that makes use of plant stems.

The Surgeon General first warned of the dangers of smoking in 1964. Since then, the average amount of tar in a cigarette made in the United States has been cut from thirty-seven to twelve milligrams. The cough and excessive phlegm production most smokers experience are, however, sure signs that the irritation caused by cigarettes is still significant.

Carbon Monoxide

You can't see or smell carbon monoxide, the potentially deadly gas produced by car engines, gas heaters, and burning tobacco. At high doses of carbon monoxide, death by asphyxiation results. When people commit suicide by breathing car exhaust in a poorly ventilated area, carbon monoxide is the killer.

Normally, red blood cells carry oxygen all over the body in specialized molecules called *hemoglobin.* But when carbon monoxide enters the bloodstream, it grabs the hemoglobin and hangs on tight. That keeps the oxygen from coming onboard. The more carbon monoxide there is traveling in the bloodstream, the less oxygen gets to body organs.

In nonsmokers breathing clean air, carbon monoxide takes over less than one in every one hundred oxygen-carrying spots. In smokers, the amount of carbon monoxide constantly rises, often two to fifteen times higher than in nonsmokers. In heavy smokers, body organs must do without 15 percent of their normal oxygen supply.

The heart and the brain are most sensitive to oxygen deprivation. Carbon monoxide makes the heart work harder to accomplish less. With chronic carbon monoxide exposure, the body tries to make up for the lack of oxygen by creating more hemoglobin. This makes the blood thicker and increases its tendency to form blood clots. In people who already have heart disease, even relatively low levels of carbon monoxide can result in angina, the chest pain that occurs when the heart muscle is not getting enough oxygen. In some patients, carbon monoxide exposure leads to heart attack, irregular heartbeat, or even sudden death.

Carbon monoxide impairs vision, judgment, and hearing. At the levels present in heavy smokers, changes in brain-wave patterns and poorer scores on mental tests have been documented. By reducing the oxygen getting to leg muscles, carbon monoxide makes walking and other exercises more difficult. Carbon monoxide is especially dangerous during pregnancy, when hemoglobin must supply oxygen for the developing fetus.

Other Toxic Gases
Among the ingredients in tobacco smoke are a variety of gases that would carry strong "do not take internally" labels if you bought them individually. Cigarette smoke includes ammonia, formaldehyde (used in embalming fluid), cyanide (used in gas chamber executions), and acetone (used in fingernail polish remover). Breathing in these gases produces irritation, coughing, and a narrowing of the bronchial tubes.

I'D RATHER SWITCH THAN QUIT

In an attempt to protect your health without giving up smoking, you might be tempted to opt for alternative products that sound safer. Unfortunately, the idea of safe tobacco is largely an illusion.

The Light Smoke
As more and more people have become aware of the dangers of smoking, tobacco companies have heavily promoted cigarettes with less tar

and nicotine. Believing that these so-called low-yield cigarettes are safer, many people have tried to switch rather than quit. However, the health advantages are largely illusory. Low-tar, low-nicotine cigarettes produce just as much carbon monoxide as regular cigarettes. They also result in the same risk of heart attack.

Moreover, the levels of tar and nicotine that actually enter your body are often far higher than the amount touted on cigarette packages. Machines calculate the measurements for the labels. The Centers for Disease Control and Prevention (CDC) warns that a cigarette listed as containing one to five milligrams of tar can become a fifteen-to-twenty-milligram tar cigarette. That occurs if the smoker inhales more deeply or more often than the average smoker or holds the cigarette in a way that closes the ventilating holes on the filter.

In addition to the known tobacco toxins they bring with them, low-yield cigarettes often contain extra chemical additives to try to make up for a lack of flavor. Manufacturers have not given the public or independent scientists complete lists of the additives they use, so it is possible that low-yield cigarettes may be even more harmful than regular cigarettes.

The Cool Smoke

If the cigarette maker added enough menthol to a cigarette, your throat can feel cool when you inhale. The smoking experience is less harsh, but the health effects are not. Menthol smokers are able to take longer and deeper drags off cigarettes, so they get even more of the damaging components of smoke than do nonmenthol smokers.

The Noncigarette Smoke

As a group, pipe and cigar smokers have shown a less striking increase in lung cancer and other tobacco-related illnesses than have cigarette smokers. This may be because pipe and cigar smokers smoke less and are less likely to inhale than cigarette smokers. However, pipe and cigar smokers who used to be cigarette smokers smoke more tobacco and are more likely to inhale the smoke deep into their lungs than those who did not previously smoke cigarettes.

Pipe and cigar smokers still have an increased risk of mouth cancer and can still be exposed to dangerous levels of tobacco smoke. If they inhale consistently, they may suffer adverse health effects comparable to those of cigarette smokers.

The Smokeless Smoke

Unlike the consumption of cigarettes, which has been decreasing in recent decades, the consumption of smokeless tobacco (also known as spit tobacco) almost tripled during the 1970s and 1980s. Today, about five million adults use chewing tobacco or snuff. So do 1 in 5 male high school students.

Many of these people believe that snuff and chewing tobacco, because they release no smoke, can't create the same damage as cigarettes, pipes, and cigars. Unfortunately, that simply is not true. Smokeless tobacco contains nicotine that is absorbed into the bloodstream through the lining of the mouth. Dipping two cans of snuff weekly exposes you to as much nicotine as smoking thirty cigarettes a day.

Compared with a cigarette smoker, the average snuff user takes in more than ten times the amount of nitrosamines. These cancer-causing chemicals are also found in certain cured and fermented foods, such as bacon and beer. The amount in smokeless tobacco is by far the highest, however. In some brands, the nitrosamine level is as much as twenty thousand times higher than the legal limit permitted in foods.

A trail of cancer follows the path that tobacco juices take in the body. First, they bathe the mouth and gums. When you swallow the juice, it exposes your throat and digestive tract to all its carcinogens. Snuff has been linked to cancers of the mouth, throat, voice box (larynx), and esophagus.

ANATOMY OF A SMOKER

From head to toe, smoking changes the way the body looks, functions, and ages.

Face

Because vessels are constricted, your skin is colder and gets less oxygen from your blood. After you have smoked for years, your skin will become dry, discolored, wrinkled, and leathery in texture.

In England, patients can be medically diagnosed with "smoker's face." These people have deep crow's-feet wrinkles around their eyes, excess wrinkling around their mouths, sunken cheeks, and grayish skin tones.

Brain

Nicotine causes immediate changes in brain chemistry and is addictive. Over the years, oxygen deprivation from smoking results in brain-wave changes and poorer scores on mental tests.

If you smoke, you're two to four times as likely as nonsmokers to have a stroke caused by an obstructed artery into the brain or by bleeding from a blood vessel on the brain's surface.

Mouth

The inside of your mouth is directly irritated by, and is exposed to carcinogens in, smoke and smokeless tobacco. Most cancers in the mouth are smoking related. If you smoke, you're at increased risk of gum disease and thus more likely to lose teeth. Also, your ability to taste is impaired.

Eyes and Ears

Tobacco may impair night vision and peripheral vision. If you're a heavy smoker, the levels of carbon monoxide you're exposed to can cause hearing problems. Children exposed to tobacco smoke develop more ear infections.

Throat

You may get hoarse, and your colds tend to last longer. Smoking causes cell damage, local cancers, and invasive cancers of the voice box and the throat (pharynx).

Bronchial Tubes

If you smoke, less air gets through the branching airways that connect your windpipe (trachea) with your lungs. Smoke narrows the passages, and you can't clear mucus effectively because smoke paralyzes *cilia,* tiny hairs that should move it along. You may develop chronic bronchitis.

Lungs

Smoking reduces lung capacity and damages the lungs' self-cleaning ability. Particles in tobacco smoke pile up in the lungs. Lungs lose their elasticity, and *emphysema* may result. Smoking causes 87 percent of all lung cancers.

Heart

Each puff of nicotine temporarily increases your heart rate and blood pressure. Carbon monoxide increases angina. Smoking encourages platelet clumping or stickiness in the blood vessels feeding your heart, a condition conducive to thrombosis or a blood clot. As a result, hardening of the coronary arteries is more common and more severe in smokers. If you smoke, you're more prone to develop an irregular heartbeat. That, in turn, makes a heart attack much more complicated and life-threatening.

Breasts

Nicotine gets into breast milk. You produce less breast milk.

Esophagus

Smoking causes three out of four cancers of the esophagus.

Arms and Hands

Diminished oxygen supply reduces the strength of your arm muscles. Smoking constricts the arteries that deliver blood to your arms. Your hands may be abnormally cool.

Stomach

More stomach acid is produced. Ulcers form more often, do not heal as well, and are more likely to recur.

Intestines and Lower Digestive Tract

More duodenal ulcers and more anal cancers occur. Food passes through your digestive tract more quickly, resulting in poorer nutrition and more diarrhea.

Urinary System

Smoking doubles your risk of bladder cancer and may increase your chance of kidney cancer.

Female Reproductive Organs

Toxic components of smoke are present inside the ovaries and in secretions of the cervix. The chance of cervical cancer increases, estrogen production is altered, and menopause occurs a year or two earlier if you smoke. Infertility is more common. Your chance of a tubal pregnancy, miscarriage, or stillbirth is greater. Furthermore, smoking can cause babies to be born too soon and too small.

Male Reproductive Organs

If you're a man who smokes, you may have lower sperm counts and more difficulty having an erection. Smoking can increase your risk of cancer of the penis.

Legs and Feet

Leg muscles get less oxygen and have reduced strength if you smoke. More leg pain and weakness from impaired circulation, a condition known as *intermittent claudication,* occur. When vessels are diseased, you're more likely to need amputation.

Bones

Bones may become less dense, increasing the risk of osteoporosis and bone fracture later in life.

Close-up on Heart Disease

"I was talking to a doctor about cholesterol and my heart. She pointed out that I was asking the wrong questions if I was focused on pizza and cardiovascular disease while I was still smoking."

Smoking is one of the four risk factors of heart attack that you can control, along with high blood cholesterol, high blood pressure, and physical inactivity.

Smoking even one cigarette a day raises your risk of heart disease. Smoking a pack a day more than doubles your risk of heart attack; it triples if you smoke two or more packs. If you do suffer a heart attack, your chance of survival is much less if you are a smoker.

Tobacco smoke damages the inside of blood vessels and encourages arteries to clog. Smoking makes the heart work harder to accomplish less—less oxygen-rich blood circulates, even though blood pressure goes up temporarily and the heart beats more often. The heart muscle itself is starved of oxygen.

Combined with other heart disease risk factors, the effect snowballs. If you have high cholesterol or diabetes, you are at risk; smoking makes your risk much higher. Women who take birth control pills and also smoke cigarettes increase their risk of heart attack many times over.

Because both substances constrict arteries, people who combine tobacco smoking with cocaine use greatly heighten their risk of chest pain or heart attack.

"I smoked for two-thirds of my life, until I was forced to stop because of a heart condition."

Is it ever too late to stop? Never.

The earlier you stop smoking, the better it is for your heart. But there are still documented benefits to giving up smoking after many years—and even after the onset of heart disease.

In one study of more than four thousand smokers with proven heart disease, those who quit smoking were 32 percent more likely to be alive in five years than those who kept smoking.

Even if you have already suffered a heart attack, giving up smoking can cut your risk of sudden death or a second attack as much as 50 percent.

If you have *peripheral vascular disease* (a narrowing of the vessels that carry blood to the hands and feet), stopping smoking can make the disease less severe. If you keep smoking, the vessels are more likely to become totally blocked. That can invite infection or tissue death in the unnourished areas.

If you are a heart disease patient and give up smoking, the treatments will work better. If you have *angioplasty*, stopping smoking will make your newly dilated artery less likely to become constricted again. Bypass grafts will be less likely to close up. Some medicines for high blood pressure, *arrhythmias* (abnormal rhythm of the heart), and angina will be more effective.

CLOSE-UP ON THE CANCER CONNECTION

"One of my best friends, probably the heaviest smoker I've ever met, was diagnosed with cancer. The whole 'smoking equals cancer' equation was smack in my face. At that point, smoking totally lost its appeal, but I still had the physical addiction."

Smoking is the major cause of cancer death in the United States.

In 87 of each 100 cases, smoking is the cause of lung cancer, the leading cancer killer. If you are a smoker, you may be more than twenty times more likely to die of lung cancer than if you are a nonsmoker. Because of the increased use of cigarettes among women, since 1987 more women have died of lung cancer than of breast cancer.

Solid evidence shows that smoking can cause cancer of the mouth, throat, voice box, esophagus, and bladder. Smoking also increases your risk of cancer in the cervix, penis, kidneys, and pancreas.

By itself, tobacco smoke contains dozens of carcinogenic chemicals. If you are also exposed to other carcinogens, smoking makes the risk many times worse. For example, a recent Swedish study indicated that exposure to high levels of *radon* is five times as dangerous in smokers. If you're exposed to asbestos, a lung-irritating material once widely used as insulation and for fireproofing, you are far more likely to develop lung cancer if you smoke.

Can the risk of cancer be reversed? Yes, but it is a process that occurs gradually over many years after you stop smoking. After five years without smoking, the extra risk you took on while smoking has been cut in half. After ten years, your risk of cancer approaches what it would have been had you never smoked.

Even if you have cancer, you can benefit by stopping smoking. One study indicates that patients with life-threatening small-cell lung cancer live longer if they stop smoking. If you require chemotherapy, your risk of infection will be lower and you will have less mouth and throat discomfort during treatment if you stop smoking.

LIFE AND DEATH CIGARETTE ROULETTE

When you envision your future, say fifteen or twenty years from now, what do you see? Do you anticipate still being active? Still in good health? Still alive?

No one can guarantee life or health in anyone's future. At age forty, you have a 1-in-20 chance you will die in the next seventeen years; at fifty, the chance creeps above 1 in 10. However, if you're a smoker, the likelihood doubles in either case If you're sixty-five and a nonsmoker, the odds are still slightly in your favor that you can look forward to being alive in seventeen years. But if you're a smoker, it's safer to bet you'll be dead—a 2-out-of-3 chance.

ANATOMY OF A FORMER SMOKER

"After a hiking accident, I was housebound and totally sedentary. It seemed like the worst possible time to give up cigarettes. Then, when knee surgery was scheduled, my doctor said the surgery and the healing process

would go much faster if I stopped smoking. The admonitions were strong enough to get me to stop."

Does it seem impossible that you heal better when you don't smoke? It isn't. Within eight hours after your last cigarette, the amount of oxygen your blood carries will have returned to normal. From two weeks to three months after you quit, your circulation will have improved, so healing from any surgery or injury will be faster. Lung function will have increased by almost one-third, so you'll have less chance of a complication during anesthesia.

When you need motivation to stop smoking or stay smoke-free, check the following box. It shows all the visible and invisible ways your body will thank you.

WHAT HAPPENS AFTER YOUR LAST SMOKE

20 minutes
- Your blood pressure returns to its usual level.
- Your pulse rate slows to normal.
- Your circulation has improved enough that your hands and feet warm to a normal temperature.

4 hours
- Half the carbon monoxide from your last cigarette has left your bloodstream.

8 hours
- The carbon monoxide from your last cigarette is now gone from your bloodstream.
- Your blood now carries a normal amount of oxygen.

24 hours
- Your chance of a heart attack is lower.

48 hours
- Damaged nerve endings start to regrow.
- Your senses of smell and taste have improved.

2 weeks to 3 months
- Your circulation is better.
- Walking is easier.
- Lung function increases up to 30 percent.

1 to 9 months
- You cough less.
- Your sinuses are clearer.
- You have more energy.
- You don't become short of breath as easily.
- The cilia regrow in your lungs, so you will have less phlegm and less infection.

1 year
- Your heart attack risk has fallen to the halfway mark between that of a current smoker and that of someone who never smoked.

5 years
- If you used to smoke a pack a day, you have now cut your risk of dying of lung cancer in half.
- Your risk of heart attack and stroke is approaching that of a non-smoker.
- You have cut your risk of mouth, throat, and esophageal cancer by half.

10 years
- Your chance of dying of lung cancer is almost as low as a non-smoker's.
- Your risk of mouth, throat, esophageal, bladder, kidney, and pancreatic cancer continues to fall.

10 to 15 years
- Your risk of dying from any cause is almost the same as that of someone who never smoked.

Beyond Personal Health:
Other Reasons People Quit

If you're reading this book, you are probably committed to protecting your health and reducing your risk of heart disease or cancer. Nevertheless, you may find a needed boost in motivation elsewhere—in love, money, politics, or your concern for the health of others.

THE NONSMOKING INVESTMENT PLAN

"When I quit, I kept telling myself I'm going to be saving more than $300 a year—and it would be a lot more now. I didn't reward myself by buying anything special, but thinking about the money I'd save was one of the strategies I used to reinforce my intention to quit."

Smoking is getting more expensive all the time. In the 1950s a quarter could buy a pack of cigarettes. Now prices routinely top $2. Cigarette companies are racking up record profits in spite of the customers they have lost because the smokers quit or died.

To a small extent, the price hike results from taxes levied to offset some of the nation's financial burden in paying for smoking-related illness. *A recent estimate indicates that for every pack of cigarettes smoked, $2.17 is paid for health care.* However, taxes levied on cigarettes at the federal and state levels combined pay only a small fraction of the cost of smokers' medical care that is borne by the government. Public health experts approve of the taxes because the money is used in antismoking educational efforts and because high prices discourage money-conscious children and teens from taking up the habit.

If you're feeling money conscious, figure out what you'd save if you quit smoking for a year. If you smoke a pack and a half a day and pay $2 a pack, you'd save well over $1,000. That is enough for a health club membership, holiday bills, an IRA contribution, or maybe a well-deserved vacation.

BREATHING FOR TWO

"If I hadn't gotten pregnant, I'd still be smoking. I knew smoking was really bad, so I willed myself to think my morning sickness made me too sick to want a cigarette."

Almost 17 percent of all pregnant women smoke throughout pregnancy.

Of all the changes you can make to boost the chance that your baby will be born healthy, stopping smoking is one of the most important.

Each time a pregnant woman puffs on a cigarette, the blood supply to her fetus is restricted, so less oxygen and nutrition are delivered. Even so, the poisons nicotine, carbon monoxide, and cyanide manage to pass through the placenta and reach the fetus.

Smoking during pregnancy doubles the risk that the smoker's baby will be born early and will weigh less than five and one-half pounds. Babies whose growth is stunted by tobacco are not just short on baby fat—their brains and other vital organs are smaller. Prone to breathing problems, low blood sugar, jaundice, and anemia, low-birthweight newborns are forty times as likely as larger babies to die in the first month. Even the full-size infants of smoking mothers are more likely to die of respiratory problems or sudden infant death syndrome (SIDS) than the infants of nonsmokers.

After a baby leaves infancy, damage from prenatal exposure to tobacco smoke can still be fatal. While the fetus is in the womb, tobacco components can permanently damage its DNA. That may be why children are 50 percent more likely to develop cancer, particularly leukemia or lymphoma, if their mothers smoked ten or more cigarettes a day during pregnancy.

If babies are in your plans, the earlier you stop smoking the better. Some of the reasons are listed below.

- Stop before you try to become pregnant and lower the chance that you'll have trouble conceiving.
- Stop before you become pregnant and you reduce the chance that a pregnancy will be lost because the egg has implanted in the fallopian tubes or elsewhere outside the uterus.
- Stop by the third month of pregnancy and your baby has a better chance of being normal in size.
- Stop by the thirtieth week and your baby will be bigger than if you continued smoking.
- Stop at least forty-eight hours before delivery and your baby will have more oxygen available during the stress of labor.

Studies show that the risk of stillbirth or low birthweight increases as women smoke more heavily. Nevertheless, to protect against most smoking-related complications, it is important to stop, not just to cut back.

NOT SMOKING AS A POLITICAL ACT

"I stopped smoking because it makes me mad that tobacco companies target inner-city kids and try to hook them into smoking."

Each day, just to replace the customers who have quit smoking or died, tobacco companies must lure 5,000 new people into smoking.

To entice them, these companies spend more than $6 million a day. More and more, their campaigns target the people most likely to become addicted to tobacco. The companies also reportedly think these people will be the least likely to quit smoking.

When tobacco companies introduce slim, perfumed cigarettes and sponsor sports and artistic events that appeal to women, they're not weeping over the more than 145,000 women who die each year from smoking-related diseases. These companies know that each day 2,000 young women try their first cigarette and that women are smoking more heavily. They surely also know that, once hooked, women smokers are more likely to keep smoking. Compared with men, a higher proportion of women smokers want to quit, but a smaller proportion succeed.

When tobacco companies put up billboards, chances are 5-to-1 that they aren't in predominantly white areas. The companies don't seem to flinch when 50,000 African-Americans die of smoking-related causes each year. Among adults who ever smoked, 62 percent of African-Americans and 65 percent of Native Americans have held onto the habit, compared with 48 percent of white Americans. In addition, recent research shows that, for unknown reasons, lung cancer death rates among African-American men who smoke are higher than rates for white men who smoke.

Former District of Columbia Health Commissioner Reed Tuckson bluntly laid out his opinion about the political ramifications in an editorial in the *Journal of the National Medical Association.* "The tobacco industry is subjugating people of color through disease," he stated. "You cannot educate people if you get sick. You cannot keep your job if you are ill. You do not function, you do not challenge, you do not confront the status quo if you are ill."

Tobacco companies also like young people with little education. Government statistics indicate that half of all smokers start the habit before age fourteen, with one in four beginning while still in elementary school. Only 10 percent of smokers start after they turn twenty-one.

Among smokers alive today, almost two-thirds of college graduates have been able to quit, but most high-school dropouts are still smoking. Although most states set eighteen as the legal age to buy tobacco products, advertising campaigns still entice children. Each day, cartoons, coupons, and other youth-oriented campaigns help convince 3,000 children to light their first cigarette. Many of them will be customers for years. And many of them will develop significant lung damage while they are still in their teens.

IS YOUR SMOKE KILLING SOMEONE ELSE?

"I thought I didn't have the willpower to quit. What finally made me? It was like when a combination of planets and stars comes together. My office announced they would soon ban smoking, and at the same time I became

involved in an intense new relationship with someone whose opinions and feelings I really cared about. She didn't nag or push, but she said she was worried about the consequences of my smoking. I thought, 'The time has come.' "

If you are smoking while living or working with a nonsmoker, you are endangering that person's life.

Involuntary smokers are nonsmokers who breathe the smoke wafting from your cigarette and the smoke you exhale. This sidestream smoke is diluted in large volumes of air. Therefore, nonsmokers are exposed to less smoke than are smokers. Nevertheless, involuntary smokers still get most of the cancer-causing components in the smoke.

The spouses of pack-a-day smokers are twice as likely to develop lung cancer as nonsmokers with spouses who don't smoke. The spouses of heavy smokers have three times the risk.

If you smoke near a nonsmoker at work or in a car, you expose that person to carbon monoxide levels as much as ten times higher than federal safety guidelines allow. Four hours after the nonsmoker says good-bye, half of the carbon monoxide will still be in his or her bloodstream. That carbon monoxide came from your cigarette.

All in all, involuntary smoking results in an estimated 53,000 deaths each year in the United States. Most are from heart disease. Lung cancer claims about 4,000.

"One of the best things about stopping was how happy it made my little niece and nephew."

If you think that kids don't notice the smoke, think again. Long before they go to school, children are forming clear ideas about smoking. And most of their perceptions depend on the adults they look up to. This may be why children of parents who smoke are more likely to become smokers than are children of nonsmokers.

Children also depend on adults for the very air they breathe. If a parent, baby-sitter, or day-care teacher smokes around them, their young lives will be affected. Because young children breathe faster, on a pound-for-pound basis they take in more than twice the air pollutants as adults do.

Children exposed to smoke in the home cough more, and their lungs don't work as well. They have more colds, asthma, bronchitis, pneumonia, and ear infections. For example, the Environmental Protection Agency estimates that up to 300,000 infants a year develop smoke-induced bronchitis or pneumonia. Of these, about 15,000 have to be hospitalized.

"I started dating a nonsmoker, and I know he found my smoking distasteful. Also, I didn't like the idea that I smoked. I wanted to be physically fit and clean. Smoking, to me, doesn't represent those things."

Sometimes the commitment to a relationship or the exhilaration of a new romance can be a powerful incentive to stop smoking.

If you stop smoking, you may look better. You, your home, and your clothes will smell fresher. Your teeth will be cleaner. Your breath will be more pleasant. Your senses of taste and smell will improve. And if your special person asks what you're thinking or why you have that far-away look in your eyes, the answer won't be that you need to go find a cigarette!

Getting Started Stopping

As you look forward to the challenge of giving up smoking, take some time to review your personal smoking saga. A clear-eyed look back will help you get ready. It should also maximize the chance that your next attempt will be the last time you have to go through the demanding process of quitting. This time you can finally give yourself a smoke-free future.

First, really observe the details of your life as a smoker.

Some aspects of your smoking patterns can give you a good idea of whether you have a strong addiction to nicotine.

- Do you smoke immediately after you wake up?
- Is your first cigarette of the day the most satisfying?
- Is it hard for you to go more than a few hours without smoking?
- Do you smoke even when you are sick in bed?

If your answer is "yes" to most of these questions, you may need help in easing your withdrawal from nicotine when you quit smoking.

Next, think about all the things you like about smoking. Do you appreciate the whole ritual—lighting and holding the cigarette, watching the smoke drift into the air? Do you rely on cigarettes as an energy booster? Something to put in your mouth besides dessert? A way to soothe anger or tension? A treat after a hard day?

You will be better prepared to stop smoking if you have other rewards, activities, or stress-reducing methods ready for all the times when it will seem natural to reach for a cigarette. You are likely to be surprised at how many healthful choices you have.

Next, think back to times you have tried to quit smoking. Think about the difficulties you had. What strategies could you use to deal with those problems without cigarettes? You will have a head start on quitting this time if you know the likely obstacles ahead and plan how to cope with them.

What Happens When I Quit

1. Which of these symptoms did you have when you tried to quit smoking before?

___ Anxiety	___ Depression	___ Disorientation
___ Sleep difficulty	___ Mood swings	___ Hostility
___ Lethargy	___ Nervousness	___ Lightheadedness
___ Irritability	___ Headaches	___ Lack of concentration
___ Frustration	___ Shakiness	___ Sense of loss
___ Anger	___ Impatience	___ Increased appetite
___ Dizziness	___ Cravings	___ Constipation

2. How many *short-term* quits (no cigarettes for less than four weeks) have you made in the past five years? ___

For your last short-term quit, how did you go about quitting? (Check all that apply.)

___ Went cold turkey	___ Used hypnosis
___ Tapered off	___ Used acupuncture
___ Tried on my own	___ Got individual counseling
___ Used book or tapes on my own	___ Used nicotine gum
___ Tried with a friend	___ Used nicotine patch
___ Attended a group stop-smoking program	

What were the most difficult situations or most disturbing symptoms?

What seemed to help you during the time you were not smoking?

What did you try that seemed not to help?

Where were you when you started smoking again?

    ___ At work
    ___ At home
    ___ At a bar
    ___ At a restaurant
    ___ At a friend's/relative's home
    ___ Other _____

Who were you with?

    ___ Alone
    ___ Spouse/family
    ___ Roommates
    ___ Co-workers
    ___ Friends
    ___ Other _____

How were you feeling right before you smoked?

    ___ Angry
    ___ Tense
    ___ Bored
    ___ Celebratory
    ___ Happy
    ___ Relaxed
    ___ Stressed
    ___ Confident
    ___ Lonely
    ___ Other _____

What were you doing?

    ___ Drinking
    ___ Finishing a meal
    ___ Working
    ___ Socializing
    ___ Other _____

3. How many *longer-term* quits (no cigarettes for more than four weeks) have you had in the past five years? ___

For your last longer-term quit, how did you go about quitting? (Check all that apply.)

___ Went cold turkey	___ Used hypnosis
___ Tapered off	___ Used acupuncture
___ Tried on my own	___ Got individual counseling
___ Used book or tapes on my own	___ Used nicotine gum
___ Tried with a friend	___ Used nicotine patch
___ Attended a group stop-smoking program	

What were the most difficult situations or most disturbing symptoms?

What seemed to help you during the time you were not smoking?

What did you try that seemed not to help?

Where were you when you started smoking again?

     ___ At work

     ___ At home

     ___ At a bar

     ___ At a restaurant

     ___ At a friend's/relative's home

     ___ Other _____

Who were you with?

     ___ Alone

     ___ Spouse/family

     ___ Roommates

     ___ Co-workers

     ___ Friends

     ___ Other _____

How were you feeling right before you smoked?

     ___ Angry

     ___ Tense

     ___ Bored

     ___ Celebratory

     ___ Happy

     ___ Relaxed

     ___ Stressed

     ___ Confident

     ___ Lonely

     ___ Other _____

What were you doing?
___ Drinking
___ Finishing a meal
___ Working
___ Socializing
___ Other _____

The more checks you made in the first section, the more likely it is that physical dependency on nicotine will make your first few days without cigarettes particularly challenging. Nicotine dependence is often the reason for relapse when smokers try to quit. The problem is not weakness of character; it is a documented medical phenomenon called *nicotine withdrawal syndrome.* In a person addicted to nicotine, the symptoms of nicotine withdrawal start almost immediately after the last cigarette and usually ease after three or four days (for common symptoms, see page 58). People who are physically dependent on nicotine may benefit from strategies for quitting that include the use of nicotine replacement therapy (see pages 48 to 50). It may help if you understand that the discomfort is predictable and temporary. Many former smokers have used prescription aids to taper off nicotine. Other smokers get enough relief from nonmedical support and nonmedical strategies.

As you read about the options for quitting and the advice of former smokers, keep in mind what's helped you in the past. Also note what people and places seem likely to tax your resolve.

"It's like a war. You have to attack on as many fronts as you can."

If you expect no difficulties in quitting this time, that's great. Do, however, give yourself a chance to think about past problems and how you dealt with them. Be aware that no particular technique is likely to provide the magic solution to your past quitting problems. If you think one special strategy will work, ask yourself why or discuss it with a professional. To give yourself the best chance at success, former smokers and professionals advise that you should anticipate possible problems and have a plan ready to deal with them. If quitting is easy this time, great. If not, you won't be taken by surprise.

The American Cancer Society and the American Heart Association want you to stop smoking. Period. Most people who have quit smoking did it cold turkey, quitting all at once on their own. But many types of help are available, and many former smokers find that medical and emotional support can mean the difference between relapsing and becoming a nonsmoker permanently. The ACS and the AHA don't ascribe to any one approach. Nor do they try to discourage smokers from looking into any strategies or aids they think will work. However, the two organizations do have a great deal of experience in helping people quit smoking. Your local ACS chapter or AHA affiliate is a good source of advice about the range of options available in your area (see pages 301–304).

The discussion below describes some types of support.

Help from Your Physician

ADVICE AND REFERRALS

Your doctor should ask whether you smoke and should advise you to stop if you do. There is an important gap in your health care if that doesn't happen.

After your checkup, your doctor can help assess your nicotine dependency and suggest whether prescription nicotine replacement therapy would help you quit smoking.

Almost all doctors who used to smoke have quit. Some doctors have a lot of experience helping patients who smoke. These professionals may be able to translate your answers to the "What Happens When I Quit?" questionnaire into valuable advice for your next attempt. But your doctor may not be your best source of advice about *how* to quit or where to get help. If this is not an area of his or her expertise, ask for a referral.

NICOTINE REPLACEMENT THERAPY

To help people withdraw from nicotine gradually while they stop smoking altogether, many doctors and dentists prescribe nicotine replacement therapy. When scientists compiled the experiences of 18,000 smokers who participated in many different studies of this approach, they found that nicotine replacement therapy significantly boosted the chance that a smoker would quit. This happened when the therapy was the cornerstone of a person's plan to quit and when it was used with stop-smoking groups or other types of support.

Nicotine replacement therapy is prescribed in two forms: with a patch or chewing gum.

Nicotine Patches

"I consider the nicotine patch one of the greatest gifts technology has brought in my lifetime. For me, it made all the difference in the world. While it takes the edge off the nicotine addiction, you can learn to deal with all the other aspects of quitting smoking."

—Smoker who used patch and stop-smoking group to quit

In 1991 the Food and Drug Administration approved a new product, the nicotine patch, to help ease the symptoms of nicotine withdrawal during the first few weeks a person is giving up smoking. A doctor or dentist must prescribe the patch.

Placed on the skin, the nicotine patch delivers a steady and predictable amount of nicotine—with none of the tar or dangerous gases that are found in tobacco smoke. You change your patch each day. Patches come in various doses. If you start with the highest dose, after several weeks your doctor or dentist will prescribe a lower dose. Eventually, usually in less than twelve weeks, you'll no longer need to use one. The patches cost about $350 for a twelve-week supply. That's roughly equivalent to what a two-pack-a-day smoker would spend during the same period if cigarettes cost $2 a pack.

Remember that the patch can help only with physical dependency on smoking. You will still need to address other aspects of your smoking. Even if you are strongly addicted to nicotine, it's likely that you smoke many of your daily cigarettes just out of habit. Some doctors like to have heavy smokers cut back first, then use the patch to quit smoking entirely.

Nicotine patches are strong medicine and can cause side effects. Most critical: *You cannot use the patch and smoke.* If you do, levels of nicotine in your bloodstream can become higher than they ever were with smoking alone. The combination may cause heart problems or a nicotine overdose. Pharmaceutical companies direct some people, including pregnant women and most people with unstable heart conditions, not to use the patch.

Some people experience itching, a rash, or a burning feeling where the patch is applied. A few people have to stop using it because of these allergic reactions. While using the patch, some people report having trouble sleeping. Those people can take off the patch at night. Others report headaches, dizziness, upset stomach, diarrhea, weakness, blurred vision, or vivid dreams or other sleep disturbances.

If you have a slight build or smoke less than half a pack per day, your physician may want to start with a lower-dose patch.

Nicotine Gum

"In taste, I'd rate nicotine gum like slippery elm gum from my childhood. Not really awful, but not pleasant either. It helped me not miss nicotine, and it was incompatible with smoking. Whenever I tried a cigarette, it didn't taste as good."

—Smoker who quit solo by using gum

Prescription chewing gum containing nicotine can ease withdrawal symptoms when you quit smoking. You must chew the gum slowly, pausing often and holding it between your teeth and cheek, for the nicotine to be absorbed. Many physicians prefer to prescribe the patch because it provides a more predictable, constant dose of nicotine.

You may prefer the gum because it keeps your mouth busy and lets you control your nicotine stimulation. On the other hand, you might dislike its dry texture and lack of sweetness.

Your physician may suggest that you chew a set number of pieces of gum each day, tapering down over several weeks. You will need to plan when you may need the gum, since it takes about twenty minutes to get the peak effect. The mistake most people make is not using enough gum when they begin and not using the gum to prevent urges. They may start to feel the effects of nicotine withdrawal and give up, thinking the gum isn't working properly. Medical experts emphasize that nicotine gum should be used *only* to help you quit smoking altogether. Some people have fallen into the trap of using nicotine gum at work or in social settings where smoking is taboo—only to continue lighting up in private. Maintaining both a nicotine addiction and a smoking habit is fiendishly expensive as well as unhealthy.

Other Prescriptions

Instead of replacing nicotine, some doctors prescribe antidepressants or other medications to help ease the symptoms of withdrawal. Talk to your doctor about whether these might be right for you.

Companions in Examining and Breaking the Smoking Habit

Do-It-Yourself Programs

"I just made an appointment with myself to quit."

—Smoker who quit cold turkey after medical warning

"My partner and I stopped simultaneously. In many ways it was great support, but we were both pretty edgy. I remember one scene driving in the fog, trying to read a map. We were both yelling, and the lack of cigarettes intensified the whole experience of being lost. It's a situation where, in the past, both of us would have lit up."

—Smokers who stopped as a couple, one cold turkey, one by tapering off

Many smokers quit on their own or with a friend. Either way, a variety of aids can help you put your commitment into action.

Most bookstores sell guides to stopping smoking. Contact your local American Cancer Society, American Heart Association, or American Lung Association to find out about self-help booklets, quit kits, and video- and audiotape programs.

By following the exercises and hints they contain, you can better understand your own smoking pattern, set a quit date, and cope with the challenges of making a major change in your lifestyle.

"The urge and desire to smoke never left enough to give me any peace of mind. It's rather embarrassing to be so obsessed with something like that. I could face anything in the world as long as I had a cigarette."

—Smoker who got individual counseling after trying alone

If you run into difficulties or have trouble on your own, don't be embarrassed to ask for help. The ultimate goal is to become a non-smoker and begin to enjoy a healthful new lifestyle, not to show you can tough it out alone.

Group Programs

"In other areas of my life I can be very willful and disciplined. With smoking, I need the classes and the peer pressure."

—Smoker who joined a group after trying alone

Leaders and other participants in group programs can provide you with a combination of information, practical advice, and emotional support. Your area may offer several to choose from—some sponsored by religious organizations, some run as profit-making businesses, and some set up by health organizations. Many are led by trained facilitators who are former smokers.

Programs usually meet once or twice a week for a total of five to ten sessions. Prices vary widely; so do the approaches. Some programs emphasize the negative aspects of smoking, using exercises such as placing all your cigarette butts in a jar of water so you can think about their nasty look and smell. Others focus on substituting healthful behaviors such as deep-breathing techniques and exercise in place of cigarettes. Such skills also will be valuable in other areas of your life.

In general, former smokers report that they appreciate programs that treat them like adults. Those using proven behavioral strategies without preaching or spending time on unnecessary homework assignments or games are popular.

Most of the programs include the elements described below.

♦ They help you become more conscious of your current smoking behavior. You may be asked to give every cigarette your full attention—not reading, not drinking coffee, and not working while you smoke. The leader may suggest that you wrap your cigarette pack so it takes more time and thought to remove a cigarette. You may be told to keep a log for a while of every cigarette you smoke, along with notes on the situation, your mood, and the smoking experience.
♦ They encourage you to set a quit date and plan whether you will quit cold turkey or taper off.
♦ They use a number of ways to help you get through nicotine cravings, learn to cope with tension and stress as a nonsmoker, and keep your hands and mouth busy without cigarettes. Some programs shake up your usual routine. They might suggest specific menus and physical activities to help unlink the daily activities you associate with smoking.
♦ They provide emotional support. At each session, you and the other participants give progress reports and talk about any difficulties that came up. You may be paired with a buddy to talk to between sessions.

"Cigarette smokers are like junkies. We twist things around to get off the hook. But my group leader was nobody's fool. She couldn't be conned, and the group members wouldn't let anyone avoid confronting the problem."

—Smoker who used group and nicotine patch

Individual Counseling

"Talking to someone one-on-one, along with using the patch, was really helpful to me. The nicotine urge pulls you to the cigarette so hard. But after that, trying to quit is still very psychological. Every time you get the least bit tense you want a cigarette."

—Smoker who used patch and individual counseling

Groups aren't for everybody. You may want to meet privately with a trusted counselor to discuss problems and emotions that arise as you stop smoking. You can probably get the most comprehensive help from a counselor who deals specifically with smoking issues, is trained in behavioral techniques, and understands the physical dependency of smoking.

"Smoking is like a smoke screen. When you don't have it, you are forced to look at yourself in the mirror. I talked to a therapist about things that were coming up around the loss of the cigarettes. When I think about quitting, I don't think about just giving up cigarettes or getting healthy. For me it really was a growth experience. It was a way to give up that smoke screen and ask, 'What is it about this emotion or this situation that makes me want to smoke?'"

—Smoker who used patch, individual counseling,
and group smoking cessation program

When you stop smoking, you are doing more than giving up an unhealthful habit. You may be saying good-bye to a companion that has helped you through many uncomfortable feelings and situations. You may find that stopping smoking gives you an excellent chance to examine bigger issues and patterns in your life. It also may help you feel and understand your emotions more clearly.

Live-in Programs

You may be one of those people who needs a complete change in environment, plus lots of professional support, to stop smoking. Some hospitals and clinics offer live-in programs that provide information, counseling, and support in a structured, nonsmoking environment. Participants usually are heavy smokers who are strongly addicted to nicotine.

Live-in programs last several days or more and can be quite costly. Participants are likely to need follow-up support to ease their way back into routine life. They also may need further help in coping with the issues that come up after the initial withdrawal period from cigarettes.

ONGOING AS-NEEDED SUPPORT

"People in your life quickly forget that you smoked for fifteen years and it's only been four months since you quit. They forget you need the encouragement. But the Stay Off Smoking group is always there, once a week, just so you can get support and talk about how you're doing."

Another choice is an unstructured support group. These groups meet regularly and are open to anyone who wants to join in just once or every week. One such organization is Smokers Anonymous. It uses the twelve-step approach that has helped many people stay off alcohol or drugs and face other destructive patterns in their thoughts and behavior. Local chapters of the American Cancer Society may offer support groups. Other groups may meet in your area.

At the meetings, you can listen, ask for specific advice, or vent your feelings to other people who know what it is like to get off and stay off cigarettes. You should be welcome at an ongoing support group no matter where you are in the process of quitting.

Changing the Way Your Body Reacts

ACUPUNCTURE

In traditional Chinese medicine, nerve endings at specific points just under the skin are believed to be connected to the function of various organs in the body. Acupuncture stimulates certain nerve endings in order to ease pain, treat some medical conditions, or counter addictions. Some health professionals believe it can help calm the urge to smoke, but others doubt its effectiveness.

During a treatment, slim acupuncture needles or staples are generally placed into the outer ear for about twenty minutes. The treatments cause little pain. Several sessions may be needed.

The Office of Alternative Medicine at the National Institutes of Health has funded several projects studying the value of acupuncture in treating a variety of medical problems. The Centers for Disease Control and Prevention has emphasized that acupuncture may have a psychological, rather than a physical, effect on stopping smoking.

Hypnosis

"I know I can stop cigarettes, but I have a much harder time controlling the need for oral gratification. I'm going to try hypnosis to help me not substitute food for cigarettes."

—Smoker planning a new attempt to quit

Many psychologists, psychiatrists, and social workers have had specialized training in hypnosis. They use relaxation techniques to help you enter a state that superficially resembles sleep. While hypnotized, you may be given suggestions that will stay in your subconscious mind even after you are fully awake. The suggestion may remind you of your reasons for wanting to quit, encourage you to relax and resist when the urge to smoke hits, or intensify your remorse if you do smoke. If hypnosis works for you—and not everyone can be hypnotized—these suggestions will linger in your mind after the session ends. They'll be there to help you avoid smoking in the future.

According to the CDC, your chance of quitting smoking after just one hypnosis session is fairly low. The chance may improve if you have several individual or group sessions. However, the CDC stresses that there is little evidence that hypnotic suggestion itself—above and beyond the effects of the counseling the therapist provides—helps people quit smoking.

Several sessions are usually needed for hypnosis to be effective.

Negative Conditioning

"My son's band was playing music in a smoky bar. I went to see him four nights in a row and smoked enough to make myself feel really sick. I never smoked again."

—Smoker who quit on her own

As anyone who has ever had food poisoning can testify, the link between a particular food and the nausea that followed can last a lifetime. Forever after, your stomach turns at the thought of the seafood delight or cream pie you used to love.

Conditioning methods try to help smokers quit by forging a visceral link between feeling ill and the thought of smoking. By inhaling every few seconds until you become ill or by suddenly doubling or tripling your intake, you may make yourself sick enough to stop smoking.

Negative conditioning alone doesn't work for most people who try to stop smoking permanently. Also, temporarily pushing your intake of tobacco smoke, even to reach a healthful goal, could have health risks. Talk to your doctor before trying this approach.

On the other hand, some people can create the negative smoking association effectively without smoking more.

"I got very relaxed and then imagined the most distasteful situation—to sit in a car with the windows rolled up and smoke a whole carton until my eyes and throat were burning and I felt trapped, like I wanted to break out of the car. I repeated this experience in my mind two or three times a day. On the fourth day, I woke up and realized that it was time for me to let go."

—Smoker who quit cold turkey

Timeline for Quitters

CHOOSING A PACE

Whether you are quitting on your own or in a stop-smoking program, you will usually be the one to decide whether to quit cold turkey or cut back gradually.

It's partly a matter of personality. Are you someone who likes to plunge headfirst into a swimming pool or enter it by the stairs, getting used to the chilly water in stages?

Each approach has its advantages. Cold turkey jump-starts the process and is the way most successful former smokers used. If you decide to use the nicotine patch, you *must* be prepared to quit smoking entirely the day you put it on.

"To me, it's more of a burden just to have three or four cigarettes a day than to have none at all."

Speed isn't the only upside to quitting cold turkey. Many people find it more difficult to cut back on cigarettes than to stop smoking. Tapering keeps you concentrated on smoking, counting the number of cigarettes or waiting until you can have the next one; cold turkey lets you shift your focus immediately to your smoke-free future.

You can gradually approach your quit day by tapering off, allowing yourself fewer cigarettes each day, or by postponing your first cigarette until later and later in the day. You may choose to make the cigarettes you value most the ones you give up last—increasing your awareness of when your vulnerable times may be in the early nonsmoking days. Or you may prefer to stick to a set schedule or use an alarm to know when it's time to smoke. Another way to start is to taper off by switching to a brand of cigarettes with less nicotine. If you're trying to quit using smokeless tobacco, remember that different brands contain very different amounts of nicotine. If you now dip the strongest brand, change to a milder chew a few days or weeks before your quit date.

"Quitting gradually gives you a time of saying farewell. You almost get a little romantic about it. And you understand the addiction better when you taper off."

Even if you plan to use prescription nicotine replacement therapy, some experts suggest that you first taper down to half your usual number of cigarettes. You may be able to do this by omitting the cigarettes you smoke out of habit but do not really need. Don't turn tapering into a delaying tactic, though. If you taper, make a specific plan for how it will lead to total cessation. Generally, it's helpful not to taper below ten cigarettes. That's because the last precious few often become very reinforcing and hard to let go. At ten, quit entirely.

"When I got down to six cigarettes a day, I thought a lot more about my smoking. How every cigarette seemed so important and then—poof—it's gone in a minute anyhow. In a lot of ways, it was easier once I stopped altogether."

The Early Days off Cigarettes

BODY ADJUSTMENTS

You may feel fine from the moment you stop smoking. However, it is more likely you'll feel some unfamiliar, sometimes uncomfortable, sensations in your body as it readjusts for life without smoking.

Even if you feel miserable at times, keep the following things in mind.

- The discomfort will not last forever. A nicotine urge is over in minutes; most withdrawal symptoms will disappear within two weeks.
- The symptoms are not hurting you. In fact, we know that most of them are signs that the body is returning to normal.

◆ You can do healthful things to ease the sensations (see "The Five *D*s" on pages 59–61).
◆ If you don't return to smoking, you won't ever have to go through this again.

WHAT'S SO GOOD ABOUT FEELING BAD?

Instead of tensing up when withdrawal symptoms emerge, try to relax and greet them as messengers of the very positive changes taking place in your body.

◆ *Tingling in your arms and legs.* When your foot falls asleep, you don't notice the lack of circulation as much as the temporary buzzing and tingling that occur when you finally shift your position and blood rushes back into the area. Something similar happens when you stop smoking: Tingling is the sensation of normal circulation returning to the oxygen-starved muscles in your arms and legs. Moving around and using your muscles may speed the process.
◆ *Lightheadedness.* When you smoked, your brain was deprived of oxygen. When the supply increases, you may experience a euphoric feeling or a sensation of dizziness until your brain adjusts. Such symptoms will last only a day or two. During that time, get up slowly from sitting or lying down.
◆ *Coughing.* Since tobacco smoke temporarily paralyzes them, the tiny hairs that should cleanse your respiratory tract used to work only when you slept (hence, your morning cough as a smoker). Now they are on the job full-time and for a while will be working overtime, sweeping debris from your system. Drink plenty of water and use cough drops as needed to soothe your throat.
◆ *Constipation or stomach pain.* Nicotine speeds the passage of food through the digestive tract. When you stop using nicotine, your digestion may seem sluggish for a week or two as it readjusts to normal speed. Drink plenty of water, exercise, and make sure your nutrition plan contains fiber-rich foods.
◆ *Hunger.* Sometimes the craving for a cigarette feels like hunger pangs. Wait a few minutes and see if the craving eases. If you want to put something in your mouth, try a healthful snack or beverage.
◆ *Poor concentration.* Over time, your brain got used to frequent hits of the stimulant nicotine. It will need two to four weeks to readjust after

the stimulant is gone. You may need to juggle your workload or write notes to yourself so you can function well during the transition.

♦ *Tiredness.* Nicotine withdrawal may leave you feeling less energetic for a while. Plan time for naps and plenty of sleep for the first few weeks after you quit smoking.

♦ *Insomnia.* Tobacco smoke changed your brain waves. For a week or so while normal rhythms return, you may have trouble sleeping. Nicotine cravings can also temporarily disturb dreams and sleep. Later, however, your sleep will become more peaceful than it was when you smoked.

Coping with Cravings

An intense, recurring hunger for a cigarette may shove all other sensations and thoughts to the background. This is an entirely predictable symptom of your withdrawal from an addictive drug.

"I had a little counter that I used for my job, so I made a study of my urges for a cigarette. The first day there were three hundred sixty; the second, one hundred eighty. I still felt like I was craving a cigarette all day long, but the numbers showed me I was getting better."

Each craving, or nicotine urge, will last only a few minutes. Day by day, their number will rapidly diminish. Most will be gone in two weeks, but you may be surprised by an occasional strong urge for a cigarette even months after you quit smoking.

Most stop-smoking programs incorporate a few of the following techniques to quell cravings. They are simple and almost always available. You can use and adapt any or all of them.

The Five Ds

♦ *Distraction.* A craving will run its course in a few minutes, whether you respond to it or not. Creating momentary distractions can keep your mind and body occupied and help you ignore the call to nicotine.

Make a telephone call, sharpen pencils, walk to the drinking fountain, check the mail, play with the dog, splash water on your hands and face, or cruise through the channels on the remote control. Do anything to keep yourself busy and not smoking.

◆ *Deep breathing.*

> *"Learning to breathe deeply was very calming. I realized that, in the past, the only time I ever took a good, deep breath was when I inhaled a cigarette."*

Breathing deeply is a known tension reducer that you can apply anywhere.

Draw a smooth, full breath down into your abdomen, then exhale slowly through your nose. Repeat a few times, at whatever pace seems comfortable. Focus on the relaxation that simply breathing can allow. If you want, let your eyes close. Notice how easily tight shoulders and jaws begin to loosen as you exhale.

To be certain you are breathing deeply, gently place your hands on your abdomen. It should expand as you inhale and return to its normal position as you exhale. If this seems awkward at first, lie on your back and notice how natural deep breathing feels.

By the time you've taken six or eight deep breaths, the urgency of your nicotine craving may have passed.

An alternative technique is to imitate how you breathed when you smoked. You can inhale through a cocktail straw or a cinnamon stick, letting your head fall back a little as if you were enjoying a drag on a cigarette, then exhaling slowly. Without props, you can get the same effect by putting your mouth in a small circle, as if you were going to whistle but inhaling instead of exhaling. Repeat as often as you like.

◆ *Drinking water.*

> *"It helped me to drink lots of water, to feel like I was cleansing my body."*

Enjoy a tall glass of ice water when the urge to smoke hits. It will keep your mouth occupied and help to soothe your throat, as well as to thin sticky mucus and begin to cleanse built-up toxins from your body.

◆ *Doing something physical.*

> *"When I had an attack of withdrawal symptoms, it felt like terrible anxiety and restlessness. I headed out the door of my office and ran up and down the stairs until it passed. Then I was able to go back to work."*

◆ Exercise eases tension and that fidgety feeling. It boosts your metabolic rate and can help counter the fatigue and sluggishness you may feel when you're no longer getting nicotine stimulation.

For a quick fix, climb the stairs, do jumping jacks, or do arm circles. Exercise for three minutes on a stationary bicycle or walk briskly around the block. Exercise can combine the elements of deep breathing and distraction to get you through a nicotine urge. If you haven't already made regular exercise part of your life, the weeks after you stop smoking are a wonderful time to do so. You may be rewarded by quick advancement, thanks to your improved circulation and expanded breathing capacity as you stop smoking.

♦ *Deepening awareness.*

> *"Use the knowledge that the immediate desire to smoke will be gone in no time. You think it will last forever, but it never does. It goes in no time, and you can appreciate the freedom of not responding to it."*

When you have an urge for a cigarette, don't try to drive it away. Quietly observe the urge as if you were a tourist watching a natural phenomenon, such as the sun going down, a wave approaching the shore, or a cloud passing overhead. Notice how the urge starts, how strong and dense and irresistible it seems for a few moments—and how it lightens and passes on, even if you do nothing at all.

Some spiritual teachings make a meditation practice out of observing our desires as they come and go—just observing without grasping for the object the mind wants so much, without getting hooked into thinking that we would be happy if only we could light a cigarette, taste a pizza, or get the approval of a spouse or co-worker. Part of the lesson is that desire itself, by keeping us busy reaching for objects that promise future happiness, can rob our enjoyment of the present moment.

TIME ON YOUR HANDS

> *"If you remove a demon, you have to put three angels in its place. Part of the process was realizing that a void was there and needed to be filled in some way."*

It's no wonder your hands and taste buds feel neglected when you first stop smoking. If you smoked two packs a day, you may have lifted a cigarette to your mouth more than four hundred times a day.

That's a lot of time on your hands when you first put cigarettes down. Ultimately, that time becomes one of the most exciting gifts you give yourself by quitting. You can have three or more hours of extra time each day for worthwhile activities.

Early in the quitting process don't worry about choosing the perfect activity to occupy your idle hands. Keep an assortment of "angels" by your side, ready to fill the void in your hands or mouth. Instead of smoking a cigarette, try squeezing a rubber ball, playing with clay, popping a rubber band, or clicking a ballpoint pen. Or you might prefer doodling, mending, knitting, fiddling with worry beads, playing solitaire or a hand-held computer game, working a crossword puzzle, writing a note, or manicuring your nails.

Worried about annoying your loved ones with your fidgeting? Hold someone's hand, massage his or her temples or feet, or challenge that person to a game of cards.

When your taste buds cry out for stimulation, try jolting them with mints, sugarless gum, sour or spicy hard candies, gingerroot, breath spray, herbal teas, or a licorice- or herb-flavored toothpaste. Keep your mouth busy with a straw, toothpick, or cinnamon stick.

MOOD MANAGEMENT

Many smokers use tobacco to help control tension and unpleasant moods. They may reach for a cigarette when they are depressed, angry, or stressed out.

The truth is, cigarettes don't really ease tension and stress. Six months after quitting, most former smokers report they feel calmer and more in control of their emotions than they did when they were smoking.

"When I was chairing a meeting at work and feeling like I was going to lose it, I wanted to light a cigarette. Instead, I asked for a five-minute break."

If smoking used to give you a few minutes of relief from tense situations, find ways to give yourself the break without the smoke. Walk around the block. Put on earphones and listen to a tape you enjoy. Do some deep-breathing exercises. Look out the window.

If you are used to smoking a cigarette instead of telling people how you feel, you may be entering a whole new era of dealing with your moods. It may take a while for you even to identify how you feel. You know you want a cigarette, but is the distress you're experiencing coming from embarrassment, anger, or fear? Are your gripes with family members and co-workers legitimate or just withdrawal-induced crabbiness? Can you describe your emotions and your expectations of others without crying, exploding, or denying what you are feeling?

When your emotions seem confused or overwhelming, take some time alone before confronting people. Vent your frustration, or get a reality check from a friend on the telephone. You may want to talk to a therapist or attend an assertiveness training program.

STEPPING ON THE SCALE

"I gained about ten pounds at first, but I didn't go back to smoking. I told myself that then I'd be a smoker who weighed ten extra pounds. I lost most of the weight, but I definitely substituted more eating as I gave up cigarettes. I know other people who got into a total health kick and actually lost weight while they were stopping smoking."

Fear of gaining weight keeps many people smoking long after they know it is dangerous for their health. Quite simply, smoking is a destructive strategy for trying to control your weight.

On average, it *is* true that smokers weigh six or seven pounds less than nonsmokers. But keep this fact in context: Each of those pounds costs the smoker about a year in life expectancy.

The reality of weight gain after giving up smoking isn't as hefty as many people fear. Eighty percent of former smokers will gain weight, but during the same period so will more than half of those who kept smoking. The average postsmoking weight gain is only five pounds, with women no more likely to gain than men.

If you are concerned about weight, focus on the low-calorie, low-fat, high-action options among the strategies for coping with nicotine cravings, empty hands, and mood swings. A celery stick, a glass of seltzer, or a cinnamon stick fills an empty hand just as well as a cigarette or a high-fat snack.

"I felt a sluggishness in my body and started gaining weight, even though I had been working out regularly. I found that I had to increase my aerobic exercise to compensate for the change in metabolism. Later I was able to return to my usual three-times-a-week workout."

Increase your exercise: It will speed your metabolism and allow you to eat more without gaining weight. Boosting exercise before your quit day—establishing a first-time exercise routine or making your workout more rigorous as you taper off cigarettes—can help you keep your weight under control.

Most people suggest that you should not try to lose weight at the same time you are giving up cigarettes. However, you may find that it's the perfect time to go to a weight management class or make some of the changes in your nutrition plan discussed in chapter 3.

Stepping Over the Lapse Traps

"When my father died, the first thing I thought was that I needed a cigarette. Then I reminded myself how proud he had been that I'd stopped smoking and how disappointed he would be if his death made me start again."

Long after the physical cravings have stopped, you may be surprised when the desire to smoke suddenly bursts forth.

Expect it. Whether it has been ten months or ten years since you quit smoking, something is guaranteed to happen that will test anew your ability to continue making the healthful choice. Plan in advance how you can cope with difficult situations as a nonsmoker and what to do when your mind starts to play devious and subtle tricks.

Are you ready for the common lapse traps discussed below?

PAINFUL FEELINGS AND SITUATIONS

A loved one dies. A marriage or a job ends. Something happens that leaves you so heartbroken that you are tempted to try anything—especially a cigarette—that might dull the pain momentarily.

For reinforcement, you might carry in your wallet a reminder card with your personal reason for never wanting to smoke again. Or you might prefer a strong message such as, "No matter how bad things are, smoking will only make them worse."

Painful feelings need to be felt. Remind yourself that it's a cruel lie when a voice inside your head says, "Have a cigarette. You'll feel better." Your grief won't be any less if you add regret on top of it. Seek support from family, friends, clergy, a support group, or an individual therapist.

ENTERING NEW NONSMOKING TERRITORY

Special occasions, and even not-so-special activities that are outside your everyday routine, can bring up the urge to smoke. Every few days, look at your calendar and think ahead to situations that you know will challenge your resolve. Also think about any activities you may be doing for the first time since you quit smoking. Is it your first nonsmoking car trip? Board meeting? Birthday party? Weekend without the kids? Card game? Super Bowl? Visit to your family?

By planning ahead how you will respond if the urge arises, you can remain in control of new situations. What will you say if someone offers you a cigarette? What will you do until the urge passes? Look back at the strategies you used during the first few days after you quit smoking. Select one that feels right for the occasion and make following it a conscious plan. Then, if the urge strikes—and you may be pleased to find that it doesn't—put your plan into action.

HAVING A BABY

Women who have stayed away from tobacco throughout pregnancy, and may not even have missed it much, are often surprised that they're tempted to celebrate the blessed event with a smoke. With a newborn in the house, you may think that a cigarette would be just the thing to soothe your sleep-deprived body, lift the postpartum blues, or ease nervousness over the responsibilities of parenthood.

Reach for the telephone instead of a cigarette. Ask friends to watch the baby for a short time so you can pamper yourself in healthful ways— a nap, a leisurely shower, an adult conversation, or a sympathetic ear.

Reread the litany of health problems that children suffer when they're exposed to smoke. Remind yourself that a smoke-exposed baby—who may have colic and more colds and ear infections—is even harder to take care of than a baby who is not around smoke.

NOSTALGIA

Sometimes the smoking days may seem like the good old days, when you were always calm, had lots of energy, were successful at work, and said just the right thing at parties—when every drag of your cigarette smelled great and was totally satisfying.

"I always loved smoking. After ten months, the pleasure of it does not diminish in my mind."

Nostalgia for smoking is a mind trap that is likely to emerge when you're especially vulnerable, feeling bored, depressed, or hopeless. It can be a letdown when simply getting through a day without cigarettes is no longer a victory. The thrill of your achievement may start to seem a little humdrum, no longer generating praise from yourself or others. Now's the time to reward yourself for your nonsmoking life and to remind yourself that the good old days weren't really so good. Remember how your clothes smelled? How stained your teeth became? How it could ruin a whole dinner if you had to sit in the nonsmoking section? How your mouth tasted in the morning?

OVERCONFIDENCE

When you stop feeling hooked on cigarettes and are proud of your success in quitting, it may seem like you've changed so much that one cigarette can't hurt. For most people, that's not true.

"For fun, I decided to have just one cigarette and that was fatal. After months away from cigarettes, I went right back to smoking."

Nicotine addiction is strong, and many people are led back into steady smoking after one cigarette taken just out of curiosity or to prove that cigarettes have lost their power over them.

If you have given up cigarettes, you have a lot to be proud of. It's no wonder that you have heightened confidence in your ability to take on many challenges. Make your challenge that of staying off cigarettes totally, not testing yourself to see whether you can try just one.

ALCOHOL

"The longest time I ever stopped smoking, almost a year, I had stopped drinking. Then I started drinking casually. My resolve broke down when I was around friends smoking and drinking. This time I know my limits: I can have a glass of wine with dinner and not smoke, but I virtually can't go into a bar. When I do try it, I'll tell the people I'm with that I need help not to smoke."

Alcohol is a triple whammy. Not only is the drink-and-a-cigarette connection a strong one for many smokers, but bars often are filled with smokers. As the alcohol takes effect, resolve can dissolve in a beer or a cocktail glass.

You may find you need to forgo drinking with friends who smoke or even give up alcohol totally for a while. Before you go to events where you know there will be a lot of drinking, tell your companions that you intend not to smoke.

When you come close to any of the lapse traps, remember the Five *D*s (see pages 59–61) that you used during the first weeks of quitting. Now add a sixth *D* for delay. If you have an urge, promise yourself to wait at least another day before starting. Then extend the interval.

Remember how long it took you to decide to quit smoking? Give yourself plenty of time to consider what you are doing before deciding to start again.

If You Lapse, What Then?

Don't turn a onetime lapse into a total relapse.

So you had a cigarette. You don't deserve to die for it, although that's where you're headed if you start smoking again.

Instead, learn what you can from the experience. Is there a situation you could be better prepared for? Do you need to ask for more support from friends and relatives? Is it time to attend a support group or listen to the tapes from your stop-smoking program?

Once you understand what happened, let it go, and make a fresh commitment to a future without cigarettes.

Given enough time and recommitment, you'll realize one day that you have finally crossed the threshold and become a nonsmoker for life. Congratulations!

> *"A few months ago I started a new job. I had a horrible, stressful day where I almost quit. Walking home I realized I had this horrible, disgusting day and not once had I thought about having a cigarette. And all at once it was an amazing day."*

CHAPTER 3

Eating Well to
Discourage Disease

"Every week, you hear about something new that might cause cancer or give you a heart attack. First you get scared. Then you say, 'I can't win, so I might as well eat what I want.'"

IF YOU WATCH ENOUGH NEWS REPORTS, YOU MIGHT START TO FEEL that food is your enemy—harboring dangerous germs, cancer-causing chemicals, and artery-clogging fats and cholesterol. And if you watch enough commercials and read enough ads, you might start to feel as if you are the fraying rope in a huge game of dietary tug-of-war. Half the ads seem to yank you toward gooey desserts and greasy fast foods. The other half pull you toward pricey weight-loss programs and regimens that substitute diet drinks for real food.

Food does *not* have to be your enemy. Quite the opposite. Tasty, plentiful food can be your ally in preventing disease. The American Cancer Society and the American Heart Association want you to enjoy meals that taste good, provide plenty of energy, and leave you less prone to cancer and heart disease. By applying a few simple guidelines, you can create a healthful cuisine that suits your lifestyle and your taste buds.

If you are fed up with dieting, extravagant food promises, and onerous restrictions, you should be pleased with the promises in the nutrition plan in this chapter.

You *don't* have to eat like everyone else.
You *don't* have to swear off your favorite food.

You *don't* have to feel hungry.

You *don't* have to eat the same thing day after day.

You *don't* have to spend more for groceries.

You *don't* have to give up dining out.

You *don't* have to eat fake foods.

You *don't* have to trade protection against one disease for protection against another.

The last point may be the best news of all about eating healthfully. Although the biological reasons may be quite different for heart disease and for cancer, the nutrition findings add up to virtually identical advice.

1. Eat foods that are low in fat and cholesterol.
2. Eat a high-carbohydrate diet, rich in fiber.
3. Eat a variety of foods, with lots of fruits and vegetables.
4. Limit your consumption of salt and of salty and certain cured foods.
5. If you drink alcohol, drink moderately.
6. Maintain a desirable weight.

Each of the next three major sections of this chapter—"Understanding How Eating Right May Help Prevent Cancer and Heart Disease," "Getting Started: How Do You Rate Now?" and "Putting the Guidelines into Action"—will deal with all six of these areas individually.

If you need to work on only one area, follow the advice about it in each of the three discussions. If you need to improve in more than one area, start making changes in the way that is most comfortable for you. You may want to pick the most urgent first, master it, then move on to the one that's next in importance to you. Alternatively, you may find that it's easier to make the most appealing, easiest-sounding changes first. Or you can combine several guidelines to adopt an entirely new menu. For instance, if you are trying to cut down on certain foods, look at the suggestions on fruits and vegetables, plus the ones on other high-fiber foods to find items you can eat more of.

Understanding How Eating Right May Help Prevent Cancer and Heart Disease

For about thirty years, the American Heart Association has recognized that a large body of scientific evidence links dietary factors with heart disease. The way you eat helps to determine not only whether you will become obese but also whether you will develop high blood cholesterol and high blood pressure. Overall, considerably more than half of all heart disease occurrences can be attributed to eating habits.

Evidence indicates that what you eat, and whether you are at a healthful weight, can play a significant role in whether you'll develop certain types of cancer. Some experts have estimated that one in every three cancers in the United States can be attributed to nutrition.

Here is the science behind the specific guidelines.

1. EAT FOODS THAT ARE LOW IN FAT AND CHOLESTEROL

Jack Sprat and his wife made all-or-nothing decisions about fat. She ate it all, he ate none, and that was that. If they lived in a 1990s fairy tale, the divisions might not be so simple.

For one thing, we now know that all fats are not equal. Chemically, they come in a variety of shapes—and the different structures are important in how they alter health risks.

In the body, fat has important jobs to do. Fats are needed for the manufacture of many hormones. Fats carry essential vitamins that do not dissolve in water. Fats are an indispensable part of cell membranes. Fats keep your skin supple. Fats store energy.

However, fat is much *less* important as part of proper nutrition. Your body can make most of the fat it needs. Your food needs to supply only a small amount of fat building blocks. But although we need very little fat, most Americans consume it in large amounts.

Part of the problem with too much fat and too many calories on your dinner plate is that they can easily become rolls of fat on your body. Each gram of fat contains nine calories. Gram for gram, fat contains more calories than protein, sugar, starch, or alcohol.

The undesirable health effects of obesity are clear (see page 83). However, even if you are not overweight, fat plays a role in your health. To understand the science of the dietary fat/health relationship, and to decipher food advertisements and labels, it helps to know some of the lingo of fat chemistry and the varieties that fat comes in.

All fats are made up of small units called *fatty acids*. The basic skeleton of a fatty acid is a string of carbon atoms. Depending on the type of chemical bonds that attach the atoms, there is more room or less room for hydrogen atoms to hook onto the carbons. Fats are divided into three basic types, depending on the chemical structure of their fatty acids. These types are *saturated, monounsaturated,* and *polyunsaturated.*

In a saturated fat, every available spot on the carbon chain is taken up by a hydrogen atom. At room temperature, most saturated fats are usually solid. That is why a stick of butter left on your kitchen counter on all but the hottest days will retain its form. Meat and other animal products, such as dairy foods, contain high levels of saturated fats. A few plant oils—coconut oil, cocoa butter, palm, and palm kernel oil—are high in saturated fats. Because you are an animal, your body can create its own saturated fats. Therefore, you don't *need* to add any saturated fats from your food.

In a monounsaturated fat, two carbon atoms in the chain are hooked in a double bond at one spot on the carbon skeleton. That means one pair of hydrogen atoms is missing. Monounsaturated fats are liquid at room temperature. They start to solidify when they are chilled. They are found in various proportions in many vegetable oils. Avocados, olive oil, and canola (rapeseed) oil are particularly rich in monounsaturated fats.

In a polyunsaturated fat, carbon atoms are double-bonded at two or more spots on the skeleton. Therefore, many hydrogen atoms are missing. Polyunsaturated fats are usually liquid at room temperature and stay that way when chilled. At least half the fatty acids in most vegetable oils are polyunsaturated. Safflower oil, sunflower oil, soybean oil, and corn oil are the richest sources of polyunsaturated oil.

The two basic types of polyunsaturated fatty acids are named for where the double bonds are located along the line of carbons. *Omega-6 fatty acids* are found in cooking oils, such as safflower, corn, sesame, soybean, cottonseed, and sunflower. *Omega-3 fatty acids* are most concentrated in fish oils. They also are found in some plant sources, such as walnut, canola, and linseed (flax) oils.

The only fatty acids your body can't make are three varieties of polyunsaturates. These so-called *essential fatty acids* are linoleic, arachidonic, and linolenic. If your eating plan furnishes a little linoleic acid (found in corn oil and other vegetable oils), your body can use that to make the other two.

Polyunsaturated fats are not as stable as butter and other saturated fats. They easily combine with oxygen in the air to become rancid. To increase the time foods made with polyunsaturated fats will stay fresh, manufacturers use a process called *hydrogenation.* It's also the process used to make a solid margarine out of vegetable oil. Hydrogenation adds hydrogen atoms to fill in some of the natural spaces. Stick margarines and canned vegetable shortenings are good examples of partially *hydrogenated oils.*

Both monounsaturated and polyunsaturated fats may help lower your blood cholesterol level if you use them in place of saturated fats. The important thing is to be moderate in your use of all types of fat.

In recent years, attention has been focused on both the number of hydrogen atoms in a fatty acid and how the hydrogens are attached. When nature attaches hydrogen to the carbon backbone of polyunsaturated and monounsaturated fatty acids, most of the hydrogen atoms stick out the same side of the line of carbons. These atoms are called *cis* (meaning "on the same side") *fatty* acids. In contrast, when manufacturers attach hydrogen atoms to unsaturated fatty acids, as they do in making shortening, some of the hydrogens are added on opposite sides of the molecule. These are called *trans* (meaning "across") *fatty* acids. There has been concern that trans fatty acids act more like saturated fats in the body. The AHA Nutrition Committee continues to monitor research in this area. However, its members believe that margarine still is preferable to butter, which is rich in both saturated fat and cholesterol. Trans fatty acids are lower in tub or liquid margarines than in stick margarines. If you limit your daily intake of fats and oils to five to eight teaspoons, you aren't likely to consume an excess of trans fatty acids.

Cholesterol is a waxy, lipidlike substance, but its structure is different from that of fat. (See page 242 for a detailed discussion of cholesterol.) The cholesterol in your diet comes from two separate sources. You eat some cholesterol directly, in meat, eggs, and other animal products. Some cholesterol is produced in the liver, using, in part, the breakdown products of fat. A food can be low in fat but high in cholesterol, such as shrimp. A food can be high in fat but contain no cholesterol, such as peanut butter or margarine.

Heart Disease Science

Scanning different parts of the world, you'll find huge differences in the amount of fat eaten. In some regions, people eat a diet in which about 10 percent of the calories comes from fat. Some people in the United States eat more than 50 percent of their calories in fat. The average amount for an American is 34 percent.

If you had a world map showing where fat is eaten and superimposed it on a world map of heart disease, you would notice an astounding overlap. International studies document the simple relationship. The more fat, especially saturated fat, you eat, the higher the blood cholesterol levels and the more severe the atherosclerosis.

Genetics alone cannot account for the country-to-country comparisons. When people migrate to new countries and change their food habits, cholesterol levels and the risk of heart disease change, too. In one study, the amount of saturated fat that Japanese ate depended on where they lived. They ate little in Japan, more in Hawaii, and still more in San Francisco. Along with these diet changes came a higher death rate from heart disease. Compared with the rate in Japan, it was almost twice as high in Hawaii and almost three times as high in San Francisco.

Even when people start out in a country accustomed to a moderate level of fat, moving to the American eating plan can bring problems. In an Ireland-Boston Heart Study, Irish men living in Boston ate more fat and were more likely to die of heart disease than their brothers and cousins who stayed in Ireland.

In the American diet, *saturated fat* is the number-one culprit in raising blood cholesterol, particularly low-density lipoprotein (LDL) cholesterol. (See page 243 for a detailed discussion of LDLs.) Exactly why saturated fat has this effect isn't clear, but it seems to interfere with the body's methods of getting rid of LDLs. If you want to lower your cholesterol level, it is very important to reduce the amount of saturated fat that you eat. By doing so, you'll also reduce the amount of cholesterol you eat. That's because it is found in many foods high in saturated fat. In volunteers in the research ward of a hospital where diet can be rigorously controlled and analyzed, levels of LDL cholesterol decrease as the amount of saturated fats in the food decreases. This occurs even if monounsaturated or polyunsaturated fats are substituted so that the total amount of fat stays the same.

Some studies show that besides raising cholesterol, an excessive intake of saturated fat increases the amount of the proteins in blood that form blood clots.

It is thought that eating cholesterol-rich foods reduces the number of receptors that act as doorways for LDL cholesterol to leave the bloodstream. That results in higher blood LDL levels and a higher heart disease risk.

Polyunsaturated fats do not raise blood cholesterol. In fact, they may help the body dispose of newly formed cholesterol, keeping it out of the blood and off artery walls.

Among the different polyunsaturated fats, the effect on cholesterol varies. Omega-6 fatty acids lower both total blood cholesterol and LDL cholesterol. This is particularly true when omega-6 fatty acids are used in place of saturated fats. Omega-3 fatty acids seem less effective than omega-6 in lowering the most worrisome lipoproteins, LDLs, but they do lower triglycerides. Omega-3 fatty acids also inhibit the tendency of blood to clot, which is another benefit in preventing heart disease.

Monounsaturated fats also may help reduce blood cholesterol, especially if they are part of an eating plan with low levels of saturated fats.

Cancer Science

Eating too much fat increases your risk of colon cancer. It may also increase your risk of breast cancer and prostate cancer. In studies of Japanese who migrated to Hawaii or the mainland United States, the rate of all three cancers goes up as fat intake increases.

Studies in many countries have shown that the rate of colon cancer is higher in people who eat more total fat, saturated fat, and calories. In this country, the fat/colon cancer link has been demonstrated in African-Americans and in Americans of Bohemian ancestry in Nebraska. One group of Americans, Seventh-Day Adventists, enjoys a much lower than average rate of colon cancer. For religious reasons, these people follow a vegetarian diet that contains less fat and protein, and more carbohydrates and fiber, than the typical American diet.

Fat is thought to be related to both the inception and the growth of colon cancer. Bacteria that live in your colon interact with fat that you eat, modifying it into carcinogens. They, in turn, damage the lining of the colon. This can eventually cause colon cancer. Because it takes a long time for cancer to form, reducing the amount of fat eaten (and hence the level of carcinogens in the colon) may help prevent colon cancer.

Fat also seems to encourage tumors in the colon to grow faster. When you eat fat, your body secretes bile acids. The acids help you digest the fat, breaking it down into fatty acids. However, certain fatty acids, as well as the breakdown products of the bile acids, seem to spur abnormal cells in the colon to divide. The result: more and bigger tumors.

In studies linking fat and GI (gastrointestinal) tract cancers, saturated fats have raised the greatest concern. The omega-6 type of polyunsaturated fatty acids also have been implicated in promoting the growth of tumors.

Prostate cancer—particularly in its faster-growing, more aggressive forms—has been related to fat intake in several studies comparing the diets of groups of men. In West Africa, men traditionally eat little meat or fat, and they have very low rates of prostate cancer. In the United States, African-American men have the highest risk of prostate cancer of any group.

The amount of fat, rather than whether it comes from meat, may determine the prostate cancer risk. In one study, men who drink whole milk were found to have nearly double the risk of prostate cancer of men who drink either 2-percent-fat milk or no milk at all. Among Seventh-Day Adventists, men who eat lots of cheese and eggs are more likely to die of prostate cancer than Adventists who eat no animal products.

The speed at which prostate cancer advances also may be related to the amount of fat a man eats. By the time they are over fifty, one out of three men will have some tumor growth in the prostate. This may or may not ever pose a threat to life or health. In a study that looked at more than 50,000 men with various eating habits, those who ate the most red meat and the most fat were more likely to develop advanced prostate cancer.

Dietary fat has long been a suspect in the risk of breast cancer. A world map of breast cancer rates, like one of heart disease, would mirror a world map of fat consumption. In studies trying to directly compare the eating patterns of women who develop cancer and women who don't, the findings have been inconsistent. Some studies have strongly implicated fat as a risk factor. Others have shown no relationship. In the long-term Harvard study tracking almost 90,000 nurses, no relationship was found between fat intake and the chance that a woman will develop breast cancer. Some scientists wondered whether a fat link might be disguised in this study because even the women consuming lower amounts of fat still got more than 30 percent of their calories from fat.

Another analysis, which compiled data from twelve smaller studies, agreed with the nurses' study in finding no relationship with breast cancer before menopause. However, it found that the risk of developing cancer after menopause went up if women ate higher levels of fat and saturated fat.

Although they lack proof, scientists believe that a link between fat and breast cancer makes biological sense. Animals fed a high-fat diet are more likely than other animals to develop breast tumors when exposed to carcinogens. Fatty foods, and a greater amount of body fat, alter the amount of hormones and hormone receptors in the body— and hormones influence tumor growth. Another possibility is that fat is not causing the problem. Instead, the foods that are eaten *instead* of fat—primarily fruits, vegetables, and grains—may be protective.

The AHA and the ACS recommend that you follow a nutrition plan with less than 30 percent of your calories coming from fat. Less than 10 percent of your calories should come from saturated fats. Do you already follow this guideline but your cholesterol is still too high? Eat less fat and reduce your saturated fat to less than 7 percent of your calories. If you can't reduce cholesterol to the normal range by proper nutrition alone, talk to your doctor for advice about medication. See page 87 to learn how to calculate the percentage of your calories that comes from fat.

2. EAT MORE HIGH-FIBER FOODS

The cell walls of animals contain cholesterol. The cell walls of plants contain *fiber*, a variety of substances that humans don't find very digestible. Fiber in foods is usually divided into two types: fiber that falls to the bottom of a glass of water and fiber that forms gels in water. The first kind, *insoluble fiber*, doesn't dissolve in water. An example is the wheat bran in whole wheat bread. The second kind, *soluble fiber*, dissolves in water and has a gummier consistency. The pectin in fruit, as well as a small component of oat bran, is soluble fiber. When jellies gel, that's the action of the pectin.

Heart Disease Science

When eaten regularly in a low-fat nutrition plan, soluble fiber can help lower blood cholesterol, particularly LDL cholesterol. Exactly why has not been established. Fiber may reduce the amount of dietary fat and cholesterol that is absorbed into the body. It also appears to increase the loss of cholesterol breakdown products (bile acids) in the bowel movement. Both these effects may spur the removal of LDL from the bloodstream and into the liver.

Eating more fiber helps people adjust other heart disease risk factors in a positive direction. Calorie for calorie, high-fiber foods are more filling and help people trying to reduce their weight. High-fiber foods are often lower in fat as well. Eating foods that are both high-fiber and low-fat may lower cholesterol.

Cancer Science

Eating plenty of fiber is associated with a lower risk of cancers of the digestive tract. Worldwide, thirteen studies from the 1970s and 1980s tried to document whether eating fiber-rich grains, vegetables, and fruit helped lower the risk of colon cancer. They also looked at whether the true protection comes because these eating plans usually happen to be lower in calories, meat consumption, and fat. Fiber was clearly protective. The lesson for making menu changes is that you are better off eating more fiber, even if you have not yet shifted to lower-fat eating or achieved the weight you want.

Why is fiber so helpful? So far, no specific ingredient has been given credit for the protection fiber provides. Part of the benefit may be that fiber is a neutral product just along for the ride through the digestive tract. As filler in the digestive tract, fiber may dilute the concentration of carcinogens in the bowel, reducing the amount that the GI-tract lining is exposed to. Fiber may give carcinogens less time to cause damage. When you eat a diet high in fiber, food speeds through your digestive tract faster.

The ACS and the AHA recommend that you eat lots of high-fiber foods, such as whole grain cereals, breads, pastas, fruits, and vegetables.

3. EAT PLENTY OF FRUITS AND VEGETABLES

Heart Disease Science

Fruits and vegetables are high in fiber, rich in vitamins and minerals, low in calories, and virtually fat free. They are the cornerstone of proper nutrition that can help you achieve and maintain a healthy weight and reduce cholesterol and blood pressure.

Two nutrients found in many fruits and vegetables, vitamin C and *beta-carotene,* seem to deactivate a process that can turn LDL cholesterol into a more artery-damaging form. Other specific nutrients may turn out to be equally heart healthy.

Cancer Science

In comparisons between countries, the 25 percent of the world's population who eat the most fruits and vegetables have roughly half as many cancers as the 25 percent who eat the fewest. In one review of 156 studies, 128 provided evidence that eating fruits and vegetables helps to protect against cancer.

People who eat vegetables and fruits every day have a lower risk of lung, prostate, bladder, esophagus, colorectal, and stomach cancers. No particular ingredient gets the credit. Vegetables and fruits contain varying amounts of vitamins, minerals, fiber, and other compounds. Alone or in combination, these may be responsible for reducing cancer risk.

Certain aspects of fruits and vegetables have gained special attention as possible cancer preventives.

1. Beta-carotene, found in dark green and deep yellow fruits and vegetables, may reduce the risk of esophagus and larynx cancers. Studies of its possible benefits are ongoing (see page 281).

2. Vitamin C prevents nitrites from combining with proteins to form cancer-promoting chemicals that increase the risk of stomach, esophagus, and larynx cancers. Citrus fruits and many green vegetables are rich in vitamin C.

3. Cruciferous vegetables have long been thought to have cancer-preventive properties. The best-known members of this family are broccoli, brussels sprouts, cabbage, and cauliflower. In the liver, these vegetables produce powerful enzymes that may break down cancer-promoting chemicals. The enzymes may also beneficially alter the way that hormones are metabolized. Cruciferous vegetables may reduce the risk of esophagus, stomach, colorectal, lung, and bladder cancers.

To make sure you get the fullest array of these nutrients, it makes sense to include a variety of vegetables and fruits in your menu. Five or more servings are recommended each day. Such a food plan may also provide other protective factors that haven't been identified yet.

4. LIMIT CONSUMPTION OF SODIUM AND CERTAIN CURED FOODS

One of the world's earliest industries produced sodium chloride, ordinary table salt. When salt is scarce, it has been considered a life or death situation. Wars have been fought over it, and in the Old West you might have traded a tiny stash of salt for clothing or even a horse. The word *salary* actually comes from a Latin word for the salt that was used to pay soldiers.

Why is salt so important? Because it is 40 percent *sodium,* and humans need a little sodium to sustain life. For the equilibrium of your body chemistry, you need a minimum of about 500 milligrams of sodium every day. That's the amount about a quarter of a teaspoon of salt contains. Sodium lets your body maintain the right amount of fluid and helps shuttle nutrients in and out of your cells. Sodium and water work together to maintain the right fluid balance in the body. Too much sodium or too much water upsets the balance.

Salt's other lifesaving function is as a preservative. Throughout history, salt has been invaluable in preserving foods to sustain people through cycles of scarcity and to prevent the disease and waste that spoilage can cause. Modern cuisines reflect the foods that are plentiful in the local area, as well as available methods of cooking and preserving food both today and historically. How food is prepared and stored may account for some variations in the rates of cancer and heart disease occurrence in different areas of the world.

Heart Disease Science

The average American eats twenty to thirty times more sodium than is needed to sustain life. That excess shows up in a greater risk for high blood pressure for some people. High blood pressure, in turn, increases the risk of stroke, heart attack, and kidney failure.

For any one person, it is difficult to predict whether eating too much salt will cause high blood pressure or whether restricting salt can bring it back to normal. Some people are highly sensitive to the amount of sodium they consume; others are not.

However, when scientists compare groups of people who routinely eat different amounts of salt, they find definite differences in blood pressure. In places where people don't eat much salt, high blood pressure is rare. In these places, blood pressure doesn't rise as people get older. (The rise is significant in the United States.) If we reduced our salt enough so that blood pressures fell an average of a few points, the result would be thousands fewer strokes each year.

Dozens of medical studies have tested whether people can lower their blood pressure by reducing the sodium they eat. Researchers analyzed compiled data from seventy of those studies and concluded that the impact of reduced sodium intake on blood pressure was significant. That's particularly true in older people and people with high blood pressure.

Cancer Science

Eating lots of salt-cured and pickled foods seems to increase the risk of cancer of the stomach and the esophagus. For example, stomach cancer has been linked to the consumption of pickled vegetables in Japan and the consumption of salted fish in Norway. In the United States, the rates of these cancers are low compared with those in some other parts of the world. Consumption of these foods generally is not high here.

Another type of preservative, nitrites, has been used widely for both cosmetic and health reasons. Nitrites give bacon and ham a fresh-looking red color. They also deter the growth of the bacteria that cause botulism, a deadly type of food poisoning. However, once in the body, nitrites can be converted to *nitrosamines,* chemicals that have been found to cause cancer. In response to information about this link, food manufacturers have learned how to cut back on the use of nitrites. Food labels now state whether nitrites are used, letting you minimize your exposure.

When foods are smoked or grilled, they absorb some of the tars that result from incomplete burning of wood or charcoal. These tars contain carcinogens that are chemically similar to those in tobacco smoke. Eating smoked foods occasionally does not pose a substantial risk. However, diets high in naturally smoked foods have been linked to cancer.

In general, the American Heart Association recommends that sodium intake should be limited to a maximum of 3,000 milligrams a day. That's the amount of sodium contained in about one and one-half teaspoons of salt. Be sure to count sodium from prepared foods and other sources as well. Doctors may suggest sodium levels of under 3,000 milligrams for some people with high blood pressure.

In the United States, fresh foods are available year-round and the amount of salt-cured, pickled, and smoked foods eaten is fairly low. Limit these foods to occasional use.

5. LIMIT ALCOHOL CONSUMPTION

With visions of happy Parisians sipping wine and eating cheese into an apparently healthy old age, many Americans were glad to read that moderate consumption of alcoholic beverages can be healthful and good for the heart. Still, most physicians are cautious about endorsing alcohol use and do *not* recommend that nondrinkers take up the habit.

Why not? Because alcohol consumption is the ultimate good news/ bad news story in nutrition. Alcohol can have some very beneficial effects. It also has so many dangers and side effects that a new medication with the same ratio of benefits to risks would never gain approval from the Food and Drug Administration (FDA).

Heart Disease Science

Depending on the individual person and the amount of alcohol consumed, alcohol can seem like either a blessing or a curse to the cardiovascular system.

First, the good news. People who drink moderately—a drink or two a day—reduce the risk for a heart attack compared to people who don't drink, according to a few large studies. That seems to be because alcohol raises your HDL. But it's also possible that moderate drinkers differed from other people in another protective factor that was not apparent.

Laboratory studies do offer one hint about how alcohol might help protect. It can increase the levels of beneficial HDL cholesterol. Taking a large group of nondrinkers and prescribing moderate alcohol consumption to half of them, then seeing if the heart disease and death rates of the two groups were different, would really convince scientists. Such a study has not been done, however.

Now the bad news. In some people, moderate alcohol consumption causes unwanted changes in risk factors for heart disease. Alcohol can raise blood pressure and/or the level of triglycerides in the blood.

A heavy intake of alcohol is no more healthful for the cardiovascular system than it is for the rest of the body. At high levels, alcohol usually raises blood pressure. Excessive drinking can poison the heart muscle and cause abnormal heart rhythms or even heart failure. Constant excessive alcohol intake or binge drinking can lead to stroke.

Cancer Science

No matter what your alcoholic beverage of choice, heavy alcohol use raises the risk that you will develop cancer of the mouth, larynx, throat, and esophagus. These risks multiply manyfold if you smoke or use smokeless tobacco in addition to drinking heavily.

Cirrhosis of the liver (from drinking too much or as a result of a medical condition) makes you forty times more likely to develop liver cancer than is a person without a damaged liver.

Drinking one or two drinks a day is a less clear cancer risk. Some evidence suggests, but has not proved, that regular alcohol consumption increases the risk of breast cancer in women.

Exactly how alcohol use may lead to cancer isn't certain. In laboratory tests, pure alcohol (ethanol) does not seem to be carcinogenic. Nevertheless, alcoholic beverages have many properties that are worrisome.

One of these properties is that alcohol weakens the body's protection. Alcohol provides lots of calories but no nutrition. In heavy drinkers who get most of their calories from alcohol, malnutrition may be the underlying health robber. The liver, which is responsible for the breakdown and removal of many drugs and toxins from the body, is also the primary place where alcohol is metabolized. If alcohol overburdens the liver, other toxins may have more of a chance to cause damage.

Also quite worrisome is that alcohol lets carcinogens into the body. Alcohol may irritate the surface of the mouth and throat and make it easier for carcinogens in tobacco to enter the cells lining these areas. Alcohol is also a solvent. Therefore, a particle of tar might get into a cell when dissolved in alcohol. If alcohol were not present, the same particle might instead have rested on the surface of the mouth or throat until it was coughed away.

It's also possible that the carcinogens alcohol lets in the door are present in the drink itself. Alcoholic beverages include more than 400 substances besides ethanol. In a few isolated instances, cancer in a specific locale has been linked to ingredients in the alcoholic beverages that are popular there.

Beyond cancer and heart disease, it is well known that alcohol can contribute to diseases of the liver, pancreas, and nervous system. Alcohol use sometimes results in serious social, psychological, and emotional problems. All these things have been taken into consideration when physicians decide not to encourage drinking despite its possible benefits to the cardiovascular system in some people.

In summary, the American Cancer Society and the American Heart Association do not encourage drinking alcohol. They recommend that if you do drink, you do so sparingly. Limit your consumption to no more than one ounce of ethanol per day (see page 98 for equivalents).

6. MAINTAIN A DESIRABLE BODY WEIGHT

Overweight people as a rule don't live as long as people who maintain a healthful weight. They die disproportionately from heart disease, strokes, cancer, diabetes, and digestive diseases. The more overweight someone is, the higher the risk.

Heart Disease Science

If you are 20 percent or more over your ideal body weight (see pages 101–103), you are at higher risk to develop coronary heart disease. If you glance below at how obesity increases a full range of heart disease risk factors, it is clear why the total impact on heart disease is significant.

◆ Obesity can raise your blood cholesterol. If you are obese, you have a 50 percent higher chance of developing high cholesterol than does a person at normal weight.

◆ Obesity can raise your triglyceride level.

◆ Obesity lowers protective *high-density lipoproteins* and can raise *low-density lipoproteins*. In large studies tracking heart disease risk factors, an average weight gain of just eight pounds lowers HDLs by about three milligrams per deciliter.

◆ Obesity usually raises your blood pressure. Being overweight increases the chance of high blood pressure two- to sixfold.

◆ Obesity can predispose you to adult-onset diabetes. Four out of five people who are diagnosed with this disorder are more than 15 percent over their desirable body weight. Some scientists predict that if people didn't become overweight in middle age, the number of new diabetes cases would be cut in half.

If you have any of these risk factors, losing weight may help. Losing weight can help reduce cholesterol, LDLs, and triglycerides while boosting HDLs. Since the 1920s, doctors have recommended weight loss to treat high blood pressure. If you are overweight and have high blood pressure, a ten-pound weight loss may reduce your blood pressure significantly. This may be true even if you are still well above your ideal weight. If your blood pressure is high normal, losing weight can cut your risk of developing high blood pressure by 50 percent.

Even if your latest checkup revealed none of these risk factors, obesity is still raising your heart disease risk. This is particularly true if you are a woman or if you are under the age of fifty. Excess weight increases strain on the heart. Obesity increases your risk of having a stroke by raising blood pressure and increasing the risk of heart disease.

The available evidence supports the wisdom of keeping your weight under control. The risks from elevated blood pressure and cholesterol start to emerge before they would be medically diagnosed. In the same way, you don't need to be obese for extra pounds to begin to increase heart disease risk.

"We called my father 'hollow hips' because no matter how much weight he gained, he had a little rear end and pants that sagged in the back."

In trying to tease apart the influence of various risk factors, several researchers have concluded that the distribution of body fat—being an apple rather than a pear shape—poses a risk factor for heart disease. That risk factor is distinct from the risk of obesity.

Where is your fat most prominent? Are you top-heavy? That would give you prominent rolls of fat above your waist, a beer belly on top of small hips, or the profile of an apple. Heart experts are more concerned about this distribution than about extra body fat below your waist. Fat in the abdominal area has an active impact on body metabolism, increasing the risk of diabetes, high triglycerides, and cardiovascular disease. On the other hand, your extra weight might stick mostly to your hips, thighs, and rear end, giving you saddlebags or a pear-shaped physique. That kind of weight gain is less likely to influence your metabolism and poses less of a heart-disease risk.

Where you gain weight isn't really under your control. As a general rule, men are more likely to be shaped like apples and women are more likely to be shaped like pears. If you are gaining weight around your upper body and waist, losing weight is more important to your health than it is to someone equally overweight who has put on fat primarily below the waist.

Whether cycles of losing and then regaining weight, so called yo-yo dieting, bring with them an extra heart-health risk is a controversial issue. Some recent studies claim yo-yo dieting is harmful. However, a task force convened by the National Institutes of Health reviewed the existing research as of 1994 and found no compelling evidence that weight cycling adversely affects health or makes it harder to lose weight in the future.

Cancer Science

If you are more than 40 percent overweight, you are at markedly higher risk of colon, breast, prostate, gallbladder, ovarian, and uterine cancers. According to the ACS's twelve-year Cancer Prevention Study I, obesity raised women's cancer risk by about 55 percent and men's by about 33 percent.

Many studies have pegged obesity as a risk factor for breast cancer in older women. They disagree about the amount of danger, however. Gaining weight as an adult female increases your risk of developing cancer after menopause. In one study, gaining seventy extra pounds meant a two-and-a-half times greater risk; gaining forty pounds brought about half that increase.

In summary, the AHA and the ACS recommend that you should achieve and maintain a desirable weight. If you need to lose weight, follow this chapter's guidelines for low-fat, high-fiber eating and increase your physical activity (see Chapter 4 for lots of tips). Always eat enough calories to maintain your recommended body weight.

IS IT TOO LATE TO CHANGE HOW YOU EAT?

"The first birthday after my heart attack, my family served me a loaf of French bread with candles on it."

It is never too late to gain some health benefits from good nutrition. If you have been diagnosed with high cholesterol or other *lipid* problems, the first line of medical treatment is likely to include changes in what you eat. For many people, making nutrition and lifestyle changes is enough to bring the risks under control.

Some people are very sensitive to changes in what they eat. Their cholesterol falls significantly when they follow advice for low-fat eating. In other people, cholesterol levels seem resistant to diet changes. If you are one of them, you may need to take advantage of other strategies, such as medication, to bring down your risk. The only way to know about your response is to make eating changes and see what happens. When people with high cholesterol follow a low-fat nutrition plan, studies show that they can, on average, reduce cholesterol about 10 to 15 percent. Every 1 percent drop in cholesterol lowers your heart attack risk by at least 2 percent. Even if you've been diagnosed with atherosclerosis, you can reduce the chance of a heart attack by reducing your LDL and total cholesterol with healthful eating and other lifestyle changes.

If you have had a heart attack, your physician will want to reduce the chance of another. He or she will help you achieve the lowest LDL cholesterol and the highest HDL cholesterol that you can. Low-fat eating, not smoking, and exercising are likely to form the cornerstones of your treatment. You may also need medications to bring your lipids under control.

If you have been diagnosed with cancer, eating nutritious foods will make it easier to keep up your strength and fight infection while you undergo cancer treatment. However, no nutrition plan, specific food, vitamin, or dietary supplement has been scientifically shown either to cure cancer or to stop it from coming back.

Getting Started: How Do You Rate Now?

Now you know about the six most important aspects of proper nutrition and why you should pay careful attention to each. It's time to see how your current eating plan measures up.

1. DO YOU EAT TOO MUCH FAT AND CHOLESTEROL?

Fat

The American Heart Association and the American Cancer Society recommend that all adults limit the total fat they eat daily to less than 30 percent of calories. Saturated fats should be less than 10 percent, and cholesterol shouldn't be over 300 milligrams. If you are an average American, about 34 percent of your calories comes from fat and 12 percent from saturated fat. If so, to be within the recommendations discussed in this chapter, you need to cut out about 15 percent of the total fat and 25 percent of the saturated fat you eat.

The AHA has two eating plans to help you lower your blood cholesterol: the Step-One Diet and the Step-Two Diet. The nutrition plan that corresponds to this chapter's guidelines is the Step-One Diet. It is recommended for everyone. The Step-Two Diet is suggested if you need to lower your cholesterol more than you can with the Step-One Diet. The Step-Two Diet restricts saturated fats to less than 7 percent of calories and daily cholesterol to 200 milligrams. For a copy of a brochure outlining these nutrition plans, contact your local American Heart Association (see pages 301–302).

How much fat are you eating? Here are two ways to assess your fat sta-tus. The first one helps you calculate the percentage of your calories that comes from fat. In the second method, your answers to questions about common sources of fat in your eating plan give you a rough idea of whether you meet the guidelines.

Computing the Fat
To check whether too many of your calories are coming from fat—par-ticularly from saturated fat—write down everything you ate on any typ-ical day.

Next, add up the number of fat grams you consumed. The FDA requires packaged foods to display a "Nutrition Facts" label that lists the number of grams of total fat and saturated fat they contain. Or you can consult the American Heart Association *Brand Name Fat and Cholesterol Counter* or a similar publication. Be sure to check the serving size on the label or in the book and adjust the amount of fat if you ate a larger or smaller portion. For dishes you eat at home, use the chart below to esti-mate the amount of fat. Remember to include any fat used in cooking. After you have estimated your total fat, figure out the saturated fat.

FAT, SATURATED-FAT, AND CALORIE CONTENT OF COMMON FOODS

Food Description/Portion	Fat g	Saturated Fat g	Calories
Breads, Pasta, and Starchy Vegetables			
Breads, Pancakes, and Waffles			
English muffin, plain (half)	0.6	—	69
Pancake, with egg, milk, 6" diameter × ½" thick (1)	5.3	1.9	164
Pasta and Rice, Cooked			
Noodles, egg, cooked in unsalted water (1 cup)	2.4	0.5	212
Rice, white, cooked in unsalted water (1 cup)	0.6	0.2	264
Starchy Vegetables			
Corn, lima beans, green peas, white potato (½ cup)	0.0	0.0	80
Dairy Products			
Cheese			
Cheese, Cheddar, Parmesan, Roquefort, Swiss (1 oz)	9.4	6.0	114

Food Description/Portion	Fat g	Saturated Fat g	Calories
Dairy Products (cont.)			
Dairy Toppings			
Sour cream, real (1 tbsp)	2.5	1.6	26
Milk			
Milk, skim or nonfat (1 cup)	0.4	0.3	86
whole (1 cup)	8.2	5.1	150
Eggs			
Egg, whole, raw (1)	5.6	1.7	79
white, raw (1)	trace	0.0	16
Fruits			
Apple, raw, 2¾" diameter (1)	0.5	0.1	81
Banana, 9" long (half)	0.3	0.1	53
Strawberries, raw, whole (1½ cups)	0.7	0.0	56
Meat, Poultry, and Seafood			
Beef			
Beef, lean, average all grades, cooked (1 oz)	2.9	1.1	63
Ground beef, extra lean, broiled (1 oz)	4.5	1.8	75
Chicken			
Breast, with skin, stewed (4 oz)	8.2	2.3	202
fried with batter, with skin (5 oz)	18.5	4.9	364
Finfish			
Fish sticks and portions, frozen and reheated (1 oz)	3.4	0.9	76
Flounder or sole, cooked, dry heat (1 oz)	0.4	0.1	33
Tuna, white, canned in water, drained solids (1 oz)	0.7	0.2	39
Tuna salad, prepared with light tuna in oil, pickle relish, salad dressing, onion, celery (½ cup)	9.5	1.6	192
Lunch Meat			
Frankfurter, beef and pork (1 oz)	8.3	3.1	91
chicken (1 oz)	5.5	1.6	73
Pork			
Bacon, pan-fried, 4½ slices (1 oz)	14.0	5.0	163
Ham, boneless, extra lean, roasted (1 oz)	1.6	0.5	41
Pork tenderloin, roasted (1 oz)	1.4	0.5	47
Shellfish			
Shrimp, cooked (1 oz)	0.3	0.1	28
Fast Food			
Pizza, pepperoni (1 slice—⅛ of 12" diameter)	5.2	1.7	135

Food Description/Portion	Fat g	Saturated Fat g	Calories
Mixed Dishes with Meat, Poultry, and Seafood			
Macaroni and cheese, homemade (1 cup)	22.2	11.9	430
Spaghetti with meatballs and tomato sauce, canned (1 cup)	10.8	2.2	258
Stew, beef and vegetable (1 cup)	10.5	4.4	218
Soups, Canned			
Cream of mushroom, prepared with water (1 cup)	9.0	2.4	129
Vegetarian vegetable, prepared with water (1 cup)	1.9	0.3	72
Vegetables			
Broccoli, fresh, chopped, cooked (½ cup)	0.1	0.0	25
Green beans, fresh, cooked (½ cup)	0.2	0.0	13

Once you have totaled the fat grams and saturated fat grams you eat each day, see where you fall on the chart below. The calculations are based on each gram of fat containing nine calories.

FAT GRAMS BY CALORIE LEVELS

Calorie Level	Maximum Total Fat Grams (30% of calories)	Saturated Fat if Step-One Diet (10% of calories)	Saturated Fat if Step-Two Diet (7% of calories)
1,200	40	13	9
1,500	50	17	12
1,800	60	20	14
2,000	67	22	16
2,200	73	24	17
2,500	83	28	19
3,000	100	33	23

If your fat grams are below the maximum, you are within the suggested guidelines for fat intake.

The Quiz Approach

To see quickly whether you are eating more fat than is good for your health, try the quiz below. It's adapted from a MEDFICTS questionnaire doctors use as part of the National Cholesterol Education Program. Keep in mind that this particular test is concerned only with your consumption of high-fat foods that are common in the American diet. You must be aware that low-fat foods can be as high in calories as their high-fat counterparts. Just because a food is low in fat doesn't mean you can eat it without using your common sense.

High-Fat Foods Quiz

M is for Meats

1. How many times a week do you eat any of these meats?

Beef: Ribs, steak, chuck blade, brisket, ground beef, meat loaf, corned beef.

Processed meats: Regular hamburger, fast-food hamburger, bacon, lunch meat, sausage, hot dogs, knockwurst.

Pork and others: Pork shoulder, chops, or ribs; ground pork; regular ham; lamb steaks, ribs, or chops; organ meats; poultry with skin.

> *Rarely or never:* give yourself 0.   _____
>
> *3 times a week or fewer*
>> If your daily portion totals about six ounces (or about the size of two decks of playing cards), score 6.
>>
>> If your daily portion is smaller than that, score 3.
>>
>> If your daily portion is larger than that, score 9.   _____
>
> *4 times a week or more*
>> If your daily portion totals about six ounces (or about the size of two decks of playing cards), score 14.
>>
>> If your daily portion is smaller than that, score 7.
>>
>> If your daily portion is larger than that, score 21.   _____

2. Do you choose lean cuts of meat, low-fat processed meats, poultry without skin, or fish?

> If yes, and you eat small or medium amounts of these foods, score 0.   _____
>
> If your daily portion is large (more than six ounces), score 6.   _____

E is for Eggs

1. How many times a week do you eat whole eggs or egg yolks?

> *Rarely or never:* give yourself 0. _____

> *3 times a week or fewer*

>> If you eat one egg each time, score 3.

>> If you eat two eggs each time, score 6.

>> If you eat three or more eggs each time, score 9. _____

> *4 times a week or more*

>> If you eat one egg each time, score 7.

>> If you eat two eggs each time, score 14.

>> If you eat three or more eggs each time, score 21. _____

D is for Dairy

1. How many times a week do you use whole milk, 2% milk, 2% buttermilk, or yogurt made with whole milk?

> *Rarely or never:* give yourself 0. _____

> *3 times a week or fewer*

>> If you drink or eat less than a cup each time, score 3.

>> If you drink or eat about a cup each time, score 6.

>> If you drink or eat more than a cup each time, score 9. _____

> *4 times a week or more*

>> If you drink or eat less than a cup each time, score 7.

>> If you drink or eat about a cup each time, score 14.

>> If you drink or eat more than a cup each time, score 21. _____

2. How many times a week do you use cheeses made with whole milk?

These include cream cheese, Cheddar, Monterey Jack, Colby, Swiss, American processed, blue cheese, mozzarella, cottage cheese, and ricotta.

> *Rarely or never:* give yourself 0. _____

> *3 times a week or fewer*

>> If you eat about one ounce each time (or about a half-cup of cottage cheese or ricotta), score 6.

>> If you eat a smaller portion, score 3.

>> If you eat a larger portion, score 9. _____

4 times a week or more
> If you eat about one ounce each time (or about a
> half-cup of cottage cheese or ricotta), score 14.
> If you eat a smaller portion, score 7.
> If you eat a larger portion, score 21.   _____

3. How many times a week do you eat regular or pre-
mium ice cream or milk shakes made with ice cream?
> *Rarely or never:* give yourself 0.   _____
> *3 times a week or fewer*
>> If you have less than a half-cup each time, score 3.
>> If you have about a half-cup each time, score 6.
>> If you have more than a half-cup each time, score 9.   _____
> *4 times a week or more*
>> If you have less than a half-cup each time, score 7.
>> If you have about a half-cup each time, score 14.
>> If you have more than a half-cup each time, score 21. _____

F is for Fried Foods

1. How many times a week do you eat French fries; fried
vegetables; fried chicken, fish, or meat?
> *Rarely or never:* give yourself 0.   _____
> *3 times a week or fewer*
>> If you eat about a half-cup of French fries or fried
>> vegetables or three ounces of fried meat each
>> time, score 6.
>> If you eat a smaller portion, score 3.
>> If you eat a larger portion, score 9.   _____
> *4 times a week or more*
>> If you eat about a half-cup of French fries or fried
>> vegetables or three ounces of fried meat each
>> time, score 14.
>> If you eat a smaller portion, score 7.
>> If you eat a larger portion, score 21.   _____

I is for In Baked Goods

1. How many times a week do you eat a doughnut, biscuit,
butter roll, muffin, croissant, sweet roll, Danish, slice of
cake, piece of pie, slice of coffee cake, or cookie? (Don't

count special low-fat baked goods, angel food cake, fruit bars, or homemade baked goods made with vegetable oil.)

    Rarely or never: give yourself 0.   _____

    3 times a week or fewer

      If you eat fewer than one each time, score 3.

      If you eat one each time, score 6.

      If you eat more than one each time, score 9.   _____

    4 times a week or more

      If you eat fewer than one each time, score 7.

      If you eat one each time, score 14.

      If you eat more than one each time, score 21.   _____

C is for Convenience Foods

1. How many times a week do you eat canned, packaged, or frozen meals or dinner items such as pizza, macaroni and cheese, potpies, or cream soups? (Don't count special low-fat dinners or side dishes.)

    Rarely or never: give yourself 0.   _____

    3 times a week or fewer

      If you eat a potpie, slice of pizza, frozen entrée, or about a cup of soup or macaroni and cheese each time, score 6.

      If you eat a smaller portion, score 3.

      If you eat a larger portion, score 9.   _____

    4 times a week or more

      If you eat a potpie, slice of pizza, frozen entrée, or about a cup of soup or macaroni and cheese each time, score 14.

      If you eat a smaller portion, score 7.

      If you eat a larger portion, score 21.   _____

T is for Table Fats

1. How many times a week do you use butter, stick margarine, regular salad dressing, mayonnaise, or sour cream? (Don't count low-fat versions of these products or tub margarines.)

Rarely or never: give yourself 0.   _____

3 times a week or fewer

    If you eat one pat of butter or margarine or one to
two tablespoons of the other toppings each
time, score 6.

    If you eat a smaller portion, score 3.

    If you eat a larger portion, score 9.   _____

4 times a week or more

    If you eat one pat of butter or margarine or one to
two tablespoons of the other toppings each
time, score 14.

    If you eat a smaller portion, score 7.

    If you eat a larger portion, score 21.   _____

S is for Snacks

How many times a week do you eat these snack foods:
potato, corn, or taco chips; cheese puffs; snack mix; nuts;
regular crackers; regular popcorn; candy? (Don't count air-
popped popcorn, nonfat or low-fat crackers, fat-free chips,
hard candy, licorice, fruit rolls, breadsticks, pretzels, or fruit.)

Rarely or never: give yourself 0.   _____

3 times a week or fewer

    If you eat an average serving (check the package)
each time, score 6.

    If you eat a smaller portion, score 3.

    If you eat a larger portion, score 9.   _____

4 times a week or more

    If you eat less than the average serving each time,
score 7.

    If you eat an average serving each time, score 14.

    If you eat a larger-than-average serving each time,
score 21.   _____

                                               TOTAL   _____

Your Test Score

Is your total score *higher than 70?* If so, you are eating too many foods
high in fat or cholesterol. For your eating choices to contribute to a disease-preventive lifestyle, you will need to cut back.

A score *between 40 and 70* indicates you may not need to reduce the amount of fat you eat *if* you maintain a desirable weight and follow the other guidelines for healthful nutrition. The amount of fat allowed depends on how many calories you eat. If you are smaller than average, you may want to aim for the low end of this range. If your doctor has suggested that you follow the Step-Two Diet to lower your cholesterol, make food choices that bring your score below 40.

Did you score *below 40?* Congratulations! You probably do not need to reduce the amount of fat you eat. If your doctor has suggested that you follow the Step-Two Diet to lower your cholesterol, choose foods that keep your score below 40.

Cholesterol

One thing you don't have to worry about is getting enough cholesterol to be healthy. But it is easy to get too much. You don't need to eat a speck of cholesterol, because your body makes all you need.

To assess whether you're eating too much cholesterol, answer the following questions:

♦ *Do you eat meats fried in grease or more than six ounces of meat every day?* If prepared without lard, six ounces keeps you well within your daily cholesterol allowance.

♦ *Do you eat organ meats?* They are extremely high in cholesterol. Just three ounces of chicken giblets or beef kidney or liver contain a day's allotment of cholesterol. One ounce of beef brains has a two-day maximum!

♦ *Do you eat either high-fat cheese and dairy products or lots of low-fat cheese?* Besides having more fat, high-fat cheeses have twice as much cholesterol as cheeses made from part-skim or skim milk. One ounce of regular cheese, a cup of whole milk, one and one-half tablespoons of whipped cream, or a half-cup of ice cream has about 30 milligrams of cholesterol. You can see how quickly the milligrams can add up in your daily intake.

♦ *How often do you eat a whole egg or baked goods prepared with egg yolks?* A single egg yolk has about 213 milligrams of cholesterol. Eating one egg for breakfast makes it tough to keep under the daily cholesterol maximum of 300 mg without giving up all other animal foods. You should eat no more than three to four egg yolks a week. Be sure to count any yolks you eat as part of another food, such as cake or casseroles.

♦ *Do you eat many high-cholesterol shellfish?* Although low in fat, shrimp and crayfish have lots of cholesterol. A five- to six-ounce portion of either one uses up a day's cholesterol allotment. Scallops, clams, lobster, and oysters are lower-cholesterol choices. Because these shellfish are so low in total fat and saturated fat, it's okay to enjoy them now and then. Just don't fry them or dip them in melted butter!

2. Do You Eat Enough Fiber?

The average-size person should consume twenty-five to thirty grams of fiber each day. If you eat five or more servings of fruits and vegetables and six or more servings of grain products each day, you probably get the recommended amount of fiber. To be sure, ask yourself the following questions about your specific food choices:

- *In general, do you choose whole grain cereals and breads over more-refined products?* Most people need to increase their consumption of complex carbohydrates. These foods help do that.
- *Do you eat foods high in soluble fiber, the type that has been shown to reduce cholesterol?* Examples are oatmeal and oat bran, beans, peas, brown rice, barley, psyllium, citrus fruits, strawberries, and apples. Psyllium, used as a stool softener, is almost pure soluble fiber but has little other nutritional value. It's available at drug stores and grocery stores.
- *Do you eat foods high in insoluble fiber?* This also helps the bowel work well, although it doesn't lower cholesterol. Examples are whole wheat breads, wheat cereals, wheat bran, cabbage, beets, carrots, brussels sprouts, turnips, cauliflower, and apple skin.
- *Are you often constipated?* Fiber is important for your bowel to function properly. If your stools are hard or constipation is a problem, it is likely you are not getting enough fiber. Fiber works well only if you are drinking enough water. (The suggested amount is six to eight eight-ounce glasses of water a day.)
- *Do you eat lots of fruits, vegetables, and grains?* The American Heart Association recommends that at least half of your calories should come from carbohydrates, particularly complex carbohydrates with lots of fiber. Most Americans need to shift their food choices more toward carbohydrates and away from animal foods that include no fiber at all (eggs, milk, cheese, seafood).

3. Do You Eat Enough Fruits and Vegetables?

Are you eating at least five servings of fruits and vegetables each day? Only one in four adults does, but it's easy. Each serving doesn't have to be a separate vegetable—an entrée-size green salad may count as three servings, or a big slice of watermelon as two.

For your daily vegetable count, one serving equals one cup of salad greens, one-half cup of other vegetables, or three-quarters of a cup of vegetable juice. A medium-size piece of fruit, a half-cup of berries or cut-up fruit, or a half-cup of fruit juice counts as one serving. If you already eat more than five servings a day, keep it up! Five servings is a minimum, just enough to ensure that you will get needed nutrients.

Is your family in a fruit and vegetable rut, eating the same foods day after day? Then you are not getting the full health benefits that this part of your nutrition plan can provide. Look more closely at which fruits and vegetables you eat and how often you eat them.

- *Do you eat foods high in vitamin A and related nutrients that may reduce your cancer risk?* Broccoli, carrots, pumpkins, sweet potatoes, cantaloupes, peaches, prunes, and other dark green and deep yellow fruits and vegetables are some choices.
- *Do you eat some fruits and vegetables high in vitamin C every day?* Oranges, cantaloupes, berries, tomatoes, greens, and potatoes are examples. They may prevent the formation of some cancer-causing substances.
- *Do you eat cruciferous vegetables several times a week?* Try some broccoli, brussels sprouts, cabbage, cauliflower, and other dark green vegetables. They produce enzymes that may help protect against cancer.

4. DO YOU EAT TOO MANY SALTY OR CURED FOODS?

You don't have to eliminate smoked and cured foods from your diet. Instead, just shift to occasional use and appetizer portions. If any food listed below is a staple of your dinner table or lunchbox choices, think about serving it less often.

Anchovies	Salted and dried venison
Bacon	Sausage (liverwurst, pepperoni
Beef jerky	salami, Polish, bratwurst, pork)
Corned beef	Smoked cheeses
Dried chipped beef	Smoked chicken
Herring	Smoked ham
Pastrami (beef or turkey)	Smoked and cured pork
Pickled pigs' feet	Smoked seafood (cod, salmon,
Processed meat (bologna,	oysters, whitefish)
frankfurters, lunch meats)	Smoked turkey

Manufacturers have added vitamin C compounds to some foods to help prevent the nitrites and proteins from forming carcinogens. To find such protective compounds, check the food labels. Look for foods that list these ingredients: ascorbic acid, sodium ascorbate, or sodium erthrobate. Eaten in moderation, these foods should cause less concern than do other foods with nitrites. If the label on a smoky-tasting food lists liquid smoke, the food may be less hazardous than a naturally smoked product.

Almost all of us eat many times more sodium than we need, at least double the recommended maximum of 3,000 milligrams a day. That's the amount in about a teaspoon and one-half of salt. You can easily estimate how much salt you add during cooking and at the table. However, that usually represents little more than a third of the sodium you eat. The rest comes from processed foods.

If you have high blood pressure, your physician may advise you to restrict sodium to a lower level. He or she will want you to try this at least long enough to determine whether your blood pressure seems to be salt sensitive.

5. IS YOUR DRINKING WITHIN RECOMMENDED GUIDELINES?

If your lifestyle includes wine, beer, or other alcoholic beverages, keep track of what you drink on a typical day. Then figure the amount of ethanol (pure alcohol) you are consuming.

One ounce of ethanol is contained in:

2 ounces of 100-proof whiskey
3 ounces of 80-proof whiskey
8 ounces of wine
24 ounces of beer

If you drink more than one or two ounces of ethanol a day, you surpass the amount of alcohol that may have overall protective benefits. Drinking more is usually not healthful for your cardiovascular system or the rest of your body, and the health problems mount up as consumption increases.

Some people should *not* drink alcohol, even moderately. The National Institute of Alcoholism and Alcohol Abuse suggests that you abstain from alcohol completely:

- If you are pregnant or trying to conceive;
- If you will be driving or doing other activities that require you to be attentive or have unimpaired muscular coordination;
- If you are taking antihistamines, sedatives, or other medications that can magnify the effect of alcohol;
- If you are a recovering alcoholic;
- If you are under the legal drinking age.

Some people should approach alcohol use with more caution than others. Ask for professional advice about how—and whether—you can safely drink alcohol

- If you have peptic ulcers;
- If you have diabetes;
- If you have a strong family history of alcoholism;
- If you have been told your triglyceride level is high.

6. ARE YOU AT A HEALTHFUL WEIGHT?

Life insurance companies make their money by predicting how long a customer is likely to live. Using their analysis of the weights and death rates of policyholders, for many years the insurance industry has published tables of "ideal" or "desirable" weights. These are the weights of the people with the lowest mortality rates.

To help you determine whether you are at a healthful weight, use the appropriate table on pages 101–103. The ACS and the AHA use these tables, published by the Metropolitan Life Insurance Company in 1959. In 1983 the insurance industry revised its tables, raising the weights by about 10 percent to reflect their experience that even obese policyholders live longer than they used to. However, the ACS and the AHA are concerned that the heavier weights may not be beneficial to health. The two organizations therefore stick by the older guidelines.

Following the steps below will help you figure out your desirable weight.

- *Find your frame size.* You probably already have a sense of whether you are big boned, average, or slight in build. Metropolitan rates people by a simple measurement:

    1. Get a ruler.
    2. Extend your right arm in front of you, palm facing up.
    3. Bend your right arm at the elbow, lifting your forearm straight up.

4. With your left hand, place your thumb on the bone sticking out on the inside of your right elbow and place your index finger on the bone sticking out on the outside.

5. Without changing the distance between your left thumb and index finger, move your right elbow out of the way.

6. Measure the distance between your left thumb and index finger and compare it to the chart below.

7. If the measurement falls in the range listed for your height, use the medium-frame listings for desirable weight. If it is below the range, use the small-frame listing. If it is higher than the range, look for your desirable weight in the large-frame listing.

- *Weigh yourself.* Leave on your shoes and regular indoor clothing. Heights on the charts assume you are wearing low-heeled shoes.
- *Find the right chart for your frame size and see where your weight falls on the "Desirable Weight" column.* If it is in the desirable range for height and gender, help to keep it that way through a program of exercise and healthful eating. If the body weight exceeds the desirable weight by 20 percent or more and the excess weight is fat rather than water, muscle, or bone, you are at increased risk for heart attack and stroke. If it is in the 40 percent overweight range, you are at increased risk to develop several different types of cancer.
- *If the chart reading doesn't make sense to you, ask your physician about your weight and health risks.* Because muscle tissue weighs more than fat, if you are a very athletic, muscular person, you may be above the desirable weight range but still have little fat and be at a healthy weight. On the other hand, if you have little muscle tone, you may be falsely reassured by a weight reading that doesn't take into account the amount of fat on your body.

FRAME SIZE

Men		Women	
Height	*Elbow measure*	*Height*	*Elbow measure*
5'2"–5'3"	2½"–2⅞"	4'10"–4'11"	2¼"–2½"
5'4"–5'7"	2⅝"–2⅞"	5'0"–5'3"	2¼"–2½"
5'8"–5'11"	2¾"–3"	5'4"–5'7"	2⅜"–2⅝"
6'0"–6'3"	2¾"–3⅛"	5'8"–5'11"	2⅜"–2⅝"
6'4"	2⅞"–3¼"	6'0"	2½"–2¾"

DESIRABLE WEIGHT: MEN, SMALL FRAME

Height	Desirable Weight	20% Overweight	40% Overweight
5'2"	112–120 lb	134–144 lb	157–168 lb
5'3"	115–123	138–148	161–172
5'4"	118–126	142–151	165–176
5'5"	121–129	145–155	169–181
5'6"	124–133	149–160	174–186
5'7"	128–137	154–164	179–192
5'8"	132–141	158–169	185–197
5'9"	136–145	163–174	190–203
5'10"	140–150	168–180	196–210
5'11"	144–154	173–185	202–216
6'0"	148–158	178–190	207–221
6'1"	152–162	182–194	213–227
6'2"	156–167	187–200	218–234
6'3"	160–171	192–205	224–239
6'4"	164–175	197–210	230–245

DESIRABLE WEIGHT: MEN, MEDIUM FRAME

Height	Desirable Weight	20% Overweight	40% Overweight
5'2"	118–129 lb	142–155 lb	165–181 lb
5'3"	121–133	145–160	169–186
5'4"	124–136	149–163	174–190
5'5"	127–139	152–167	178–195
5'6"	130–143	156–172	182–200
5'7"	134–147	161–176	188–206
5'8"	138–152	166–182	193–213
5'9"	142–156	170–187	199–218
5'10"	146–160	175–192	204–224
5'11"	150–165	180–198	210–231
6'0"	154–170	185–204	216–238
6'1"	158–175	190–210	221–245
6'2"	162–180	194–216	227–252
6'3"	167–185	200–222	234–259
6'4"	172–190	206–228	241–266

DESIRABLE WEIGHT: MEN, LARGE FRAME

Height	Desirable Weight	20% Overweight	40% Overweight
5'2"	124–141 lb	149–169 lb	174–197 lb
5'3"	129–144	155–173	181–202
5'4"	132–148	158–178	185–207
5'5"	135–152	162–182	189–213
5'6"	138–156	166–187	193–218
5'7"	142–161	170–193	199–225
5'8"	147–166	176–199	206–232
5'9"	151–170	181–204	211–238
5'10"	155–174	186–209	217–244
5'11"	159–179	191–215	223–251
6'0"	164–184	197–221	230–258
6'1"	168–189	202–227	235–265
6'2"	173–194	208–233	242–272
6'3"	178–199	214–239	249–279
6'4"	182–204	218–245	255–286

DESIRABLE WEIGHT: WOMEN, SMALL FRAME

Height	Desirable Weight	20% Overweight	40% Overweight
4'10"	92–98 lb	110–118 lb	129–137 lb
4'11"	94–101	113–121	132–141
5'0"	96–104	115–125	134–146
5'1"	99–107	119–128	139–150
5'2"	102–110	122–132	143–154
5'3"	105–113	126–136	147–158
5'4"	108–116	130–139	151–162
5'5"	111–119	133–143	155–167
5'6"	114–123	137–148	159–172
5'7"	118–127	142–152	165–178
5'8"	122–131	146–157	171–183
5'9"	126–135	151–162	176–189
5'10"	130–140	156–168	182–196
5'11"	134–144	161–174	188–202
6'0"	138–148	166–178	193–207

For women between eighteen and twenty-five, subtract one pound for each year under twenty-five.

DESIRABLE WEIGHT: WOMEN, MEDIUM FRAME

Height	Desirable Weight	20% Overweight	40% Overweight
4'10"	96–107 lb	115–128 lb	134–150 lb
4'11"	98–110	118–132	137–154
5'0"	101–113	121–136	141–158
5'1"	104–116	125–139	146–162
5'2"	107–119	128–143	150–167
5'3"	110–122	132–146	154–171
5'4"	113–126	136–151	158–176
5'5"	116–130	139–156	162–182
5'6"	120–135	144–162	168–189
5'7"	124–139	149–167	174–195
5'8"	128–143	154–172	179–200
5'9"	132–147	158–176	185–206
5'10"	136–151	163–181	190–211
5'11"	140–155	168–186	196–217
6'0"	144–159	173–191	202–223

For women between eighteen and twenty-five, subtract one pound for each year under twenty-five.

DESIRABLE WEIGHT: WOMEN, LARGE FRAME

Height	Desirable Weight	20% Overweight	40% Overweight
4'10"	104–119 lb	125–143 lb	146–167 lb
4'11"	106–122	127–146	149–171
5'0"	109–125	131–150	153–175
5'1"	112–128	134–154	157–179
5'2"	115–131	138–157	161–183
5'3"	118–134	142–161	165–188
5'4"	121–138	145–166	169–193
5'5"	125–142	150–170	175–199
5'6"	129–146	155–175	181–204
5'7"	133–150	160–180	186–210
5'8"	137–154	164–185	192–216
5'9"	141–158	169–190	197–221
5'10"	145–163	174–196	203–228
5'11"	149–168	179–202	209–235
6'0"	153–173	184–208	214–242

For women between eighteen and twenty-five, subtract one pound for each year under twenty-five.

Is Your Weight Creeping Up?

Look at where your weight five years ago or ten years ago falls on the charts. If you used to be at the lower end of the desirable range but your weight is now edging toward the top, don't let it get out of control. Exercise and eat healthfully now.

Are You an Apple or a Pear?

If you have a top-heavy, apple-shaped physique, the same number of extra pounds can pose a greater health risk than if you are bottom heavy and pear shaped (see page 84). Your mirror will give you a pretty good idea of where your fat is. You can also calculate the waist-to-hip ratio that doctors use to determine whether you have too much fat around the middle.

1. Measure your waist.
2. Measure your hips at the widest point.
3. Divide your waist measurement by your hip measurement.
4. If you are a woman, the answer should be less than 0.8 (for example, no wider than a twenty-eight-and-one-half-inch waist if you have thirty-six-inch hips). If you are a man, the answer should be less than 1.0 (for example, thirty-six-inch hips should be topped by a waist of less than thirty-six inches).

Putting the Guidelines into Action

After reading the previous sections of this chapter, you should be able to decide which of the six important areas of your eating plan needs attention first. This section will give you lots of tips about getting into action. After you pat yourself on the back for mastering one area, move on to the next area that needs some work.

1. LOWER YOUR FAT AND CHOLESTEROL QUOTIENTS

"Sometimes people hand me a gooey dessert and say, 'I made this with margarine instead of butter because of you.' They don't realize that I have to cut down on all kinds of fat."

Your answers to the quiz on pages 90–94 may reveal the perfect place for you to start to reduce fat in your diet. Look at the foods that gave you the most points. Could you eat any of them in smaller portions or trade them for a low-fat or nonfat substitute?

Serve Meat Leaner, in Smaller Amounts, and Less Often

"Two ounces of grilled chicken on a plate looks pitiful. Two ounces of grilled chicken sliced and arranged on top of a big salad or plate of pasta looks like a gourmet meal. And tastes like it, too."

Meat, fish, and poultry provide concentrated nutrition. They are dense in protein, B vitamins, and iron—and can also be packed with calories and fat.

Meat can be part of a more healthful diet, but your focus may need to shift to other foods. If a large piece of meat is usually the centerpiece of dinner at your house, try serving fish two or three times a week. Some other nights you might have a main dish featuring pasta, rice, beans, tofu, or vegetables instead of meat.

When you do serve meat, choose leaner cuts instead of those high in saturated fats. The beef found at the supermarket probably is graded Prime, Choice, and Select. For the least marbling (flecks of fat in the meat), pick Select. Sirloin tip, flank steak, round steak, rump roast, and chuck arm roast are good choices. Or try lean cuts of other meats, such as pork loin, veal, venison, lean ham, and lamb flank and leg-shank.

Instead of fatty processed meats, look for nonfat or low-fat lunch meat, low-fat hot dogs, or Canadian bacon.

Serve poultry, removing the skin and the fat under the skin before cooking. If you are roasting a whole chicken or turkey, however, leave the skin on to keep the bird from getting too dry, but remove it before serving. Do not select poultry that has been injected with fat and salt.

Fish and other types of seafood are lower in fat than meats. More of their fat is polyunsaturated. Shrimp and crayfish are higher in cholesterol than most other types of seafood but are still lower in fat than most meats and poultry.

Restrict the meat, fish, and poultry you eat to six ounces a day. Keep portions to three ounces, or about the size of a deck of playing cards. Three ounces is also about two deli-style thin slices of meat (each slice about a quarter-inch thick and three inches by three inches) or three-fourths of a cup of flaked fish. One-half of a skinless chicken breast or a skinless chicken leg with a thigh also provides about a three-ounce serving.

Eat Fewer Eggs

"I used to eat eggs because they were the quickest thing to eat that could keep me going through the morning. I finally decided to eat cereal at home and take a muffin to eat during the coffee break. Ultimately, it's more satisfying."

If you are a devotee of two eggs sunny-side up at breakfast, egg salad sandwiches at lunch, or deviled eggs as a side dish or appetizer, healthful eating is going to mean some changes.

Limit your consumption of whole eggs and egg yolks to no more than three or four a week. This amount also must take into account any egg yolks used in cooking and in store-bought foods. When cooking, you can replace one whole egg with two egg whites, or use one of the commercial egg substitutes.

Think about when you usually eat eggs and make sure you have some satisfying alternatives. Are eggs your favorite breakfast? Then save them for a weekend treat when you have time to enjoy them. During the week,

HOW "INVISIBLE" EGGS ADD UP

Foods Containing Eggs	Approximate Portion of Whole Egg
Beverages	
Eggnog (½ cup)	¼
Breads	
Cornbread (3 inches × 3 inches)	¼
Muffin (1)	¹⁄₁₀
Pancakes, 4 inches (2)	¼
Desserts	
Baked custard or crème brûlée (6 ounces)	½
Chocolate, lemon meringue, or pumpkin pie (⅛ of 9-inch pie)	⅓
Pound cake (¹⁄₁₂ loaf)	¼
Sponge cake (¹⁄₁₂ of 9-inch square)	½
Tapioca pudding (½ cup)	⅓
Yellow or chocolate two-layer cake (¹⁄₁₆ of 9-inch cake)	⅛
Main Dishes	
Cheese soufflé (1 cup)	½
Chicken salad (½ cup)	⅓
Corn pudding (½ cup)	½
Egg salad	1–2
Omelette (depends on size)	1–3
Salad Dressings	
Mayonnaise (¼ cup)	¼
Thousand Island (¼ cup)	⅓

plan some substitutes, such as hot cereal with skim milk, cold cereal with skim milk or nonfat or low-fat yogurt, muffins, toast, or fruit. Don't skip breakfast or make it any less filling—just switch from fat and cholesterol.

Then think about that weekend treat. Would you enjoy waffles or pancakes (made with one egg spread among several servings) just as much as an egg on its own? Try it. Or cut back from two eggs to one at a sitting.

At lunch and dinner, find alternatives to egg salad or sauces using eggs. Look for sources of hidden eggs you eat regularly. If they add up to more than you should consume, use egg substitutes or egg whites or select prepared foods with less fat and cholesterol.

Take the Fat Out of Dairy Foods

"I keep two types of milk in the house, 2 percent for coffee and 1 percent for everything else. My yogurt is always nonfat since I found the perfect-tasting brand."

Dairy products are excellent sources of protein, calcium, phosphorus, niacin, riboflavin, and vitamins A and D. Part or all the fat can be removed, leaving all these good features intact. As a result, the fat content of dairy foods varies widely. If you choose nonfat or low-fat varieties, you can easily include two or more servings a day and stay within the fat guidelines of proper nutrition.

Milk

If you drink whole milk, use 2-percent milk as a stepping-stone while you get accustomed to lower-fat dairy products. But don't be fooled into thinking that 2-percent milk is 98 percent lower in fat than regular. All milk is mostly water. Whole milk is about 3 percent fat by volume, so 2-percent milk doesn't cut a lot of the fat. Once you're used to 2-percent milk, try 1-percent or skim milk. All you're losing is a lot of fat, saturated fat, cholesterol, and calories.

Cheese

"I never did eat much meat, but I ate lots of cheese. It was the most surprising source of fat in my diet and the hardest one for me to change."

Cheese is a very condensed food. Cheese lovers, and even some vegetarians who routinely use lots of cheese, may find that they are eating far more fat than they should.

FAT/CALORIES IN MILK PRODUCTS

Type of Milk	Fat Grams	Calories	Percentage of Calories from Fat
Whole milk (1 cup)	8.2	150	49
2% milk (1 cup)	4.7	121	35
1% milk (1 cup)	2.6	102	23
Skim/nonfat milk (1 cup)	.4	86	4
Buttermilk (1 cup) (*Note: buttermilk is high in sodium.*)	2.2	99	20
Half-and-half cream (1 tablespoon)	1.7	20	77
Whipping cream, unwhipped (1 tablespoon)	5.6	52	97
Sour cream (1 tablespoon)	2.5	26	87

If you use cheese as a topping for vegetables, try other seasonings. When you shop, look for cheese made with skim milk and try to find nonfat or low-fat varieties (with fewer than five grams of fat per ounce). Limit your portions and use the cheese as a substitute for, not an addition to, meat and fish.

"We buy the cheese with the strongest taste. That way the smallest slivers deliver lots of flavor without much fat."

FAT/CALORIES IN SELECTED CHEESES

Type of Cheese	Fat Grams	Calories	Percentage of Calories from Fat
American (1 ounce)	8.9	106	76
Blue, Brie, Cheddar, Colby, Edam, Gouda, Gruyère, Monterey Jack, Parmesan, Roquefort, or Swiss (1 ounce)	9.4	114	74
Cream cheese (1 ounce)	9.9	99	90
Neufchâtel (1 ounce)	6.6	74	80
Part-skim mozzarella (1 ounce)	4.5	72	56
Part-skim ricotta (1 ounce)	2.2	39	50
Whole-milk ricotta (1 ounce)	3.7	49	68
Cottage cheese			
Dry (½ cup)	.3	62	4
1% fat (½ cup)	1.2	82	13
2% fat (½ cup)	2.2	101	20
Creamed (½ cup)	4.7	109	39

Dairy Desserts

It used to be the law that ice cream was high in fat. If the words "ice cream" went on a package, the product had to contain at least 10 percent fat (by volume, usually translating into more than 50 percent of calories coming from fat). Ice milk, containing 2 to 7 percent fat, was a better choice.

But you no longer have to shy away from the words "ice cream" to reduce the fat in your dessert bowl. Beginning in 1994, the labeling rules switched so that a wider range of products, some with no cream at all, can be called ice cream. Nonfat ice cream has less than a half-gram of fat in a half-cup serving. (In some cases, its creamy texture comes courtesy of an artificial fat like those described on page 155.) A serving of low-fat ice cream has fewer than three grams of fat. Reduced-fat ice creams have to contain at least 25 percent less fat than a comparable regular product. Light ice creams must cut the fat by at least 50 percent. Consult the Nutrition Facts label on the package to see the exact percentages so you know what you're buying.

Sherbet is low in fat but does contain some milk fat. Water-based sorbets and fruit ices are other good choices for a cool dessert treat, usually with no fat.

"The food that helped me cut fat the most was yogurt cheese—straining nonfat plain yogurt until it was thick and rich. I use it instead of ice cream with fruit. I even use it instead of butter on toast, cream cheese on a bagel, cheese on sandwiches, and sour cream on a potato. It's the best!"

Have a Fear of Frying

"Eating fried foods has gone from a delight to being repugnant."

"I sauté with bouillon or wine, or even with clam juice if I'm making a fish dinner. Any kind of liquid with a little flavor is good, and you don't need any fat at all. Or you can use a tiny bit of olive oil to season a monumental panful of vegetables."

Take a potato or zucchini, slice it, and deep-fry. Voilà! You have turned a beneficial no-fat food into one that is dripping with fat and calories.

A fried food is almost always higher in fat than the same food cooked another way. As often as possible, choose one of the many tasty alternatives to frying, such as those listed on the next page.

- *Using cooking sprays or nonstick cookware.* Instead of frying in fat, use a nonstick pan or a cooking spray so that food won't stick.
- *Baking.* Bake or roast meats on a rack or in a pan designed to let fat drip into indentations. Either way, your meat won't sit in fat. Baste with a nonfat or low-fat marinade instead of fat-filled pan drippings.
- *Broiling.* Broil lean meats, poultry, and fish. Instead of using an oil-based marinade, try lemon juice or dry-broil by rubbing seasonings on first and not basting.
- *Oven-frying.* Instead of plunging foods in oil in a skillet or deep fryer, use a tiny bit of oil and your oven to get the same crispy texture. The two healthful versions of favorite fried foods that follow will get you started. They're adapted from the *American Heart Association Cookbook*, 5th Edition, Times Books, 1991.

Oven French Fries

Scrub four large potatoes and cut them into strips about ½ inch wide. Drop into ice water, cover, and chill for 1 to 2 hours. Dry thoroughly. Preheat oven to 475°F. Place the potatoes in a bowl and toss the slices with 2 tablespoons of peanut or safflower oil until they are lightly coated. Spread the fries in a single layer in a shallow baking pan. Bake for 30 to 35 minutes, stirring occasinally so the potatoes brown on all sides. Season with garlic powder, lemon pepper, cumin, chili powder, freshly ground herbs, or other salt-free seasonings. Serves 8.

Crispy Baked Chicken

Preheat oven to 400°F. Line a baking pan with foil. Lightly spray foil with vegetable oil spray. Cut a 2½- to 3-pound frying chicken into serving-size pieces, removing the skin and all visible fat. Rinse chicken pieces and pat dry. Make a coating from a cup of cornflake crumbs seasoned with 1 teaspoon rosemary and ½ teaspoon freshly ground black pepper. Dip the chicken pieces into skim milk (a cup should be plenty) and then into the crumb mixture. Allow to stand briefly so the coating will stick. Arrange the chicken on the baking pan. Bake 45 minutes, or until the chicken is done and the crumbs form a crisp coating. Serves 4.

Sautéing Without Fat
Instead of sautéing in butter or oil, use bouillon, juice, wine, or even a little water.

Steaming
Steaming vegetables preserves their bright color and gives you just the right amount of crispness.

Choose Fats and Oils Wisely
Try to use no more than five to eight servings of fats or oils a day (see list below). This amount should include the margarine you put on your baked potato and on your morning toast. But don't forget the "hidden" oils used in cooking and baking, as well as what's contained in salad dressings and spreads and in prepackaged foods. Substitute unsaturated for saturated fats whenever you can.

These amounts each count as one serving of fat:

- 1 teaspoon of vegetable oil or regular margarine
- 2 teaspoons of diet margarine
- 1 tablespoon of salad dressing
- 2 teaspoons of mayonnaise or peanut butter
- 3 teaspoons of seeds or nuts
- ⅛ of a medium avocado
- 10 small or 5 large olives

In choosing cooking oils and margarine, look for those with the least amount of saturated fat (no more than two grams per tablespoon). Select one that lists liquid vegetable oil as the first ingredient. Some good choices are products made with canola, corn, olive, safflower, sesame, soybean, or sunflower oil.

All oils are 100 percent fat, but no oil is purely one type of fat. All oils contain at least a little saturated fat. Food sources containing both saturated fat and cholesterol include animal fats, such as lard and bacon, beef, chicken, ham, lamb, pork, and turkey fats. Butter, cream, and whole milk also provide lots of saturated fat and cholesterol. Other sources of saturated fat are palm, palm kernel, and coconut oils.

Margarines labeled "diet" and those in tubs may contain less saturated and hydrogenated fats than those in sticks. Buy the ones that list unsaturated liquid oil as the first ingredient. Check the labels for both fat and sodium.

HOW MUCH OF THE FAT YOU COOK WITH IS SATURATED?

Fats	Percentage of Saturated Fat	Fats	Percentage of Saturated Fat
Butter	61	Peanut oil	18
Canola oil	7	Safflower oil	9
Coconut oil	87	Sesame oil	13
Corn oil	13	Soybean oil	16
Olive oil	13	Soybean/cottonseed oil	18
Palm oil	49	Sunflower oil	11
Palm kernel oil	81	Vegetable shortening	27

Look for low-fat (no more than one gram of saturated fatty acids per tablespoon) and fat-free salad dressings, or make your own. Flavored vinegars add zip with no fat. Or use an herb-flavored or naturally stronger tasting oil, such as olive or sesame. A little of those packs more punch.

Switch to low-fat or fat-free mayonnaise or sandwich spreads. As an alternative on your sandwich, try yogurt cheese, mustard, or bean dip with no oil.

Bake the Low-Fat Way

If you love the smell and taste of fresh-baked goodies, learn to make them part of a low-fat menu. Angel food cake (no fat) and fruit bars are good choices for store-bought or homemade baked goods. At the store, look for baked goods marked "low fat." At home, try the recipes in a low-fat cookbook or use a little trial and error to adjust your favorites. Here are some helpful tips.

1. Try using half the fat called for in the recipe and see what happens. In many recipes, it won't change the taste or texture.

2. Switch from ingredients that are high in saturated fats (lard, butter, and vegetable shortening) to vegetable oils lower in saturated fats.

3. Try applesauce or mashed banana to replace oil in some recipes, such as brownies or spice cake.

4. Experiment using water to replace half the oil called for in some recipes, such as marinades and salad dressings.

TAKING THE FAT OUT OF YOUR FAVORITE RECIPES

When your recipe says . . .	. . . Try this instead
Whole milk (1 cup)	1 cup of skim or nonfat milk plus 1 table-spoon of unsaturated oil
Heavy cream (1 cup)	1 cup evaporated skim milk
	½ cup nonfat or low-fat yogurt and ½ cup nonfat or low-fat cottage cheese
Sour cream	Low-fat cottage cheese plus nonfat or low-fat yogurt
	Ricotta cheese (made with skim milk), thinned to taste with yogurt or buttermilk
	Chilled evaporated skim milk whipped with a little lemon juice
	Nonfat or low-fat buttermilk
	Nonfat or low-fat yogurt
Cream cheese	Dry nonfat or low-fat cottage cheese blended with 4 tablespoons of margarine, adding skim milk and seasonings to taste
Butter (1 tablespoon)	1 tablespoon polyunsaturated margarine
	¾ tablespoon polyunsaturated oil
Shortening (1 cup)	1 cup (2 sticks) polyunsaturated margarine
Oil (1 cup)	1¼ cups polyunsaturated margarine
Eggs (1)	1 egg white plus 2 teaspoons of unsaturated oil
	Commercially produced cholesterol-free egg substitute, according to package instructions
	3 egg whites for 2 whole eggs
	2 egg whites for 1 whole egg in baking
Unsweetened baking chocolate (1 ounce)	3 tablespoons unsweetened cocoa powder or carob powder* plus 1 tablespoon poly-unsaturated oil or margarine

*Carob is sweeter than cocoa, so reduce the sugar in the recipe by one fourth.

In many recipes, you can omit a fatty layer or topping and not notice any big change in taste. If an ingredient that pushes your fat alarm seems crucial for a favorite recipe, try a substitution for that item.

To see how easy it is to adapt recipes, look at the following lasagna recipes. One is made the traditional way, and one was adapted for low-fat eating for the *American Heart Association Cookbook,* 5th Edition, Times Books, 1991.

Traditional Lasagna

♦ **Serves 8**

1 8-ounce package of lasagna noodles	½ teaspoon pepper
	1 28-ounce can tomatoes, broken up
1 pound Italian sausage	2 6-ounce cans tomato paste
½ pound ground beef	1 egg, beaten
1 cup chopped onion	1 15-ounce container ricotta cheese
2 cloves garlic, minced	1 tablespoon dried parsley flakes
2 teaspoons sugar	½ teaspoon salt
1 tablespoon salt	1 cup pitted ripe olives, sliced
1½ teaspoons basil leaves	1 pound mozzarella cheese, grated
½ teaspoon fennel seed	¾ cup grated Parmesan cheese

Prepare lasagna noodles according to package directions. Drain. Cook sausage and ground beef; drain excess fat. Add onion and garlic; stir and cook 5 minutes. Add next seven ingredients and simmer 20 minutes. Combine egg, ricotta, parsley, and salt. Into the bottom of a 13-x-9-inch baking dish, spoon about 1½ cups meat sauce. Layer one-third of the lasagna noodles, one-third of the meat sauce, one-third of the ricotta, one-third of the sliced olives, one-third of the mozzarella, and one-third of the Parmesan. Repeat layering. Cover with foil. Bake in a 375°F oven for 25 minutes; remove foil and bake uncovered for 25 minutes longer. Let stand 10 minutes before cutting.

Nutrient Analysis

Calories	679	Cholesterol	161 mg	Saturated Fat	20 g
Protein	40 g	Sodium	2358 mg	Polyunsaturated Fat	3 g
Carbohydrate	38 g	Total Fat	41 g	Monounsaturated Fat	15 g

Turkey Lasagna

♦ **Serves 9**

Vegetable oil spray	1 pound freshly ground turkey, skin removed before grinding
½ cup chopped onion	
8 ounces fresh mushrooms, sliced	3 cups no-salt-added tomato sauce
3 cloves garlic, minced	2 teaspoons basil

½ teaspoon oregano

Freshly ground black pepper to
  taste

1 10-ounce package frozen no-salt-
  added chopped spinach, defrosted
  and squeezed dry

2 cups (1 pound) low-fat cottage
  cheese

Dash nutmeg

1 8-ounce package lasagna noodles

8 ounces part-skim mozzarella cheese,
  grated

Preheat oven to 375°F. Lightly spray a 9-x-13-inch baking dish with vegetable oil.

In a nonstick skillet over medium-high heat, combine onion, mushrooms, garlic, and ground turkey. Sauté until turkey is no longer pink. Cover pan and continue to cook until mushrooms have released juices, then uncover and evaporate juices over high heat. Add tomato sauce, basil, oregano, and pepper. Reduce heat.

In a bowl, stir spinach, cottage cheese, and nutmeg together well. Set aside.

Cook noodles according to package directions, omitting salt.

Lay one-third of noodles on bottom of dish; add one-half of spinach mixture, one-third of tomato sauce, and one-third of cheese. Repeat layers once. Finish with one layer noodles, one-third sauce, and remaining cheese. Cover with aluminum foil and bake 35 to 40 minutes.

Nutrient Analysis

Calories	326	Cholesterol	49 mg	Saturated Fat	4 g
Protein	31 g	Sodium	411 mg	Polyunsaturated Fat	1 g
Carbohydrate	32 g	Total Fat	8 g	Monounsaturated Fat	2 g

Cook Fast, Not Fat

"My first trip to the grocery store took over an hour because I was reading all the labels. Now I know which brands taste good and are low in fat and sodium."

If prepackaged dinners in the frozen food section of your grocery store are sending your fat off the charts, become a scrupulous label reader. Look for frozen dinners with less than ten grams of fat, and try to pick side dishes with little or no fat (see pages 87–9).

Also consider whether some "nonconvenience" foods might be just as convenient—and lots lower in fat. In less time than it takes to bake a TV dinner, you can boil pasta and top it with steamed vegetables, bottled nonfat or low-fat sauce, or herbs from the garden or freezer. In less time than it takes to microwave a frozen dinner, you can make a quick salad (or open a package of ready-to-serve salad) and open a can of water-packed tuna, crabmeat, or no-salt-added beans to put on top.

And remember, you can create your own healthful fast foods, even if you have time for major cooking only on weekends. Just freeze an extra portion for a fast-food dinner to eat when you will appreciate it most.

Snacks are impulse foods that can quickly derail the benefits of low-fat meals and leave you feeling guilty instead of satisfied. Prepare in advance for that snack attack. Don't keep high-fat snacks in the house. Instead, make sure you have carrot sticks, fruit, nonfat or low-fat crackers, breadsticks, pretzels, fat-free chips, or popcorn to air pop. Snacks can add to the grains, fruits, vegetables, and fiber you want to eat. They don't have to add to the fat. Keep in mind, though, that some low-fat and fat-free products have almost as many calories as similar products without reduced fat. Read the labels and avoid excess, or the pounds may sneak up on you.

Avoid Misconceptions About Low-Fat Eating

The following discussion should help you avoid the pitfalls of believing five widely held misconceptions about healthful eating.

1. You Have to Eat High-Cholesterol Foods to Raise Your Blood Cholesterol
You don't have to eat any cholesterol to raise your cholesterol. Your body can manufacture all the cholesterol it needs. If you are concerned about your blood cholesterol, you need to watch both cholesterol and fat, particularly saturated fat.

2. Eating Too Much Salt Can Raise Your Cholesterol
Although the medical advice to "eat less fat and sodium" is often delivered in the same breath, the two are not related. Sodium in food does not influence cholesterol; dietary fat and cholesterol do. Sodium influences the fluid balance in the body. In general, the risk of high blood pressure is related to the amount of sodium people eat. In susceptible people, sodium raises blood pressure and limiting sodium can reduce it.

3. Every Food You Eat Must Derive Less Than 30 Percent of Calories from Fat
Limiting your fat to less than 30 percent of your calories is an *overall daily* and *weekly goal.* You can eat some foods that have a higher per-

centage, as long as you balance them with plenty of low-fat foods. For example, you can still eat a small piece of meat with more than 30 percent of its calories from fat. Add a salad and a baked potato without high-fat trimmings, and you will have a low-fat meal.

If you want to calculate fat grams to be sure you don't go over 30 percent, look at your total grams for the day (see page 87). Don't worry about the individual food items except as they may contribute to an overall eating plan with more fat than you want.

4. It Is Hard to Get Enough Protein When Cutting Back on Fat and Animal Products

Americans often eat extra fat because they want to be sure they get enough protein. Yes, protein is crucial to proper nutrition, but most of us get 40 percent more than we need. The recommended daily allowance is fifty-six grams of protein for men and forty-four grams for women.

Meats, fish, and dairy products are highly concentrated in protein, and many starchy foods and vegetables provide protein as well.

Glance at these foods to see how easy it is to get plenty of protein:

½ chicken breast. . . . . about 40 grams
3 ounces cooked beef. . . . . about 25 grams
3 ounces cooked fish. . . . . about 25 grams
1 cup milk. . . . . about 8 grams
1 cup cooked dried beans . . . . about 15 grams
1 cup cooked spaghetti. . . . . about 5 grams
1 cup cooked oatmeal. . . . . about 5 grams
1 cup cooked brown rice . . . . about 5 grams
1 baked potato. . . . . about 4 grams
1 ounce cheese . . . . 6 to 8 grams
1 stalk broccoli. . . . . about 5 grams
1 cup cooked spinach. . . . . about 6 grams
1 cup corn kernels. . . . . about 4 grams
1 slice of tofu (about 3 inches × 3 inches) . . . . about 10 grams

What if you want to shift from large amounts of meat and dairy foods to lots of vegetables and grains? And what if you want to be a strict vegetarian? Will you be able to get enough "high-quality" or "complete" protein? You need far less protein than once believed. A vegetarian diet is well within the current guidelines for protein intake. Just be sure to

eat a varied and balanced diet. If your food plan includes dairy products along with plant foods, you do not need to worry about getting
enough complete protein.

5. It Is Hard to Get Enough Calcium in a Low-Fat Diet

Almost all the calcium in your body is found in your teeth and bones. If
you don't eat enough calcium, you're compromising the density and
strength of your bones, and you'll be at risk for osteoporosis later in life.

Many adults do not get their recommended daily amount of calcium. For most adults, that's about 800 milligrams a day. Pregnant and
lactating women need even more—about 1,200 milligrams—and postmenopausal women need about 1,500 milligrams. To support their
bone growth, people ages eleven to twenty-four need about 1,200 milligrams.

Dairy products are a rich calcium source, but they can also be high in
fat. Luckily, nonfat and low-fat dairy foods have just as much calcium as
their higher-fat relatives. One cup of milk or an ounce and a half of
cheese supplies well over a third of the calcium you need in a day.
Other rich sources of calcium are sardines or other canned fish eaten
with the bones. Collard greens are a good source of calcium. Other
dark green vegetables, including broccoli and kale, are less concentrated sources. If you're concerned that you may not be meeting your
dietary requirements, check into the range of packaged products fortified with calcium. These include milk and orange juice.

2. GET ENOUGH FIBER

*"I'm used to eating a very grainy, bulky diet. When I visit my parents, I'm
hungry all the time, even though I certainly eat more fat and calories than
I do at home. When the food is low-fat and high-fiber, you can have larger,
more satisfying meals."*

If alcohol and sugar are empty calories, providing calories without
nutrition, fiber could be considered the opposite. It provides satisfac-
tion and important health benefits without adding calories. Fiber can
help you reduce fat without feeling deprived. That means it helps you
lose weight without feeling hungry.

Getting enough fiber is easy if you base your meals on grains, fruits,
and vegetables.

You can't take a low-fiber nutrition plan and make it high-fiber merely by adding a bowl of bran cereal, an oat bran muffin, or even a fiber supplement. Because there are many types of fiber, eat an assortment of fiber-rich foods to make sure you are getting the full range of health benefits they can offer.

"For a while, I baked oat bran muffins every day. Now I try to spread out the fiber in every part of my menu."

To get enough fiber, you don't have to eat only bran cereals, brown rice, and whole wheat bread. If a French baguette is your favorite bread, enjoy it. But whenever it suits your taste buds, make the less-refined, higher-fiber food selection.

The FDA food label recommends a daily minimum of twenty-five to thirty grams of fiber, depending on how many calories you should eat. Little choices you make throughout the day will add up to this amount. On prepared food, check the Nutrition Facts labels. Don't rely on the promotional words on the front of a package. Many commercial oat bran and wheat bran products actually contain very little fiber, and they may also be high in fat and sodium.

For high-fiber grains, fruits, and vegetables, check the following lists. You can see that five servings of fruits and vegetables will give you ten to fifteen grams of fiber. Six servings of grains should give you another twelve. Then you're set or almost set for the day.

HIGH-FIBER, LOW-FAT FOODS

Breads/Crackers—1 to 2 g/serving*		Grains—2 g/serving	
Whole wheat, rye, or		Brown rice[†]	½ cup, cooked
pumpernickel		Wild rice	¼ cup, cooked
bread/rolls	1	Barley, whole[†]	½ cup, cooked
Muffins: bran, oat[†],		Bulgur	⅓ cup, cooked
corn	1	Buckwheat	1 tbsp
Graham crackers	2 squares	Cornmeal,	
Rye crackers	3	stone ground	¼ cup
Whole wheat matzo	2	Whole grain	
Whole wheat pita	1 small	flour, wheat,	
Whole wheat English		rye, buckwheat	2 tbsp
muffin	½	Whole wheat	
Whole wheat bagel	1 small	pasta	½ cup, cooked

Cereals**—more than 8 g/serving		Cereals—2 to 3 g/serving	
Bran cereals	⅓ to ½ cup	Shredded wheat	1 oz
		Wheat germ	¼ cup

Cereals—4–5 g/serving

Oatmeal[†]	1 cup
40% bran and raisin bran type	¾ cup
Corn bran	1 oz

Legumes—6 g/serving		Legumes—4 g/serving	
Cooked dried beans[†] (kidney, pinto, black, northern, navy)	½ cup	Cooked dried peas[†] (green, yellow)	½ cup
		Cooked lentils	½ cup
		Cooked lima beans[†]	½ cup

Fruits/Vegetables—3 g/serving

Apple with skin[†]	1 medium
Pear with skin	½ large
Prunes[†]	3
Raisins	¼ cup
Raspberries	½ cup
Strawberries[†]	1 cup
Canned corn	½ cup
Cooked green peas	½ cup

Fruits/Vegetables—2 g/serving

Apple without skin[†]	1 medium
Banana	1 medium
Blueberries	½ cup
Dates	4
Orange[†]	1 medium
Pear without skin	½ large
Broccoli	½ cup
Brussels sprouts	½ cup
Carrots	½ cup
Parsnips	½ cup
Potato with skin	1 medium
Spinach	½ cup

Adapted from "Eating Smart," a publication of the American Cancer Society.

*All fiber is represented as dietary fiber.

**Check labels; new cereal products with high-fiber content are being marketed.

†Rich in soluble fiber.

As you choose fiber-rich foods, make sure that some of your selections are good sources of soluble fiber. To lower your cholesterol level, put a stronger emphasis on soluble fibers while you reduce the amount of fat that you eat. Also, coordinate the total plan for your medical treatment, diet, and other lifestyle interventions with your physician. A fiber supplement may be recommended if you need a laxative to counteract the side effects of medication or if it will be extremely difficult for you to eat enough fiber.

If eating high-fiber foods is new for your digestive system, you may notice some unwelcome bloating and rumblings until you adjust. Build up slowly, and be sure to drink plenty of water.

If you have diverticulosis (pouches of the colon that can become inflamed), colitis, or a spastic colon, ask your health professional for advice about fiber. Doctors often recommend increased fiber in the diet in these conditions but sometimes suggest a low-fiber eating plan or specific food prohibitions.

FILLING IN THE FIBER

- For one cup of white flour, substitute one-half cup of white flour and one-half cup of whole wheat flour, or use ¾ cup of white flour mixed with ¼ cup of wheat bran.
- Substitute oat flour for part of the white flour in baking.
- Top a green salad with chickpeas or black beans.
- For dessert, serve fresh fruit or a fruit compote instead of custard or ice cream.
- Use brown rice instead of white.
- Leave the skin on fruits and vegetables if possible. Apples, pears, and potatoes are some foods that taste good with skins on.
- Add ¼ cup bran or oatmeal to meat loaf and casseroles.
- Instead of fruit cobbler with a flour-based topping, make fruit crisps with oatmeal topping.
- Try bulgur wheat or kasha instead of pasta or white rice as a side dish.
- Use corn tortillas instead of white flour tortillas.
- Sweeten pancakes or hot cereal with raisins or chunks of apple.
- Try a piping-hot sweet potato for a cold-weather snack or dessert.
- Enjoy air-popped popcorn with a movie.

3. EAT MORE VEGETABLES AND FRUITS

"Salads taste richer and more satisfying to me when they include something cooked. I'll chop up mushrooms or onions, grind some pepper on top, and cook them in the microwave for a few minutes. By the time the greens are washed, the cooked vegetables are cool enough to add."

"I became much more inventive with vegetables. I made different kinds of vegetable stews for dinner and then took the leftovers to work for lunch the next day. People in the office kept mentioning how great my food smelled."

Fruits and vegetables are created from the perfect combination of healthful elements. They provide lots of the vitamins, minerals, and fiber you want but little of the fat, calories, and sodium you don't want.

With the exception of coconut, olives, and avocados (which should be eaten sparingly and counted as fat), you can eat all the vegetables you want.

To get the vitamins and minerals you need, have at least five servings of fruits and vegetables a day. But don't feel like you have to stop there. More is better, and fruits and vegetables are good low-calorie, high-nutrient choices to fill you up when you reduce the amount of fat that you eat.

Make it a point to have every meal and snack you eat feature a fruit, a vegetable, or both. Instead of choosing between a cooked vegetable and a salad with dinner, have both. Have berries on your cereal and a banana on the side, or whip both with nonfat yogurt into a quick, filling smoothee. Serve bite-size pieces of baked chicken on a bed of greens. If you make a yogurt dip, load it with chopped spinach and grated carrots. Make a sandwich with pita bread, and stuff the pocket full of lettuce, tomato, peppers, shredded carrots, and sprouts. Use a scoop of leftover pasta or another grain dish to top a salad for lunch. Try carrot, apple, pumpkin, or zucchini muffins. With dark green ruffles that never lose their texture in water, kale makes a wonderful addition to soups. Vary the lettuce you use by adding or substituting spinach or other dark greens. Use fresh herbs to season vegetables and in salads— a few basil or arugula leaves add tang to salad.

For vitamin C, move beyond oranges and grapefruits to sample a whole range of fruits and vegetables rich in the nutrient. Try adding variety with some of the following:

Asparagus   Blackberries
Brussels sprouts   Cantaloupe

Cabbage
Cauliflower
Collard greens
Dandelion greens
Mustard greens
Green peppers
Potatoes (sweet and white)
Spinach
Turnips

Lemons
Limes
Papayas
Raspberries
Strawberries
Tangerines
Tomatoes

If you or your family aren't fans of vegetables in the cabbage family, try these other cruciferous vegetables:

Collard greens
Garden cress
Horseradish
Chinese kale
Southern curled kale
Sea kale
Kohlrabi
Broccoli rabe

Leaf mustard (Chinese spinach)
Mustard greens
White mustard
Radish greens
Rutabagas
Spinach
Upland cress
Watercress

4. CUT BACK ON SODIUM

"Because of medication I take, I have to follow a very low salt diet to keep my blood pressure under control. I've become very conscious of reading the label on every can, every loaf of bread, and every frozen vegetable."

The amount of salt you consume will govern how much of a challenge you will face in cutting your sodium to the recommended level of less than 3,000 milligrams, or 3 grams, a day. That's the amount in a teaspoon and a half of salt.

Most people would be better off if they cut their sodium intake in half. Your doctor may have told you a very low sodium diet is important. Or you may have decided on your own to cut back. Either way, if your palate is used to lots of salt, you may need to make drastic adjustments in how you select and spice foods.

When you eat less sodium, your ability to taste it increases. Eating a low-sodium diet leads to foods tasting saltier. This makes it easier to adhere to a low-sodium diet, once you are in the habit of avoiding salty foods.

Follow These Five Steps to Lower Your Salt Intake

1. Remove the Salt Shaker from the Dining Table
Use low-sodium alternatives in cooking, and make sure the food you serve has plenty of taste before it leaves the kitchen. A dash of salt added to the pot during cooking will end up as far less sodium per serving than a dash of salt added when the dish is ready.

On the table, put a pepper mill, lemon slices, and a shaker with well-seasoned vinegar.

2. Season Food with No-Sodium or Low-Sodium Alternatives
Salt can overwhelm the flavor of foods and other seasonings. When you start experimenting with herbs and spices, you can explore a whole new range of flavors. You can also begin to enjoy the natural flavors in unseasoned fresh foods.

As you begin to reach beyond the salt shaker, don't substitute the flavorings listed below. They usually contain lots of sodium.

Bouillon cubes	Seasoned salts
Cooking sherry or cooking wine	Soy sauce
Chili sauce	Steak sauce
Meat tenderizer	Tamari
Monosodium glutamate (MSG)	Worcestershire sauce

Before spiking a dish with salt or another high-sodium flavoring, check the list on pages 125–26 for alternative taste enhancers. It's just a starting point—lots of other combinations are possible, too.

When nothing but a steak sauce or ketchup will give you the taste you want, make your own or check for no-salt alternatives at your grocery store.

3. Limit Your Consumption of Salty Foods
If a corned beef sandwich and a pickle are on your lunch menu, you'll take in a whopping amount of sodium (more than 1,500 milligrams) without touching a salt shaker.

If you don't regularly eat high-sodium foods, cutting back on the salt you use to season food may be all that's required to get your sodium intake under 3,000 milligrams.

Check labels for the amount of sodium in packaged foods. The new food labels make it easy. They tell you what percentage of your daily

HERB, SPICE, AND SEASONING GUIDE

Dips

Caraway, dill, garlic, oregano, parsley, freshly ground pepper

Soups and Stews

Bean soup: Fresh cilantro, dry mustard powder
Vegetable soup: Sugar, vinegar
Skim milk chowders: Bay leaf, peppercorns
Pea soup: Bay leaf, coriander, fresh parsley
Other soups and stews: Basil, bay leaf, burnet, cayenne, chervil, chili
    powder, fresh cilantro, cinnamon, cloves, cumin, curry powder, dill, garlic,
    ginger, marjoram, mint, mustard, nutmeg, onion, oregano, parsley, freshly
    ground pepper, rosemary, sage, savory, sesame seeds, tarragon, thyme,
    watercress

Salads

Basil, burnet, chervil, fresh cilantro, coriander, dill, fresh lemon juice, mint,
    fresh mushrooms, mustard, oregano, parsley, freshly ground pepper,
    rosemary, sage, savory, sesame seeds, turmeric, vinegar, watercress

Seafood, Poultry, and Meat

Seafood: Allspice, basil, bay leaf, bell pepper, cayenne, fresh cilantro, curry
    powder, cumin, fennel, garlic, fresh lemon juice, mace, marjoram, mint,
    fresh mushrooms, Dijon mustard, dry mustard powder, green onion,
    paprika, saffron, sage, sesame seeds, tarragon, thyme, turmeric, white
    wine (not cooking wine)
Poultry: Basil, bay leaf, bell pepper, cinnamon, curry powder, garlic, fresh
    lemon juice, mace, marjoram, fresh mushrooms, onion, paprika, fresh
    parsley, lemon pepper, poultry seasoning, rosemary, saffron, sage, savory,
    sesame seeds, thyme, tarragon, white wine (not cooking wine)
Game: Bay leaf, garlic, fresh lemon juice, fresh mushrooms, onion, rosemary,
    sage, savory, tarragon, thyme, vinegar
Beef: Allspice, bay leaf, bell pepper, cayenne, cumin, curry powder, garlic,
    marjoram, fresh mushrooms, dry mustard, nutmeg, onion, freshly ground
    pepper, rosemary, sage, thyme, red wine (not cooking wine)
Lamb: Curry powder, garlic, mint, mint jelly, onion, pineapple, rosemary,
    sage, savory, sesame seeds, red wine (not cooking wine)
Pork: Apple, applesauce, cinnamon, cloves, fennel, garlic, mint, onion, sage,
    savory, red wine (not cooking wine)
Veal: Apricot, bay leaf, curry powder, ginger, fresh lemon juice, marjoram,
    mint, fresh mushrooms, oregano, saffron, sage, savory, tarragon, white
    wine (not cooking wine)
Various: Cayenne, chervil, chili powder, coriander, curry powder, dill, garlic,
    ginger, marjoram, onion, oregano, parsley, freshly ground pepper

Vegetables

Asparagus: Garlic, fresh lemon juice, onion, vinegar
Beans: Bell pepper, caraway, cloves, cumin, fresh cilantro, mint, onion, savory, tarragon, thyme
Beets: Anise, caraway, fennel, ginger, savory
Carrots: Anise, cinnamon, cloves, mint, sage, tarragon
Corn: Allspice, bell pepper, chili powder, fresh cilantro, pimiento, fresh tomato
Cucumbers: Chives, dill, garlic, vinegar
Green beans: Dill, fresh lemon juice, marjoram, nutmeg, pimiento
Greens: Garlic, fresh lemon juice, onion, vinegar
Peas: Allspice, bell pepper, mint, fresh mushrooms, onion, fresh parsley, sage, savory
Potatoes: Bell pepper, chives, dill, onion, pimiento, saffron
Squash: Allspice, brown sugar, cinnamon, cloves, fennel, ginger, mace, nutmeg, onion, savory
Tomato: Allspice, basil, fresh cilantro, garlic, marjoram, onion, oregano, sage, savory, tarragon, thyme
Various Vegetables: Basil, burnet, cayenne, chervil, dill, marjoram, mint, fresh mushrooms, nutmeg, oregano, parsley, freshly ground pepper, poppy seeds, rosemary, sage, sesame seeds, sunflower seeds, tarragon, thyme, turmeric, watercress

Baked Goods

Breads: Anise, caraway, cardamom, fennel, poppy seeds, sesame seeds
Desserts: Anise, caraway, cardamom, cinnamon, cloves, coriander, fennel, ginger, mace, mint, nutmeg, poppy seeds, sesame seeds

Fruits

Allspice, anise, basil, cardamom, cloves, cumin, curry powder, ginger, mint, nutmeg, poppy seeds, rosemary, watercress

Adapted from American Heart Association Cookbook, *5th Edition, Times Books, 1991.*

sodium is contained in a serving of the product, using 2,400 milligrams as a daily total to help you stay under 3,000. Be sure to check prepared meat and fish, canned fish, frozen main dishes, canned vegetables and juices, cheese, baked goods, and condiments.

Notice the huge difference in sodium totals in the daily menus that follow. These charts can help you make wise choices about sodium in your own daily food plan. They are not intended as guides for other nutrients.

Sample Daily Menus

Amount	Food	Sodium	Amount	Food	Sodium
Breakfast I			**Breakfast II**		
4 oz	Tomato juice (canned/bottled)	243 mg	4 oz	Grapefruit juice	1 mg
¾ cup	Wheat flakes	231	¾ cup	Puffed wheat or puffed rice (no salt)	trace
8 oz	Skim milk	126	8 oz	Skim milk	126
2 slices	Bread	292	2 slices	Bread	292
2 tsp	Margarine	92	2 tsp	Margarine	92
1 tbsp	Jelly	trace	1 tbsp	Jelly	trace
6 oz	Coffee	2	6 oz	Coffee	2
2 slices	Imitation bacon	153			
	TOTAL	1139		TOTAL	513
Lunch I			**Lunch II**		
1 cup	Vegetable soup (canned)	838	½ cup	Fruit cup	6
2 slices	Sandwich bread	292	2 slices	Sandwich bread	292
2 oz	Corned beef (pressed)	535	2 oz	Chicken breast (roasted)	39
1 tsp	Mustard	63	2 tsp	Mayonnaise	56
1	Dill pickle (3¾")	928	½	Tomato (3" diameter)	3
10	Potato chips	68	½	Cucumber	5
1	Apple	2	4	Vanilla wafers	36
6 oz	Coffee	2	8 oz	Skim milk	126
	TOTAL	2728		TOTAL	563
Dinner I			**Dinner II**		
4 oz	Baked ham	1027	4 oz	Halibut (broiled)	152
½ cup	Green peas (canned)	294	½ cup	Broccoli	28
½ cup	Scalloped potatoes (with margarine, skim milk, and salt)	430	2	Boiled potatoes with parsley	4
			2 slices	Italian bread	118
2 tsp	Margarine	92	3 tsp	Margarine	138
1 cup	Spinach salad	39	1 cup	Lettuce salad	trace
1 tbsp	French dressing	219	3 tsp	Oil	trace

Amount	Food	Sodium	Amount	Food	Sodium
½ cup	Instant pudding (made with skim milk)	161 126	2 tsp ½ cup 6 oz	Vinegar Sherbet Coffee	trace 5 2
	TOTAL	2388		TOTAL	447
Snacks I			*Snacks II*		
3 oz	Salted peanuts	418	3 oz	Unsalted peanuts	15
1 cup	Salted popcorn	320	1 cup	Unsalted popcorn	1
2	Celery stalks	100	1	Whole carrots	34
8 oz	Buttermilk	319	8 oz	Skim milk	126
	TOTAL	739		TOTAL	161
TOTAL I		7412	**TOTAL II**		1699

As you cut back on high-sodium foods, remember that you have a double health reason—heart disease and cancer prevention—to limit your intake of cured, pickled, and smoked foods (see page 97).

4. Bake Without Excess Sodium

Baking soda and baking powder are high in sodium. If you use them frequently in baking, or need to restrict your sodium, you can try a low-sodium baking powder (you may need to use a little more to get the same rising effect). It may be hard to find at your local grocery store, but you should be able to buy it at a health food store.

In most recipes, salt is present only for the taste. Leaving it out, or reducing it to a tiny amount (say, one-quarter of what is called for), should not influence how the dish turns out.

> *"I went to a local bakery and asked them to make me ten loaves of no-salt bread and several dozen rolls. They don't mind making a special recipe in a big order, and we have a freezer full of excellent bread."*

5. Check Your Medicine Chest

Some over-the-counter drugs contain large amounts of sodium. Inspect the label for a warning statement. One is required if a dose of the product contains more than five milligrams of sodium. If you are on a very low sodium diet and in doubt about whether a medicine is safe, ask your physician or pharmacist.

> *"Now that I've cut back on salt, I can taste it in all kinds of surprising places, like cookies and boxed cereals and even in the fancy chocolates my brother gives for presents."*

5. SAVOR A DRINK SAFELY

"After a very stressful day, I sit and sip a glass of red wine in a beautiful glass and it helps me to relax."

"After mowing the lawn or after a long bicycle ride, nothing but a beer will do."

If you don't drink, don't start.

If you do drink a moderate amount of alcohol, and it is not causing you health or social problems, make sure your alcohol use fits into the overall healthful lifestyle you are seeking. Keep these points in mind:

* *Don't overdo.* On a routine basis, don't consume more than an ounce of ethanol a day (see page 98). Above that level, the health risks mount, with disrupted social lives, more accidents, and more liver disease, high blood pressure, heart disease, and cancer.
* *Don't let alcohol undermine your weight goals.* On average, Americans who drink consume about 10 percent of their calories as alcohol— and they get no nutrition from it. Alcohol has lots of calories. Be sure to count them, along with any mixers you use, when you figure how much you are consuming. Sometimes substituting seltzer for one beer a day is easier than cutting back on food calories.

This list provides a few examples of 100-calorie alcoholic beverages:

* 8 ounces of most regular beers or ales
* 12 ounces of most light beers
* 1½ ounces of 80-proof liquor (with a no-calorie mixer)
* 1⅕ ounces of 100-proof liquor (with a no-calorie mixer)
* 1 ounce of most cordials or liqueurs
* 4 ounces of most wines or champagnes

6. FILL UP, NOT OUT

"I ate in a lackadaisical way, not eating all day and drinking beers for lunch. Then I'd come home and swallow everything in front of me. I had to change my ways when I was diagnosed with diabetes."

"I don't like to feel deprived, so I think about what I should eat instead of what I can't. I keep a mental list: six breads, two fruits, five vegetables, three proteins. When I plan dinner, I tell myself I can have anything else I want after I've finished my list. But with all those vegetables, I'm never hungry."

According to national statistics, one in every three Americans is over-weight.

If carrying extra pounds is increasing your risk of heart disease or cancer, take steps to lower your weight to a healthful level. Because dietary fat is so concentrated in calories, reducing fat is an excellent first step in changing what you eat. It may even be all you need to do to shed pounds.

"Following a low-fat diet, my extra weight came off absolutely naturally. I didn't watch quantities. In fact, I probably ate more, but I was eating more grains and beans and vegetables."

One of the joys of healthful eating is that it allows most people to achieve a healthful weight without following a formal "diet" and while eating as much as they usually do. However, no matter what foods you choose, you will gain weight if you routinely eat more calories than you use. Exercise burns calories and fat, so it is a tremendous help in keeping weight under control (see page 198).

To determine whether you are eating too many calories to achieve a healthful weight, use this formula to estimate how many calories you need each day.

1. Multiply your weight by 10. That's how many calories you need each day to support your current weight, if you do nothing at all.

2. Based on your regular activity level, multiply the calories by the appropriate number:

    Sedentary—multiply calories by 0.3;

    Moderately active—multiply calories by 0.4;

    Very active—multiply calories by 0.5.

That's how many additional calories you need to support your usual daily activities.

3. Add the two numbers, and that's how many calories you use each day to maintain your current weight. If you stay below that number, you shouldn't gain weight. If you stay right at that number or go a little higher, you will still lose weight if you add exercise.

Example: If you weigh 200 pounds, you need a base of 2,000 calories, plus 600 more for daily activities if you're sedentary—a total of 2,600. To lose weight, eat fewer calories or add exercise.

Let's say you're a medium-framed 6'0" man who weighs 200 pounds. You see on the ideal weight chart (see page 101) that your weight puts you in the range for heart disease concern. You would like to get down to 170. You can gradually do that by eating fewer than 2,600 calories a day, exercising more, or doing a combination of the two. What you should *not* do is eat fewer than the number of calories needed to support your *ideal* weight. Eating too few calories makes it difficult to get the nutrients you need and can result in an undesirable loss in muscle. For a 170-pound weight goal, you'll need 1,700 calories plus 510—a total of 2,210.

Cutting about 400 calories a day may not sound like much or feel like much when you make the change, but in a year's time you could lose more than 40 pounds. That's even more than your goal but still leaves you in the desirable range for your height and frame.

If you need to reduce the calories you take in, follow the eating guidelines in this chapter. Whenever possible, make a lower-calorie, lower-fat selection or eat a smaller portion. If you want an accurate count of how many calories you are eating, keep track of your food for a day or two. Then use the amounts supplied in the *American Heart Association Brand Name Fat and Cholesterol Counter* or some other reliable calorie counter. Look for them at your bookstore, grocery store, or library.

"I've been dieting since I was nine years old. I eat less than any of my friends and weigh forty pounds more. Food and weight are a constant struggle."

Obesity is complex. Many people still consider weight gain to be a failure of willpower. However, scientists are finding increasing evidence of genetic and biological differences that affect metabolism and the signals that make people feel hungry or full. Your biology may make it more difficult for you to lose weight, but that doesn't mean you should give up trying. Take advantage of the help you can get from health-care professionals. Losing a modest amount of weight and keeping it off, even if you never attain your ideal weight, can have important health benefits.

"I do what I call escrow dieting. If I know I'm going to a birthday party on the weekend, I'm very careful during the week so I can eat party food and not worry about it."

A nutritionist can help you plan changes in your eating habits, or you may already be aware of some personal problem-eating situations.

WEIGHT GAIN TROUBLESHOOTING

If this describes you . . .	*Give this a try . . .*
Overeating at parties	Have a low-calorie snack before leaving home.
	Don't stand near the food table.
	Keep a glass of seltzer, iced tea, or other no-calorie beverage in hand. Sip while others nibble.
	Don't go back for seconds.
Eating while watching TV	Confine your eating to one spot.
	Sit down at the table whenever you eat; don't read or watch TV while eating.
	Find something to occupy your hands while watching TV.
Can't resist a favorite high-calorie food	Bite the bullet. Do not order, buy, or make this food.
	Create a low-calorie substitute.
Eating too fast	Keep second helpings out of easy reach.
	Take only one portion.
	Chew each mouthful thoroughly.
	After three or four bites, pause and put down your silverware.
	Stop eating for a few minutes and join in the conversation.
	Swallow one bite before you pick up the next.
	Cut food into tiny pieces.
Coffee-break pastries	When the coffee wagon comes around, leave the area.
	Have a low-calorie beverage. You may be thirsty, not really hungry.
	If coffee or tea cries out for something to eat with it, switch to a different beverage.
	Bring fruit or a low-fat muffin from home. Count it as part of your daily menu.
After-dinner snacks	Do not have ready-made, high-calorie food in the house.
	Have a no-calorie beverage.
	Go for a walk.
	Go to bed earlier. You may be tired rather than hungry.
Eating when depressed or nervous	Practice deep-breathing exercises.
	Exercise instead of eating.

Do It Your Way—Five Paths to More Healthful Eating

Changing habits is always a challenge, especially when it comes to eating. Besides providing nutrition, food is often a centerpiece of interactions with family, friends, and colleagues. When you were an infant, it was your earliest source of comfort. The habits you established early in life have been repeated thousands of times.

Eating isn't like smoking. You can't give it up entirely and focus your attention on something else. You will be eating several times every day for the rest of your life. Don't expect to change your eating habits overnight unless your medical condition requires a rapid alteration in the way you eat or making a dramatic onetime shift suits your personality best. It took years for you to become accustomed to the way you eat now. Gradual changes toward a more healthful way of eating, phased in over weeks or months, can be very effective. Gradual change does *not* mean taking a wishy-washy approach to nutrition, trying one thing and then another. It means planning what you will do and doing it, taking definite steps toward the way you want to eat. Maybe the first thing you will do is regain control over your snacking habits or switch to low-fat breakfast choices or move from whole milk to 2-percent milk. Wherever you choose to start is fine.

MARIA: GETTING READY IS THE FIRST STEP

What got me started was being around people who were eating healthy food. I listened to them. And I would listen to programs on the radio that talked about eating healthfully. Even if I was sitting there eating junk food, it was getting through a little at a time.

Eventually it sinks in and you start to make incremental changes. I would go around the corner to the store for ice cream but get a banana instead. I wouldn't have meat and fried potatoes every night.

There is nothing more powerful than being around people you like and respect who are saying this stuff is no good for you. At first, the thought of me eating tofu was, "Whew, you're kidding," but now I've spent enough time around people who eat healthy to find out it's (a) not alien and (b) tasty.

Dinner and snacks were my biggest changes. I don't have potato chips anymore. And I don't eat ice cream like I used to—not that I won't occasionally, but it's rare compared to the way it was. Now I have yogurt, granola, more fruit.

Slowly I've gone from eating high-fat to trying to eat low- to moderate-fat foods. Eventually I got interested enough in good food to join a food co-op.

As I eat less meat at dinner, I notice how much energy it took to digest. That was very startling to me. What I noticed is if I eat grains or other stuff, I'm not as lethargic or weighted down, as opposed to eating meat and feeling like cement.

Eating the old way, I had slightly high blood pressure. Now it is under control. I've lost four or five pounds, and my body is a little tighter. And feels a lot better.

I say just be around people who eat healthy, and see that as a goal. Slowly you will make the changes, and your taste will change, too. Occasionally I still order ribs and then I say, "Yuck, why did I order that?" I don't even like the smell.

Reading about eating healthfully or paying attention to what you put in your mouth and how it makes you feel is an important first step in changing your eating habits.

Your next step may be to analyze your past and present eating plans more closely. Have you tried to make changes before? What happened? Could you do some things differently this time to avoid being stymied by the same problems? Perhaps you need to make changes in smaller steps or have certain foods in the house. Maybe you need to get specific advice from your doctor or ask for more help from family and friends.

No matter what your eating habits have been in the past, you can do something today to make them more healthful.

MAY: PAY CLOSE ATTENTION TO JUST ONE THING

My mother had a bad heart and died of a heart complication. My cholesterol is just a little bit over what I'd want, but not really serious. I'm conscious of my weight and of wanting to stay alive longer.

I saw an ad in the paper and signed up for a free class in following a low-fat diet. It was part of a research study, so we counted our fat grams very carefully. Depending on our weight and calories, we were given a limit for how many fat grams to eat in a day. Using a little chart, we marked how many grams were in each dish. We could see how they were adding up.

Some things I had never allowed myself turned out not to have fat at all. Sugar, I thought, was very high in fat, but I learned different. I can have a glass of fruit drink or eat a slice of toast with a little jelly or jam. Neither one is going to make or break my diet as long as I use a low-fat margarine on the toast.

The basic trick is just finding substitutes for the things that are high in fat in your diet. Salad dressings are a good example of something that just a short time ago were not available in nonfat. Now just about every company makes one.

I also cook for my son, who has a ravenous appetite. He doesn't want his food altered, but when I change a recipe to reduce the fat, I don't mention it. That way, it tastes fine to him.

I enjoyed keeping track of the fat grams, and I will keep that up after the class. We're also planning to keep meeting informally for the support and enjoyment.

When people ask me for advice about eating, I say, "Just watch one thing, and fat grams are a good thing to watch." I don't follow a set menu. I think if that's not your usual way of doing things, you won't keep it up for long.

If you think counting fat grams would help you change your eating habits, follow these two steps:

1. See page 130 to figure out how many calories you need to stay at your desired weight.
2. Check the chart on page 89 for the number of fat grams allowed each day for that calorie level.

This is a maximum, an amount that healthy Americans should find readily achievable. If you want to go lower, that's fine, within reason.

JAMAL: JUST GIVE ME A FEW SIMPLE RULES

My doctor wanted me to cut down on fat. I'm willing to follow a prescription, but I'm not willing to spend much time thinking about food. So on a prescription pad, the doctor wrote, "Avoid: hamburgers, cheeseburgers, meat loaf, whole milk, cheese, beef steak, roast beef, hot dogs, ham, lunch meat, doughnuts, cookies, cake, eggs."

The list had some foods on it that I like a lot and used to order all the time when I was traveling. Now when I see them on a menu, I look for something not on the list that would taste just as good. At home, we use skim milk and don't keep high-fat food around. And that's that.

The foods that Jamal's doctor prescribed against are the foods that make up half of the saturated fats in what Americans eat.

If Jamal's strategy sounds helpful for you, write the foods on a card and keep it with you when you grocery shop or eat out. These foods may or may not be your major sources of fat. It is not necessary to exclude any specific food from your menu. Just eat high-fat foods less frequently and in small amounts. Then fat won't have too prominent a role in your nutrition plan.

VIOLET: BECOMING A VEGETARIAN

I work at home, where food is always there as a distraction. Between the ages of thirty and thirty-five, my weight crept up twenty pounds. I didn't seem able to lose the extra weight by eating less. My relatives have lots of the illnesses overweight people seem to get more of—gallbladder attacks, diabetes, cancer, strokes, and heart attacks. My cholesterol wasn't high yet, but when I got a checkup at age thirty-five, it had gone up thirty points from my last visit. I figured it was just a matter of time until I got high cholesterol like both my parents.

After a vacation where every meal featured meat, I decided to take a break from meat and see what it felt like. It was no big deal. I looked at my diet and realized that meat was the one source of fat that I didn't miss. I decided if I gave it up, I wouldn't have to be very rigid about other sources of fat and calories. I could still have cheese and a piece of pie now and then.

Since I still eat fish and dairy products, every restaurant has plenty for me to eat. Just giving up meat and doing more exercise, I lost that twenty pounds without ever dieting. The last time my cholesterol was checked, it was lower than it ever had been as an adult.

To me, not eating meat at all is easier than cutting back. If I go to the grocery store or a restaurant, I don't have to think, "Should I have meat today? Will it taste great? Will it be worth the fat and calories?" I don't even look at it, and I don't miss it. I like how my body looks, and I like not having to diet or ever feel hungry to stay thin.

There's no getting around it: A low-fat, low-cholesterol menu will include fewer animal products than one higher in fat and cholesterol.

Because of religious or political beliefs and food preferences, as well as health goals, you may want to eliminate entire categories of animal foods. These might be all red meats, all meat but not poultry, all meat and poultry but not fish, or all animal products, perhaps including eggs and dairy foods.

If this sounds right for you, you might want to pick one of the many excellent vegetarian cookbooks to help you get started. Older vegetarian cookbooks, which often relied heavily on cheese as a source of protein, may need to be adapted to fit your eating plan. If you decide to follow a strict vegetarian diet, be careful to find sources of calcium, iron, zinc, and vitamins D, B_2, and B_6.

As with making any other major change, a gradual evolution in eating habits may be more long lasting than a sudden revolution. Some families take a year or more to convert to a vegetarian eating plan.

GLENN: THE MAIN-DISH SHUFFLE

I grew up on a farm, working hard and eating three big meals a day. I ate meat at each one. Through middle age, especially after I retired, I gradually put on weight. Also, my blood pressure got higher. I was still eating like a farmhand but not doing the hard work. I started taking a blood pressure pill and figured that was just normal for someone my age.

Then I married a woman who had had high cholesterol and blood pressure herself but who didn't take any medicine. She exercised and kept her weight down and cooked differently from me. Not using salt. Chili using ground turkey instead of beef, and taking off the oil after the turkey browned. A thick vegetable soup with a little meat. Bean burritos. A chef salad with a little meat on top. Fish once or twice a week. When we have lamb chops, one instead of two. When we have steak, saving half for a salad the next day. I still make pancakes for Sunday breakfast, but I hardly ever have meat at breakfast anymore.

I have just as much strength and energy as I ever did. I haven't given up any of my favorite foods—just changed what's for dinner some of the time.

To maintain a low-fat nutrition plan, you don't need to follow a pre-planned menu unless that's how you like to shop and cook. What's important is for you to discover some appealing low-fat choices for meals and snacks. When you grocery shop, aim to fill your pantry with enough low-fat ingredients so that creating healthful meals will be easy.

For example, skim milk, fruit, nonfat yogurt, cereal, oatmeal, and bread, supply the makings of several different low-fat breakfasts. Each morning, pick the combination that suits your fancy.

How to Eat Well on a Budget

"At first I was really conscious of spending money on fish and vegetables. But I chose to treat myself with good foods and ultimately decided I wasn't spending any more money than I did when I wasn't eating properly. Why worry about splurging on a $2 pineapple when I used to spend $3 on ice cream?"

Can you eat healthfully without breaking the food budget? Definitely. Following an eating plan that is low in fat and built around lots of fruits, vegetables, and whole grains can actually save you money.

Foods that are high in saturated fats are some of the more expensive items that may find their way into your food cart. As you reduce the amount of fat that you use, and plan more meals based on vegetables, you should save money.

For example, the ingredients to prepare Traditional Lasagna on page 114 cost $4.50 more than the ingredients for Turkey Lasagna (pages 114–15).

Let's see how some other choices add up.

A hearty breakfast: Serving a classic high-fat breakfast—for example, two fried eggs, two strips of bacon, toast with butter and jam, and orange juice—will cost about $5 for four people. An equally hearty low-fat breakfast of oatmeal with raisins and low-fat milk, toast with fruit spread, and a bowl of blueberries would certainly be more healthful. It's better for your budget, too. You can serve the same number of people for less than $3.

A lunch salad: Let's say you want to make a meal-size chef salad to serve guests at lunch. If you buy six ounces each of ham, turkey, and cheese from the lunch meat section of the grocery store, you've spent about $7 on toppings. Instead, try turkey, kidney beans, and roasted mushrooms or red peppers and you've saved $3 or so on an equally colorful and festive lunch with a lot less fat.

Appetizers: You want to have appetizers on hand for a party. First, take your favorite cream-cheese dip recipe and create a substitute using cottage cheese (see page 113). Then pick what to dip.

A platter with potato chips, tortilla chips, and pretzels will set you back more than $4. Substitute crudités (such as dipping-size pieces of raw cauliflower, broccoli, and carrots) and you'll save money as well as fat. That leaves enough for you to splurge on a bag of fat-free baked tortilla chips, which run about 50¢ higher than fried chips.

Dessert: An angel food cake with sorbet or fresh berries costs no more than a pound cake with ice cream.

A vegetarian dinner: Moussaka is a dish worth serving at your next dinner party. The meatless moussaka recipe below will cost you about $6 less to make than a traditional moussaka that uses ground meats and lots of Parmesan and ricotta cheese. Our version has 214 calories; 11 grams of total fat, including 3 grams of saturated fat; and 548 milligrams of sodium per serving.

Meatless Moussaka

◆ **Serves 8**

Vegetable oil spray
2 pounds peeled eggplant, thickly
sliced

2 tablespoons olive oil

SAUCE

2 tablespoons olive oil
1 cup finely chopped onion
3 cloves garlic, minced
1 14½-ounce can diced, no-salt-
added tomatoes in juice
1 6-ounce can no-salt-added tomato
paste

1 cup water
½ teaspoon salt
2 teaspoons crushed rosemary
2 tablespoons finely chopped fresh
parsley
2 tablespoons finely chopped fresh
mint

FILLING

1 pound nonfat or low-fat cottage
cheese
Egg substitute equivalent to 2 eggs
1 teaspoon crushed rosemary

½ teaspoon ground oregano
¼ cup grated Parmesan cheese
½ teaspoon freshly ground black
pepper, or to taste

TOPPING

¼ cup grated Parmesan cheese

Preheat broiler. Lightly spray a 3½-quart oblong glass baking dish with vegetable oil spray.

Place eggplant slices on two large baking sheets. Brush both sides of
slices lightly with 2 tablespoons olive oil. Brown 5 minutes on each side, or
until eggplant is tender.

Set oven temperature to 375°F.

SAUCE

Heat 2 tablespoons olive oil in a nonstick skillet over medium-high heat. Add
onion and sauté until translucent. Add garlic and cook 1 minute more. Stir in
tomatoes, tomato paste, water, salt, and 2 teaspoons rosemary. Reduce heat
and simmer 10 minutes. Add parsley and mint. Remove from heat and set
aside.

FILLING

In a bowl, combine cottage cheese, egg substitute, 1 teaspoon rosemary, oregano, ¼ cup Parmesan cheese, and pepper.

Spread half of sauce on bottom of prepared dish. Arrange half of eggplant over it. Spread filling over eggplant, then lay remaining eggplant on top of filling. Cover with remaining sauce. Sprinkle ¼ cup Parmesan cheese over all. Cover casserole with foil and bake 40 to 45 minutes. Uncover and bake 10 additional minutes.

Nutrient Analysis

Calories	214	Cholesterol	10 mg	Saturated Fat	3 g
Protein	14 g	Sodium	548 mg	Polyunsaturated Fat	1 g
Carbohydrate	17 g	Total Fat	11 g	Monounsaturated Fat	6 g

From American Heart Association Cookbook, *5th Edition, Times Books, 1991.*

Specialty foods can cost extra. Egg substitute costs about twice as much as a comparable amount of real egg. Baked tortilla chips cost more than fried. No-salt-added canned foods sometimes cost no more than regular canned products. However, canned foods labeled as specific for a low-sodium eating plan often cost more than their saltier counterparts.

Still, it is less expensive and easier than ever before to make changes in how you eat. Literally thousands of nonfat and low-fat foods have been introduced, and food manufacturers are getting the word that consumers want less fat and salt without paying more money. Many manufacturers price their products exactly the same. You probably can buy no-fat refried beans for the same price as those cooked in lard. Your favorite grocery store probably stocks sorbet or low-fat frozen yogurt for the same price as ice cream, and part-skim cheeses for the same price as whole-milk cheeses. Other products are just naturally less expensive when they contain less fat. As a rule, skim milk saves you a few pennies on every quart over whole milk; margarine is less expensive than butter; pretzels are cheaper than potato chips.

Dining Out

"I am on a very low sodium diet, and I have two suggestions for people on a special diet. Number one: Get on a first-name basis with the owner or the waitresses at a restaurant you like. No matter how restrictive your diet is, they will help you if you establish a rapport. Number two: Don't be a killjoy.

If you're going out with friends, don't sit there and say, 'I can't have this or I can't have that.' Learn what you can ask for and stick with that."

"In my town, it's a popular thing to give the fat grams of dishes on the menu. But there are still some restaurants where the staff has no idea what's in the meals they serve."

Dining out can be both an adventure and a challenge if you are trying to reduce the amount of fat and salt you eat.

PLAN AHEAD

Try to select a restaurant where food is prepared to order. If you are on a strict diet and haven't been to a particular restaurant before, call and ask whether it offers foods you can eat without concern. Perhaps your food plan allows for dessert, but you're worried that none of the restaurant's choices will suit your health and taste. Plan to have dessert at home later.

COCKTAILS, ANYONE?

Think about the calories and fat in any drinks you order. Forgo drinks with cream, coconut cream, or sugary mixers.

TABLE TEMPTATION

If you're going to a restaurant you've been to before, think back to what was placed on the table when you first sat down. Which items will tempt you? Which can be a healthful part of your meal?

Assess whether you can skip the butter on the rolls. If not, set them aside or ask to have them taken away.

If chips or other fried crunchies are set before you, ask to have the basket removed or take a couple of pieces and push the rest out of reach. Use inviting-looking salsa to top your salad, or order raw vegetables and use them as dippers.

NEGOTIATING THE MENU

Before you order, make sure you understand what's in a dish and how it is prepared. You can often find excellent choices in a separate vegetable or fish section of the menu. Sometimes an appetizer makes a tasty and satisfying main course.

Focus on entrées with phrases such as those in the following list. Although such phrases usually indicate a low-fat preparation, you still need to be cautious. Perhaps the dish is indeed baked, but in a fat-laden sauce. Ask questions!

◆ steamed	◆ baked
◆ in its own juice	◆ roasted
◆ garden fresh	◆ poached
◆ broiled	◆ grilled

Avoid dishes when their names are a warning of saturated fat:

◆ braised	◆ panroast
◆ crispy	◆ creamed
◆ in cream sauce	◆ in gravy
◆ hollandaise	◆ rich
◆ buttered	◆ buttery
◆ in butter sauce	◆ sauté
◆ fried	◆ pan-fried
◆ au gratin	◆ escalloped
◆ in cheese sauce	◆ stewed
◆ basted	◆ casserole
◆ prime	◆ hash
◆ potpie	◆ with bacon or sausage

There are no absolutes here, either. Sautéed could mean lots of butter, but it could also mean a little wine or fruit juice. Again, ask questions!

When your dining companions are selecting a restaurant to try, you don't have to veto any world cuisine. Within each menu, you can order the lower-fat, lower-sodium choices.

GETTING THE FOOD YOU WANT, GRACIOUSLY

It helps to call ahead and find out what's on the restaurant's menu if you have serious diet restrictions. If necessary, you can then ask about having an off-the-menu meal cooked for you. Perhaps the chef could prepare a vegetable platter, fruit platter, or broiled fish with steamed vegetables.

EATING OUT WISELY

Stay away from these . . .	*. . . And try these instead*
CHINESE	
Egg drop soup	Wonton or hot-and-sour soup
Fried meat dumplings	Steamed vegetable dumplings
Fried hard noodles	Soft noodles
Fried rice	Steamed rice
Fried entrées or egg foo yung	Dishes that are boiled, broiled, steamed, or lightly stir-fried
High-sodium MSG and soy sauce	Dishes spiced with scallions, garlic, and ginger, and without salt or MSG
Lobster sauce	Sauces without egg yolks, such as sweet-and-sour sauce or plum sauce
FAST FOOD	
Large or double-meat sandwiches	Regular-size sandwiches
Cheeseburgers	Meat or cheese, not both
Small fried burgers	Small broiled lean burgers
Fried chicken nuggets	Broiled chicken breast sandwiches
Coleslaw	Salad with dressing on side
French fries	Rice or baked potato with low-fat toppings on side
"Secret" sauces	Lettuce and tomato
Mayonnaise	Mustard
Pizza with meat toppings or double cheese	Pizza with vegetable toppings and low-fat cheese
Breakfast sandwiches with eggs, meat, and cheese	Separate items with less fat
Croissant	English muffin
FRENCH	
Hollandaise or béchamel sauce	Bordelaise or other wine-based sauces
Sauce on the food	Sauce on the side
Appetizers with olives, capers, or anchovies	Less-salty appetizers, such as steamed mussels or salad
Traditional cream-based entrées	Lighter nouvelle cuisine or Provençal tomato-and-herb-based entrées
Complicated sauces	Simple preparations with sauce on the side
Chocolate mousse	Flambéed cherries
Crème caramel	Peaches in wine

Stay away from these . . .	*. . . And try these instead*
GREEK	
Hummus and baba ghanouj dips	Tzatziki
	Dolmas
Entrées in phyllo dough with butter baste	Entrées without buttery dough and butter baste, such as shish kebabs
	Pita bread
Moussaka and other creamy/cheesy entrées	Roast lamb
	Plaki
	Greek salad, watching the amount of feta cheese, olives, and anchovies
INDIAN	
Curries with coconut milk or cream	Curries with vegetable or dal base
	Shish kebab
	Tandoori chicken or fish
Fried breads	Baked whole wheat breads
Sauced rice dishes	Fragrant steamed rice
Samosas	Papadum
ITALIAN	
Pasta with cheese sauce or cream sauce	Pasta with marinara sauce
Pasta with meat	Pasta primavera or pasta with clam sauce
Pasta as appetizer	Pasta as entrée
Chicken parmigiana	Chicken or fish entrées without breading and cheese
Italian pastries	Italian ices
JAPANESE	
Pickled fish	Sashimi
Tempura	Sushi (fish or vegetable)
	Nabemono
Fried fish dishes	Yakimono fish
	Tofu dishes
High-sodium soup	Miso soup
	Salad
MEXICAN	
Fried tortilla chips	Gazpacho or black bean soup
Flour tortillas	Corn tortillas
Refried beans and rice	Frijoles a la charra or borracho beans and rice

Stay away from these . . .	. . . And try these instead
MEXICAN	
Dishes topped with sour cream or cheese	Garnishes on the side
Guacamole	Salsa
Creamy or cheesy sauces	Veracruz or other tomato-based sauces
Cheese or beef burrito	Chicken or bean enchilada
Nachos	Ceviche
MIDDLE EASTERN	
Lamb casserole	Shish kebab
	Couscous or bulgur wheat with vegetables or chicken
Meat-stuffed appetizers	Appetizers based on spiced rice or eggplant
Pastries	Fruit
SALAD BARS	
Predressed salads	Fresh vegetables
Chopped eggs or grated cheese on top	Beans on top
Seafood or tuna salad	Steamed shrimp
Creamy dressings	Flavored vinegars, lemon juice, or nonfat or low-fat dressings
Croutons	Whole wheat bread on side
SOUTHERN COOKING	
Fried oysters or fried shrimp	Boiled spiced shrimp
Fried fish	Baked, broiled, or grilled fish
Fried chicken	Baked, broiled, or grilled chicken
Hush puppies	Cornbread
Potatoes and gravy	Rice or potatoes without gravy
	Cooked greens (made without salt pork or lard)
STEAK/SEAFOOD RESTAURANTS	
Prime cuts of meat, such as rib eye, porterhouse, or T-bone	Lean cuts of meat, such as London broil, filet mignon, or round or flank steak
King-size cuts	Smaller cuts with visible fat removed
Clams casino	Steamed clams
Fried fish	Poached, steamed, broiled, or grilled fish
Seafood Newburg	Bouillabaisse

Stay away from these . . .	. . . And try these instead
STEAK/SEAFOOD RESTAURANTS	
French fries	Baked potato with nonfat or low-fat toppings on the side
Pie and ice cream	Angel food cake or sherbet
THAI	
Fried appetizers	Satay
Ground pork or beef appetizers	Fish or vegetable appetizers
Fried meat spring rolls	Baked vegetable spring rolls
Pan-fried noodles or soft noodles cooked in fat	Soaked bean thread noodles
Fried rice	Steamed rice
Coconut-milk sauces	Sauces with lemongrass or basil
Coconut ice cream	Fruit ice

There are lots of things you can easily do to make eating out more healthful. Ask for salad dressing or sauce on the side so you control the amount of fat that goes on your food. When you order meat, ask for it to be prepared without fat. In most instances, you can substitute unsalted vegetables or a baked potato for French fries. With a little practice, you will be able to find many more ways to cut back on your fat and sodium consumption.

AFTER THE MEAL

Don't be tempted by fat- and cream-laden desserts. Fresh fruit, fruit ice, sherbet, gelatin, and angel food cake are excellent alternatives. Or just linger over a cup of coffee. Ask for milk, rather than cream or nondairy creamer, for your coffee. A cup of espresso with a twist of lemon is gourmet fare without any fat (though it may contain calories). Bon appétit!

Feeding Your Kids Healthful Foods

"When our daughter had her second birthday, that's when the family started a low-fat diet. My wife and I weren't happy with the extra weight we were carrying. Mostly, though, we didn't want our child to grow up eating the way we did—putting butter on everything and thinking that it wasn't

okay to leave the table unless you were stuffed. We want to make eating right a regular part of her life so it won't be a struggle when she gets older."

Making healthful eating a normal and tasty part of life is truly a gift that keeps on giving. Imagine starting your children on a life where they will enjoy food without dieting, without high cholesterol, without obesity, without constipation.

The American Heart Association suggests the simple guidelines below for everyone. As children over two years of age begin to eat the same foods as the rest of the family, they may safely make the transition to this eating pattern.

- Eat foods low in saturated fats, total fat, and cholesterol. The percentage guidelines for fat, saturated fat, and cholesterol are the same for children as the ones recommended for adults.
- Choose a variety of foods to be sure you get enough carbohydrates, protein, and other nutrients.

If your family follows these guidelines, your children will get all the nutrition they need to grow and develop normally. The challenge is to do it in a way that pleases kids' taste preferences and won't turn meal-time into a struggle. Try these alternatives to help bring down the fat and increase the fruits and vegetables your child eats. In many instances, adults who eat the most fruits and vegetables were introduced to the habit as children.

Orange-Banana Fun Pops

---

2 bananas
6 ounces natural orange juice
* concentrate*
8 ounces water

1 cup plain nonfat or low-fat yogurt
½ cup nonfat dry milk

Peel and slice bananas. Place pieces in the work bowl of a food processor fitted with a metal blade or in a blender. Add remaining ingredients. Blend until smooth. Pour into ice cube trays. Put a drinking straw (cut the length in half) into each cube. Freeze several hours.

Adapted from American Heart Association Cookbook, *5th Edition, 1991.*

CHILD-PLEASING ALTERNATIVES

Instead of always serving this . . .	. . . How about this?
Ice cream cone	Frozen yogurt
	Frozen fruit-flavored ice
	Frozen banana
	Fun pops (recipe on page 147)
Soda or sugary juice drinks	Fruit juice mixed with seltzer
Soft white bread	Oatmeal bread
Hamburger	Turkey burger, veggie burger
Peanut butter and jelly	Lower-fat peanut butter and banana
Tomato or other soups made with milk	Chicken noodle, vegetable, or other soups made with water
Pudding	Yogurt, flavored gelatin, or apple sauce
French fries	Pasta, baked potato, or oven French fries (recipe on page 110)
Bologna	Lean lunch meats
Chips	Rice cakes
	Popcorn
	Pretzels
Milk shake	Smoothee blended with ice, fruit, or flavoring, and nonfat or low-fat yogurt or skim or low-fat milk
Candy bars	Raisins
Chocolate chip or sandwich cookies	Fig bars, gingersnaps, vanilla wafers, oatmeal cookies

Caterers have discovered that a simple rule helps them please young guests. Kids like to eat what they make for themselves. They're more likely to eat vegetables on pizza or tacos if they get to "build" their own food. If they've put blueberries in every crater of a waffle, they'll probably enjoy eating it. You'll find many helpful suggestions in the *American Heart Association Kids' Cookbook*. If you have space, let your children grow some carrots, lettuce, or other vegetables. Inside, children can grow sprouts from seeds in a few days and have a wonderful addition to a sandwich or salad.

Sometimes your child will refuse to eat what you're serving the rest of the family. A dinnertime battle, even if you win and your child swallows a few bites of an unwanted vegetable or fruit, is not worth it. Don't force the issue. The very same food may be quite appealing in another form or when your child is older.

AVOIDING THE VEGETABLE/FRUIT BATTLE

If they won't touch this . . .	. . . How about this?
Cooked carrots or other veggies	"Invisible" vegetables grated into soups, casseroles, spaghetti sauce, or sandwich spreads
	Raw carrots or broccoli with a dip
	Carrot-raisin salad made with a little non-fat or low-fat mayonnaise
Breakfast	Fruit smoothee
	Leftovers from dinner
	Bite-size chunks of nonfat or low-fat cheese
	Peanut butter sandwich
Salad	Dipping-size raw vegetables
	Celery with low-fat peanut butter
	Vegetable dip with lots of spinach, carrots, and water chestnuts
	Fresh fruit

As a parent, you can make healthful eating a normal part of life in your home. While doing that, counselors advise that you should not rule certain foods or restaurants off-limits or make eating a big issue. By and large, kids want to be like their friends, and that may mean letting them make an occasional trip to the ice cream truck or visit a fast-food restaurant. Proper nutrition overall is what matters. Your children may face a conflict between the healthful way they eat at home and their social lives. Help your kids plan what they might want to eat when they're out with their friends.

GIVING BABIES A HEALTHY START

Baby fat is natural and healthy—but only on babies.

Breast milk has a higher percentage of fat than whole milk, and that's for a reason. The body uses the fat in what we eat and drink to make cholesterol. When you're an adult, that's a health concern. For a baby, whose cells are exploding in number, cholesterol is absolutely necessary. Remember, your body needs cholesterol to make hormones, to form the protective wrapping around nerves, and to build the walls of every cell.

Do not put a child under the age of two on a low-fat diet. Toddlers two and three years of age may safely make the transition to the eating patterns recommended for older children.

Babies need to drink breast milk or a well-balanced formula. When your doctor says it's time to start the baby on cow's milk, whole milk is usually suggested.

Babies can tell when you put salt in their food, and they don't like the taste—at least at first. When infants are fed baby and toddler foods salted to suit the taste of adults, those babies acquire the same yen for salt. By the time kids are ready for school, a difference in preference is clear. Kids who have not been fed salted foods don't really care for the taste of salt. Kids who have gotten used to salt like it and want it.

A little salt is not going to hurt a baby, but this is one area where you definitely have the power to make it easier for your child to eat healthfully as an adult. Don't encourage the salt monster now, and your kids won't have to try to tame it later in life.

Stick to the mild, almost sweet-tasting foods that will please a baby's palate. Bananas, peaches, carrots, sweet potatoes, and peas are good choices. You may be telling your older kids the wonders of broccoli, cabbage, and greens, but these foods are a little strong-tasting for a baby. Why encourage dislikes when you can wait until the time is right to introduce such foods?

Getting the Help You Need

Perhaps you've hit a weight-loss plateau or some other snag in working toward the healthier you. You can find more support for eating healthfully than ever before. Some may come from things, some from people. This part of the chapter tells you about both.

Perhaps the new food labels will make choosing healthful foods so much easier than before that they'll be a major factor in your new eating habits. Or maybe one or two small purchases for your kitchen will get you started. This section also discusses sugar substitutes, fake fats, and diets that make choices for you. Look very closely at the claims they make. Some of the plans and products may not prove helpful as you start to make healthful changes. Finally, this section discusses the help you might want to seek from family, friends, even nutritionists. Use this book and other information sources to make changes on your own, but don't hesitate to ask others for emotional and professional support.

If you want to attain, then maintain, your desirable weight, help is available. If one way doesn't work, try another or try a combination.

TAKING ADVANTAGE OF THE NEW FOOD LABELS

In 1994 the FDA began to insist that manufacturers must be able to back any claim on labels implying that a food is good in a low-fat or low-sodium eating plan.

Learning to read the new labels is a good first step in devising your eating plan.

UNDERSTANDING FOOD LABELS

If the label says . . .	It means each serving of the product has . . .
Calorie free	Fewer than 5 calories.
Fat free	Less than 0.5 gram of fat.
Low fat	3 grams of fat or less.
Reduced fat or less fat	At least 25 percent less fat than the higher-fat version.
Low in saturated fat	1 gram of saturated fat or less, with not more than 15 percent of the calories coming from saturated fat.
Lean	Fewer than 10 grams of fat, 4 grams of saturated fat, and 95 milligrams of cholesterol.
Extra lean	Fewer than 5 grams of fat, 2 grams of saturated fat, and 95 milligrams of cholesterol.
Light (lite)	At least one-third fewer calories or no more than half the fat of the high-calorie, higher-fat version or no more than half the sodium of the higher-sodium version.
Cholesterol free	Fewer than 2 milligrams of cholesterol and 2 grams (or fewer) of saturated fat.
Low cholesterol	20 or fewer milligrams of cholesterol and 2 grams or fewer of saturated fat.
Reduced cholesterol	At least 25 percent less cholesterol than the higher-cholesterol version and 2 grams or fewer of saturated fat.
Sodium free or no sodium	Fewer than 5 milligrams of sodium and no sodium chloride in ingredients.
Very low sodium	35 milligrams or fewer of sodium.
Low sodium	140 milligrams or fewer of sodium.

If the label says . . .	It means each serving of the product has . . .
Reduced or less sodium	At least 25 percent less sodium than the higher-sodium version.
Sugar free	Less than 0.5 gram of sugar.
High fiber	5 grams or more of fiber.
Good source of fiber	2.5 to 4.9 grams of fiber.

In general, the wording follows the same pattern for each ingredient:

◆ "Free" has the least amount.
◆ "Very low" and "Low" have a little more.
◆ "Reduced" or "Less" always means that the food has at least 25 percent less of that nutrient than the standard version of the food. It may still be quite a bit higher than a low-fat or low-sodium product, however.

Even if a product doesn't brag about its low-fat status on the label, it may still be a good choice.

To see whether a prepared food could be called low-fat, check the number of fat grams against the list below. If it is the same or less, consider it low fat.

To make sure that the label information translates onto your dinner plate, check the serving size. If you usually eat twice that amount, alter

Food/Serving Size	Maximum Amount of Fat
Bread (2 slices)	3 grams
Cake without icing (3 ounces)	3
Cereal (1 cup cooked)	3
Cheese (1 ounce)	3
Cookies (2 small)	3
Crackers (6 saltines)	3
Frozen dessert (½ cup)	3
Frozen dinners (10 ounces)	10
Lunch meats (2 ounces)	3
Muffins (2 ounces)	3
Salad dressing (1 tablespoon)	3
Soups (1 cup)	3
Yogurt (1 cup)	3

your portions or double the values. Remember that a product that used to be labeled low fat or low sodium may not be considered low anymore.

The total amount of fat consumed in a day is more important than the amount in any single food dish. For example, a piece of meat or a frozen entrée containing nine grams of fat can still be part of a low-fat meal. Just be sure the side dishes you select are low fat. If, however, you combine it with fried potatoes, vegetables in cheese sauce, and salad with a creamy dressing, you'll very likely have trouble staying within your daily fat allowance.

On the food labels, the column called "% Daily Value" will help you figure out how much of your day's fat allowance you will be using if you eat the product. The entry for "Total Fat" is based on having 30 percent of your calories come from fat. All the daily allowances are based on a person eating 2,000 or 2,500 calories a day. If you are trying to keep your fat lower, or if you consume more or fewer calories in a day, adjust accordingly.

If an ice cream container shows that one serving has 50 percent of the average person's daily fat allowance, you know that is a very high fat food. Do you want that single serving of ice cream to eat up half of your fat allowance for the day? Or would you rather make a lower-fat dessert choice and have more fat left to spread throughout other meals and dishes?

FURNISHING A LOW-FAT KITCHEN

Cooking healthfully uses normal ingredients and simple cooking methods. It shouldn't require trips to specialty stores or new pots and pans. However, the implements discussed below come in handy for healthful cooking. Now that you've made the commitment to eat healthfully, you might want to treat yourself to one or more of the sampling of items below.

- *Vegetable steamer.* For a few dollars, you can buy a collapsible stainless steel steamer that expands to fit inside any pan. Steaming is delicious, nutritious, and fast.
- *Heavy nonstick frying pan.* A pan made with nonstick anodized metals or coated with a nonstick surface lets you use little or no oil and still not have food stick.

KVCC   KALAMAZOO VALLEY
COMMUNITY COLLEGE
LIBRARY

♦ *A rack that fits inside broiling or baking pans.* The rack will let the fat drain off the meat, keeping the meat from soaking in a puddle of drippings.

♦ *Lettuce dryer.* Spinning lettuce dry lets dressing cling so you get every bit of flavor. (Dressing tends to drip off moist ingredients.)

♦ *Yogurt strainer.* Strainers are cone-shaped mesh filters that you can use to drain nonfat yogurt that doesn't contain gelatin. The result is versatile, rich-tasting yogurt cheese to use in dips or on cereal, baked potatoes, or fruit. Alternatively, you can line a colander with good-quality paper towels or line a strainer or coffee-filter cone with a coffee filter or with cheesecloth that can be washed and reused.

♦ *Blender/food processor.* You can purée beans or vegetables to add thickness to soups and sauces without using cream or oil. A food processor can also be used to chop fresh herbs.

♦ *Gravy strainer or skim ladle.* Either of these lets you easily pour just the flavorful part of a gravy, soup, or sauce, without the fat.

♦ *Hot-air popcorn popper.* Popping with air instead of oil saves calories and virtually eliminates the fat.

♦ *Microwave oven.* A microwave keeps nutrients intact and bakes potatoes quickly; cooks other vegetables quickly, right in the serving dish; and makes it easy to reheat last night's healthful leftovers. Microwaves also allow you to freeze extra portions of nutritious dishes and have healthful "fast food" on hand. Many microwave-safe implements are available to help you cook healthfully.

♦ *Wok.* This implement is good for cooking food in vegetable stock, wine, or a minimum of oil. A wok can double as a steamer.

TRYING TO FOOL YOUR SWEET AND FAT TOOTH WITH FAKES

Sugar Substitutes

Each teaspoon of sugar contains sixteen empty calories. For decades, weight-conscious Americans have borrowed the artificial sweeteners created for diabetics and used them to enjoy sweet coffee, iced tea, and sodas without the added calories.

With all the sugar substitutes on the market, you might predict that the amount of real sugar we eat is going down. Not true. We are eating more sugar than ever—in addition to spending millions of dollars on sweeteners.

The American Cancer Society does not advise people either to use or to avoid artificial sweeteners. It does caution that the long-term health impact of their use has not been determined. At high levels, *saccharin* has been shown to cause bladder cancer in rats, but there is no clear evidence that moderate use by humans increases their cancer risk. The FDA has approved *aspartame,* a newer sweetener created from protein, but it hasn't been on the market long enough for its long-term effects to be studied. The sweetener carries a warning against use by people with phenylketonuria, who must avoid eating the amino acid it contains.

The use of artificial sweeteners by children should not be encouraged (see below).

Phony Fats

With Americans striving to eat less fat, the holy grail of food manufacturers became the creation of a perfect fake fat. They wanted something that would give foods a rich taste and have just the right feel in your mouth. One manufacturer has woven sugar and vegetable oil into large molecules that pass through the digestive system without being absorbed. The FDA is examining both whether this product is safe and whether it may interfere with the absorption of vital nutrients.

The FDA has approved a fake fat created from specially treated protein. It is used in frozen desserts, cheeses, sour cream, salad dressings, mayonnaise, and baked goods. With this product, one protein gram replaces three grams of fat. Such a fat substitute may provide a useful quick-fix to stave off a high-fat dessert craving. However, nutritionists are concerned that, as happened with sugar substitutes, people using fake fats won't lose their taste for fat and won't eat any less of the real stuff. Nutritionists also caution that the calorie content of foods using fake fats is usually as high, or almost as high, as their real-fat counterparts.

The AHA does not recommend the regular use of any fake foods to help you control your weight. This is particularly true for children, who should develop a taste for nutritious foods so they don't need to rely on fat or sugar substitutes. Fake fats haven't been used long enough for the ACS to evaluate their long-term risks and benefits. Therefore, the organization hasn't issued a recommendation either for or against their use.

USING COMMERCIAL DIET PLANS AND DRINKS—
DO THEY REALLY MAKE DECISIONS EASIER?

"With so many people paying a lot of money to go to diet places, I've felt fortunate to be able to lose weight on my own."

Choice is a centerpiece of a more healthful lifestyle. It's how all your small, daily decisions can bring you enjoyment while helping prevent disease, and in a way that suits your personality and your schedule.

Lack of choice is the advertised appeal of many diet plans. Making your decisions for you is how they propose to help you control your weight. Instead of choosing and cooking your own foods, you substitute diet drinks or special diet meals, or you follow a rigid, restricted diet plan. Such diets don't teach you good eating patterns to use for the rest of your life. And avoiding real food or going on a diet that overemphasizes one particular food or type of food is *not* recommended.

Some low-cost commercial diet plans ease members into sensible low-fat eating, with plenty of information, recipes, and group support to help them stay motivated. If you don't feel confident about changing eating habits on your own or you like the interaction that a group can provide, check out one of these programs.

The first principle of good nutrition is to eat a balanced diet that includes a variety of foods. No "superfoods" exist. Going on a crash diet that requires eating large amounts of a few foods causes one of two undesirable things to happen. One is that the diet is so boring or unsatisfying that you'll quickly abandon it, leaving you more discouraged than ever. The second is that you'll stick with the restricted diet and risk nutritional deficiencies, since no one type of food has all the nutrients needed for good health.

Diet powders and formulas have not demonstrated any health benefits when used by healthy people. Protein powders do not increase muscle size, strength, or performance. Low-calorie liquid protein diets surged in popularity in the 1970s. However, at least in part because of the effects of dietary deficiencies on the heart muscle, these liquid diets resulted in dozens of deaths. The formula for most diet shakes is basically skim milk and sugar with added fiber, vitamins, and minerals. Even if a food substitute includes fiber and selected nutrients, it is not the same as eating fruits, vegetables, and carbohydrates. It is not as nutritious, and it is not nearly as satisfying.

For convenience, you can occasionally drink a prepackaged beverage or eat a prepackaged diet meal. But a good "diet" is really a good eating plan—one you can follow for years to maintain your desirable body weight and your good health—and one that you create yourself.

ENLISTING FAMILY SUPPORT

"I've got news for you. My diet success all depended on my wife."

"I do the cooking for the family. When I started eating a low-fat diet, we all did. I think we are healthier because of it. So far, the only problem is that my husband and kids are not fish fans, so I eat fish more at lunchtime."

"Since my diet has changed, it's harder to visit my parents. Sometimes I'll eat the fried foods or the bacon with them and then regret it. Other times I just have to get away from their house to get away from the food."

Your main source of dietary support or sabotage is likely to be living in your own home.

Food is a prime focus of family interactions from the time we are born. In some families, we learn healthful ways to eat. In other families, however, food is the primary means of showing love or rewarding good behavior. Then we have to learn new ways to express those emotions. In some families, we learn food rules that don't suit us well later in life. Then we have to learn new guidelines.

You may find that starting to eat differently brings up unexpected emotions or creates occasional misunderstandings at home. As you seek to give support to, or get support from, family members, try to take responsibility for your own health and to be clear when you ask for help. As much as possible, try to keep family dynamics separate from food issues. Here are some suggestions:

- Plan family activities not centered around food.
- Take responsibility for your eating choices. Saying "Don't let me eat ice cream" (especially if it is soon followed by a plaintive, "Why didn't you bring me a treat?") is going to engender frustration instead of support.
- Don't tease. If someone isn't eating a second helping or the same food as the rest of the family, don't dwell on it. Also, many dieters feel their efforts are undermined if you say, "Wouldn't you like just a little? A little wouldn't hurt."
- Recognize that other family members may have different eating needs. You may be ready for a dramatic shift in the way you eat, while others may have different goals and timetables.

Luckily, the healthful eating guidelines are suitable and easily adapt-able for the entire family. Discuss openly how the family can accommo-date various food needs.

GETTING AN OUTSIDE OPINION

"When I left the hospital after my heart attack, the doctor gave me all the menus from the special diet I was on. That got me started, along with a book and a talk by the nutritionist."

"I thought I knew about nutrition. But then I had a heart attack and was sent to a series of lectures given by a nutritionist. She made things very clear and explicit, and I started to make big changes in the way I ate."

Some people love to think about food. They devise menus, plan recipes, count calories and fat grams, and think about the health bene-fits that proper nutrition can provide. If that sounds like you, there are plenty of cookbooks, magazines, and fat-, calorie-, and nutrition-counters to help you.

A qualified nutrition counselor can help you turn general eating guidelines, or your doctor's specific diet prescription, into daily menus. He or she can evaluate the way you eat now or help you figure out how to follow your new eating plan. You *can* eat with your family or in the office coffeeshop, and a few meetings with a nutritionist may be just the help you need to do that.

Finding a Nutritionist
If you are being treated for high blood pressure or heart disease, your physician may suggest a nutritionist who specializes in devising eating plans to lower the risk of heart attack. If you are looking for a nutri-tionist on your own, ask your local American Heart Association if it has a referral service. Some hospital outpatient clinics offer nutrition coun-seling or classes for specific conditions. You may want to call the nutri-tion department of your local university.

Assessing a Nutritionist
People with widely varying education, experience, and interests call themselves nutritionists. To find one who is qualified and right for you, ask questions:

◆ *Are you a registered dietitian, a licensed dietitian, or a licensed nutritionist?* Registered dietitians have been certified by the American Dietetic Association, and you can be sure they have received at least bachelor's-level training in food and nutrition, completed an internship, and passed a national examination. If someone is a licensed dietitian or licensed nutritionist, you know he or she has met the licensing requirements to work in your state.

◆ *Do you have any special training or experience in . . . ?* Like many other professionals, many nutritionists specialize. If you select one whose interests match your areas of concern, you are likely to receive more useful advice.

   Some dietitians and nutritionists have been trained to work specifically with people who have heart and blood vessel problems, diabetes, or cancer and people who need low-salt or low-fat diets. Others are experts in weight reduction, vegetarian diets, nutrition for athletes, or the special nutrition needs of children or the elderly.

◆ *Do I need a referral from my doctor?* A nutrition counselor needs to know about any medications you take, any health problems you have, and the results of your latest lab tests. Many nutritionists see only patients with a doctor's referral. Also, going through your physician or health plan may increase the chance that insurance will cover the costs of the nutritionist's services.

◆ *Will an eating plan be designed just for me?* A nutritionist should take into account your food likes and dislikes, current eating habits, and health goals.

Getting the Most from Your Sessions

Ask the nutritionist what to bring to your first session. In addition to medical information, you may be asked to keep a detailed food diary for a few days or bring a list of your favorite and least-favorite foods.

   At the first session, be forthright about how you live and what kind of food plan you can live with. Let the nutritionist know your social and work schedules, who does the cooking in the family, and what your experience has been in making eating changes in the past.

   If you don't do most of the shopping and cooking at your house, the person who does should be involved in the sessions.

Staying with the Program

Don't think of the guidelines and suggestions in this chapter as a "diet"—something that will deprive you of the foods you love and the traditions you cherish.

Instead, think of the guidelines as a way to eat healthfully for life. Eventually it will seem like second nature to enjoy foods that taste good, won't leave you hungry, and have the added benefit of helping to prevent disease.

The dishes and menus you create are limited only by your imagination. Here's to your good health!

CHAPTER 4

Let Your Body Move

DO YOU WISH THERE WAS A SECRET INGREDIENT FOR A HEALTHFUL lifestyle? Just one painless, pleasant thing you could eat or do that would be your ally in helping you live longer while you look and feel great?

If that secret ingredient was found, would you buy it? Would you use it? Get ready, because it *does* exist—and it is inexpensive and readily available.

Exercise is the invisible link in reducing several heart disease and cancer risks. It can be physical activity as simple as walking. As a rule, people who exercise on a regular basis live longer. No matter which of the changeable risk factors you look at, physically active people as a group may be better off than their sedentary neighbors. Physically active people often have lower blood pressure and less body fat and usually have more protective HDL cholesterol. Also, people who exercise regularly are less likely to develop diabetes and are more likely to cut down on, or to stop, cigarette smoking.

If those aren't reasons enough to get you moving, exercise seems also to have protective effects on the heart independent of its lowering other risks. In a series of studies involving people as diverse as San Francisco longshoremen, Harvard University alumni, Finnish men, British civil servants, and residents of an Israeli kibbutz, a consistent relationship emerged. The studies showed that people whose jobs and hobbies involve lots of physical exertion had less heart disease and fewer fatal heart attacks.

161

By 1992 the data had become so compelling that the American Heart Association declared physical inactivity a risk factor in the development of coronary heart disease.

Unfortunately, while the benefits of exercise are getting clearer, as a nation we are becoming more sluggish at work and at play. According to government surveys, less than half of American adults get any exercise at all. Only one in five people exercises enough to derive major health benefits. As much as we tout exercise clubs, home equipment, and fat-busting videos, we actually move less and less.

The Heart-Protecting Power of Exercise

"When I was younger, nice women wore girdles and didn't sweat. And because we loved our husbands, we encouraged them to slow down so they wouldn't have a heart attack."

Now we know that if you want to protect the people you care about, you should urge them to speed up their hearts with some exercise. Inactive people are almost twice as likely as more-vigorous individuals to develop coronary heart disease. Former athletes who don't keep moving have no more protection than lifelong couch potatoes.

Put in perspective, the risk of living an inactive life seems to be roughly equivalent to smoking a pack of cigarettes a day. Some researchers have estimated that stepping up the pace of the American lifestyle from sedentary to active could reduce heart disease risk by one third.

How does exercise help? Like other muscles, your heart becomes stronger when it works harder. When it is conditioned through regular exercise, it beats more slowly but each beat pumps out more oxygen-rich blood. When you rest, if your heart is well-conditioned, it delivers the same amount of oxygen with less work. When you exert yourself, you do the same amount of work with a lower heart rate and lower blood pressure.

While your heart is getting in condition, so are all the other muscles you exercise. They develop a greater number of capillaries (tiny blood vessels) and become more efficient at extracting the oxygen they need from your blood. Therefore, the same amount of movement or work will take less energy. Put a stronger heart and more-efficient muscles together and you are no longer worn out when you walk up a steep hill, mow the lawn, or lug laundry up the stairs.

Besides strengthening the heart muscle, exercise has other positive effects on your cardiovascular system. The clot-forming tendency of your blood decreases if you are well conditioned. The triglyceride level in your blood usually goes down, and your high-density lipoproteins (HDLs) usually go up. (Triglycerides are a form of fat in the blood that when present at high levels may raise heart disease risk or serve as a marker for other risk factors. HDLs are the "good" cholesterol associated with a lower risk for coronary heart disease.) Your heart undergoes physiologic changes when you exercise over a period of time. Those changes may protect against disturbances in abnormal heart rhythm.

Exercise doesn't directly protect against stroke. Exercise can, however, protect against heart disease and may reduce blood pressure, which would help reduce your risk of stroke.

CUTTING RISK FACTORS WITH EXERCISE

As impressive as its health benefits are, aerobic exercise alone cannot prevent or cure heart disease. You simply cannot ignore high blood pressure, a high blood cholesterol level, and cigarette smoking and expect exercise alone to make you healthy. But, as you'll see below, a regular exercise program *can* give you a major boost in changing those risks.

Smoking

"When I craved a cigarette, I would jump on my bicycle. After a ride, I felt better and didn't even want to smoke."

No matter how conscientiously you exercise, tobacco smoke will still put cancer-causing poisons in your body and raise your risk of heart disease. To a certain extent, exercise may help make the effects of carbon monoxide less severe (see page 29). However, exercise works best as an ally when you quit smoking.

Exercise can do lots for you besides making it easier not to smoke. It also reduces tension and insomnia, temporarily helps boost your metabolism to counter weight gain, and increases the speed at which particles and phlegm are cleared from your lungs after you stop smoking.

High Blood Pressure

"When I developed high blood pressure, my doctor put me on a diuretic and also told me to walk thirty minutes a day. Within a year, I no longer needed the medication. Eight years later, I'm still walking and still keeping my blood pressure in the normal range."

People who don't exercise are 35 to 52 percent more likely than active people to develop high blood pressure. If you have high blood pressure, studies show that you may be able to lower both your *diastolic* and your *systolic* measurements through regular exercise. (See page 239 for an explanation of diastolic and systolic measurements.) Reduce your blood pressure enough and you may be able to decrease the amount of medication you need. For example, in one study, a group of patients with high blood pressure took one-hour walks three times a week and dropped their blood pressures significantly.

No one knows precisely why exercise is helpful in reducing blood pressure. The reason given most often is that it may be because of changes in weight or body fat. Exercise also affects blood pressure by altering the hormones influencing blood pressure, keeping tiny blood vessels in the muscles more open, and helping the body get rid of sodium. Even among people who continue to have high blood pressure, those who become more fit through exercise tend to live longer.

Obesity

"I'm the kind of guy who made a deal in high school to take orchestra instead of gym. By the time I was forty, I was just a big, fat time bomb ready to go off."

Compared with people in most other countries, Americans are fat. In general, it's not because we consume so many more calories. The major problem is that more of what we eat sticks to our hips and abdomens because we burn far fewer calories through exercise. All that fat increases the chance we will develop heart disease, high blood pressure, stroke, and several types of cancer (see "The Exercise/Cancer Connection," page 167).

"I had dieted before but never kept the weight off, until this time when I added exercise. Although I had already lost lots of weight by dieting, people didn't start to say how much thinner I looked until I started working out.

I can't pinpoint all the changes exactly, but my waist has changed and my pants fit differently."

Exercise burns fat and builds muscle. Even when you are sleeping or sitting still, your muscle tissue uses more energy than fat. Replacing your fat with muscle means an overall faster metabolism for a while after you exercise. It also means you'll have an easier time losing weight.

If you are betting on whether someone will lose weight and keep it off, the best predictor isn't the kind of eating plan the person is on. It is whether that person includes exercise in his or her weight-loss plan.

Without changing a morsel of what you eat, adding enough exercise to burn 200 calories a day can take off a dress size or twenty pounds in a year. Exercise combined with a low-fat eating plan is a powerful weight- and fat-loss combination.

Many of the benefits exercise provides in reducing other heart disease risk factors seem to be related to the fat loss achieved with exercise. These include lower blood pressure, lower blood lipids, and better diabetes control. If maintained, exercise can result in long-term weight management.

Lipids

"My husband's cholesterol was 340 and mine was 247. For three months, we walked three times a week and watched what we ate very carefully to avoid fat whenever we could. His went down 100 points and mine is now 199."

If you follow a low-cholesterol, low-fat eating plan to improve your lipid levels, exercise will enhance its benefits. Exercise alone may not have much of an effect on your total cholesterol reading. However, recent studies hold that regular exercise can significantly raise the level of HDLs. Because HDLs help protect against heart disease, you are better off if your total cholesterol stays the same while your HDLs go up.

Regular exercise can also help you lower the level of triglycerides, another lipid associated with heart disease risk in some people. Triglycerides are the form that most fat is in when it circulates through your bloodstream.

Diabetes

"When I first got diabetes, I needed insulin. Now if I ride my bike, walk a lot, use the exchange program for eating, and make low-fat selections, I don't have to use any medication."

Diabetes occurs when the body's ability to process glucose (sugar) is impaired. This happens because not enough insulin is produced or because of other impairments in the body.

Whether diabetes starts in childhood or adulthood, it increases the risk of heart disease and stroke. Diabetes that begins in childhood cannot be cured, but exercise may lower the amount of insulin needed to keep it under control. That's why if you're an athlete and have diabetes, you need to lower your insulin dose when exercising.

Exercise can help prevent adult-onset diabetes. Eighty percent of the people who get this disease are at least 15 percent overweight. If you exercise, your weight is easier to control and your body uses glucose more efficiently. The glucose gets into muscle cells more easily, and you need less insulin. If you have adult-onset diabetes, you may be able to eliminate or control the disease through proper nutrition and exercise.

CAN EXERCISE MEND A DAMAGED HEART?

"Almost six years ago, I had a heart attack. It was slight but enough to throw me on my fanny. I started walking in the hospital, counting the floor tiles to measure how far I was going. At home, I would walk to the corner and then add two or three houses each day. Now I swim, use a stair-step machine, and lift weights. I think my heart attack saved my life."

In the past, after a heart attack you'd be kept in bed for several weeks or months, with your muscles getting weaker all the time. Now, almost everyone who has had a heart attack, depending on its severity, is encouraged to get appropriate amounts of exercise. Chances are good that you'll be up and walking in a few days.

Usually about six to eight weeks after a heart attack, you'll take a closely supervised exercise test to help plan your rehabilitation program. To determine the extent of heart damage, you might take an exercise test while still in the hospital.

"After I had a massive coronary, the doctor prescribed supervised exercise in the hospital's cardiac rehab program. At first I could only spend four min-

utes on a bicycle or treadmill, and they monitored my heart the whole time. Eventually, it was safe for me to exercise at the gym and monitor my own pulse."

If you recently had a heart attack, bypass surgery, or angioplasty, you will probably have medical supervision in a cardiac rehabilitation program when you begin exercising. Later, you will probably graduate to exercising at home or in a gym without a physician nearby.

Exercise won't just help you get back on your feet after a heart attack. Participating in exercise rehabilitation helps prevent a fatal heart attack. Combined data from several studies indicate that the risk was cut by 25 percent over the first three years after the heart attack.

Heart disease patients who exercise and condition their hearts also develop a buffer against the pain that can accompany exertion. As the patients become more fit, they can do more activity comfortably. It will take more exertion—with a higher heart rate and blood pressure—to bring on angina. (Angina is the pain associated with lack of blood flow and oxygen to the heart muscle.)

"At the gym, a college student started running with me one day. When she started doing sprints, I followed right along. The exercise supervisor really blessed me out: 'Don't you ever do that again!' "

Heart disease does make you more vulnerable to all kinds of physical stress, including exercise. Therefore, if you have heart disease and want to exercise, you need to take special precautions and go more slowly than someone who doesn't have a heart condition. This is especially true if you want to take up vigorous exercise, such as jogging. (You'll find special exercise considerations for people with heart disease on pages 202–204.)

The Exercise/Cancer Connection

Obesity is one link between lack of exercise and the risk of cancer. People who weigh 40 percent or more over their ideal body weight are at increased risk of colon, breast, prostate, gallbladder, kidney, stomach, ovarian, and uterine cancers. (That translates into about fifty extra pounds for a woman or sixty for a man of average height.)

If excess fat puts you at risk, you can reduce the amount of body fat through a combination of exercise and healthful eating.

Aside from the fat connection, a few intriguing hints indicate that exercise by itself may provide some protection against certain types of cancer. Some early studies seemed to show a link between physical inactivity and the overall chance that a person will die of cancer. Why exercise helps isn't completely understood. However, fifteen out of sixteen studies in men and nine out of ten studies in women indicate that people who do lots of physical activity are less likely to develop colon cancer.

> *"I started exercising out of fear of getting sick again. Now I realize that to have a good life, you have to move and exercise. I don't know that I'll live a long time, but I know I'll be at the gym forever—enjoying everything."*

If cancer occurs, physical activity can make you more comfortable and may help you return to normal activities sooner.

Is Exercise Ever Dangerous?

No matter how physically fit you are, you could still die during a workout. You also could die running for a bus, chopping wood, shoveling snow, or flying a kite. Or you could die in your sleep.

Each year, an estimated 25,000 people die from a heart attack that comes on during or just after strenuous exertion. (That leaves about 450,000 heart attack deaths *not* associated with physical activity.) Recent studies leave little doubt that sudden bursts of intense physical activity are prime heart attack times. However, your risk of an exertion-related death is much lower if you are physically active on a regular basis.

A normally sedentary person is 100 times more likely to have a heart attack during heavy exertion than when just sitting around. That exertion-related increase in risk is *80 percent less* for people who exercise once or twice a week and more than *97 percent less* for people who are used to exercising five times a week. Overall, this would seem to be a ringing endorsement for the protection that fitness brings.

Even if you shun exercise, you will encounter situations in life that demand exertion. Your car will get stuck in the snow, you will find yourself within moments of missing a train or plane, or an emergency will necessitate a full-out run. If you are sedentary and an intense activity is avoidable, pass on it. Hire a teenager to shovel the snow, or get help pushing your car. But in an emergency, don't be afraid to take necessary action. Even for a sedentary person, the chance of heart attack during a burst of high activity is still small—only about 1 in 10,000.

Getting Started

If you know you're out of shape but want to improve your fitness, start slowly. Then gradually work up to more strenuous activity. No matter what physical condition you are in, you can almost always make it better with exercise. In fact, an inactive person who starts to exercise will achieve an even bigger gain in health benefits than an already active person who picks up the pace.

If you are healthy, there's no reason you can't begin today to introduce more movement into your life. However, if you answer yes to one or more of the questions below, confer with your physician about finding the right activity and getting started safely.

DO YOU NEED TO SEE A DOCTOR BEFORE STARTING AN EXERCISE PROGRAM?

1. Have you ever had a heart attack, or has a doctor told you that you have heart trouble? Is early heart disease common in your family?
2. During or just after physical activity, do you ever feel pain or pressure in your chest, neck, shoulder, or arm?
3. Do you often feel faint or have spells of dizziness or shortness of breath during mild physical activity?
4. Do you have high blood pressure or not know whether your blood pressure is normal?
5. Do you smoke cigarettes?
6. Do you have diabetes?
7. Do you have a bone or joint problem, such as arthritis, that has been aggravated by exercise in the past or that you think might be made worse by exercise?
8. Do other physical reasons make you think you should not follow an activity program?
9. Are you age sixty or older?
10. Are you over age forty, not used to regular exercise, and planning to start a pretty vigorous exercise program?
11. Are you taking medication for your heart or lungs?
12. Have you recently developed chest pains?
13. Has your doctor ever recommended that you do only medically supervised physical activity?
14. Are you being treated for a serious illness?
15. Do you have to stop and catch your breath while climbing a flight of stairs?

Based on your checkup and a review of your medical history and risk factors, your doctor may suggest an *exercise tolerance test*. It can ensure that you don't have any hidden heart disease that should be considered as you plan an exercise program. Other benefits of the test are that it can establish your baseline values for fitness and heart rates at various stages and can serve as a standard baseline for future tests. An exercise tolerance test provides the most accurate basis for an exercise prescription.

For the exercise test, electrodes are pasted at precise locations on your chest, arm, and possibly your head. These record the electric current your heart produces as you gradually increase your heartbeat by walking on a treadmill or riding a stationary bicycle. The physician performing the test will keep a record of your blood pressure, appearance, and any pain or shortness of breath you experience as you exercise harder.

Exercise tolerance tests aren't for everyone. If a person is ill, likely to fall, or thought to be at risk for an immediate stroke or heart attack, an exercise tolerance test may not be safe. Also, this kind of test can be hard to interpret in women and in any people at lower risk for heart disease.

What Makes a Healthful Workout?

Experts divide the benefits of exercise into four components. They are strengthening muscles, increasing flexibility, conditioning the heart and lungs, and changing body composition to have less fat and more muscle. A decade ago, fitness experts held pretty rigid ideas of what it took to improve cardiovascular conditioning. They advocated activities that got the heart pumping furiously for at least thirty minutes, three times a week. Some people gave up exercising, or thought it wasn't worth even starting, because the program seemed arduous or impossible.

Now we know that any activity that gets you moving around, even for only a few minutes a day, is better than doing nothing at all. The Centers for Disease Control and Prevention and the American College of Sports Medicine issued a joint recommendation about this. They urge every American to accumulate thirty minutes or more of moderately intense physical activity throughout each day on most days of the week. Moderate activity includes things like raking leaves, dancing, or walking. Done at a comfortable intensity, these activities can be just as effective as strenuous exercise at improving your fitness.

However, those organizations found that for most Americans, regular daily activities don't add up to this recommended amount of exercise. If you're one of those people, you need to make the time for additional exercise.

If you don't have any medical restrictions and you want to take a walk today, go ahead. You *don't need to wait* while you plan a formal exercise program. However, to help you get the most health benefits in the safest way, an ideal three-part workout has been devised. Compare it with what you do now, and start moving.

The ideal workout includes:

+ A slow warm-up to get your muscles ready for vigorous activity;
+ Aerobic exercise (any activities that condition the heart to pump more oxygen-rich blood and condition the muscles to use it more efficiently);
+ A cooldown period to stretch the muscles you have worked and let your heartbeat gradually return to normal.

Don't forget to drink plenty of nonalcoholic fluids, especially water, before, during, and after your workout.

THE WARM-UP

Muscles are injured more easily when they are cold. A few minutes of gentle activity will get your blood moving and will warm your muscles for more-vigorous exercise.

Spend a few minutes moving at an easy pace. If you're going to run, walk or slowly jog first. If you're going to walk, begin at a stroll. Before you swim, take a few easy laps.

At the end of your warm-up, take a minute or two to stretch so you will stay flexible. Then you will be able to move your joints through their full range of motion and stretch your muscles completely during exercise without pulling or tearing the tissue. If you're stiff, you're more prone to injury and to have aches and pains that will make any exercise more difficult to enjoy.

Some activities, such as ballet, gymnastics, yoga, and swimming, incorporate stretching. For most others, it's up to you to stretch in every workout.

Try the basic stretches shown below and add others to prepare the muscles your favorite sport or activity uses most. As you stretch, don't hold your breath and don't bounce.

Wall Stand

For Achilles tendons, calves, and ankles. Face a wall, standing about a foot and a half away from it. Lean forward, pushing against the wall with your arms bent and your heels flat on the ground. Hold for about ten seconds, then relax and repeat once or twice.

Floor Touch

For back, hamstrings, and knees. Bend your knees slightly. Bend forward from your hips. Hang your arms down, touching the floor if you can. Hold for about ten seconds, then relax and repeat once or twice.

Standing Toe Touch

For hamstrings. Prop up one leg on a chair, railing, or other sturdy object that will raise your leg straight in front of you (lower if that isn't comfortable). Bending your other knee slightly, lean forward over your straightened leg and reach for your toes. Breathe normally. Feel the stretch up the back of your leg. Hold for about ten seconds, then relax. Repeat once or twice on each leg.

AEROBIC CONDITIONING

The most energetic part of your workout is aerobic conditioning. This part will last up to an hour. You'll want to exercise hard enough to burn fat and condition your heart but not so hard that you put undue stress on your body.

The intensity of the workout is measured by your heart rate, also called the *pulse*. It's the number of times your heart beats each minute. Based on your age and your physical condition, your doctor or exercise specialist may suggest a specific *target heart rate* for you. Otherwise, use the standard chart (page 175) *as a guide.* Keep in mind that such guides reflect averages and may not be exactly right for you.

Your target zone depends on your maximum heart rate (the fastest your heart can beat). Subtract your age from 220 to get an estimate of that number. Depending on your exercise goals, your medical condition, and what shape you're in, your target heart rate usually is between 50 and 75 percent of that number. For example, if you are twenty years old, subtract 20 from 220. Your maximum heart rate, then, is 200. Your target heart rate is between 50 and 75 percent of 200, or 100 to 150 beats per minute.

If you have been exercising *regularly* for several months and are ready to work out more vigorously, you can exercise at your optional rate, your 85 percent level. For this example, that rate is 170. However, the benefit-to-risk ratio of exercising at this high level isn't clear. Furthermore, you do not have to exercise that intensely to stay fit.

A good rule of thumb is don't exercise beyond your ability to talk effortlessly while exercising. You or your health advisor can also roughly gauge your exercise intensity by how you feel. Scales of "perceived exertion" ask you to rate how hard you are working according to the following:

 • Very, very light (just noticeable);
 • Very light;
 • Fairly light;
 • Somewhat hard;
 • Hard;
 • Very hard;
 • Very, very hard.

When people rate their exertion as "somewhat hard," they are likely to be working at the lower end of the target heart rate, or 50 percent. People who rate their exertion as "hard" to "very hard" are likely to be nearing the optional vigorous rate, or 85 percent.

During or immediately after peak exercise, you can check your heart rate by taking your pulse. Compare your heart rate with the rates in the chart on page 175.

When you start the aerobic phase of your workout, gradually increase the intensity of your exercise until your heart rate goes above the 50 percent level. After about fifteen minutes, your body will begin burning fat instead of carbohydrates. After twenty or thirty minutes, you'll be improving your cardiovascular fitness.

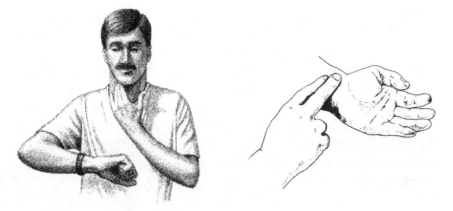

Taking Your Pulse

To be able to tell whether you are hitting your target zone, first practice finding and taking your pulse quickly. Perhaps you can easily take your pulse in your wrist. Using your first two fingers, feel the inside part of your wrist beside your wrist bone, below your thumb. (See the illustration above.) The easiest method, however, may be to place your finger-

TARGET HEART RATE *(in beats per minute)*			
Age	**Target Heart Rate Zone** **50–75%**	**Optional Maximum Rate for Regular Exercisers** **85%**	**Maximum Heart Rate** **100%**
20	100–150	170	200
25	98–146	166	195
30	95–142	162	190
35	93–138	157	185
40	90–135	153	180
45	88–131	149	175
50	85–127	145	170
55	83–123	140	165
60	80–120	136	160
65	78–116	132	155
70	75–113	128	150

NOTE ON TYPES OF EXERCISE: *If you are doing aerobic exercise that works the arms but not the legs, lower your target heart rate by ten beats a minute.*

NOTE ON MEDICATION: *If you are taking medication for angina, high blood pressure, or depression, ask your physician whether your exercise program needs to be adjusted. Some medications lower the maximum heart rate, so your target zone rate would be lower.*

tips lightly over one of your *carotid arteries*. (See the illustration on page 175.) Those are the blood vessels just to the left and right of your Adam's apple, in the lower third of your neck. Just be sure not to press on both sides of the artery at the same time or for a long period of time. Using a watch with a second hand, count your pulse for ten seconds. Then multiply by six to get the number of beats per minute. Why not just count your pulse for sixty seconds? Once you stop exercising, your heartbeat immediately begins to return to normal. Therefore, counts taken using the ten-second formula during and after exercising are more accurate.

THE COOLDOWN

After exercising within your target zone, slow down gradually to avoid dizziness. Swim more slowly or flip over for a leisurely sidestroke or backstroke. If you are jogging, slow to a walk but keep moving. After a few minutes of unhurried movement and while your muscles are still warm, repeat the stretches from the warm-up. You may find you are more limber than when you started.

How Much Is Enough?

The total amount of exercise you need depends on your goals and the activities you choose. You can gauge how much exercise you get by *how hard* you exercise, *how long* you exercise, and *how often* you exercise.

Use your target heart rate to check how hard you exercise. If your heart rate rises too quickly and goes above the target zone (more than 75 percent), you may be working too vigorously. You'll need to adjust your activity level. Exercise that is not intense enough for you to enter the target zone (less than 50 percent) is still good for you but may not give your heart and lungs enough conditioning to provide the health benefits you seek. How hard you exercise depends on your age; how fit you are; whether you have medical problems, especially cardiac problems; and how long and how often you exercise.

Generally, if you're less fit or have problems that exercise might aggravate, you should start exercising at lower intensity levels for longer periods of time or more often. You can increase the intensity later.

If you've been inactive, you might begin with a ten- or fifteen-minute walk. To condition your heart, plan to increase the length of your workout until you spend thirty minutes exercising within your target zone. To lose weight and body fat, longer, less intense workouts will help you more than shorter, more intense ones. Exercising more than an hour adds little conditioning to your heart and may increase the chance of injury if you're doing a high-impact exercise.

The usual recommendation for how often to exercise is every other day. Exercising less than twice a week provides little conditioning. Doing the same type of exercise more than five times a week doesn't improve conditioning much more than exercising every other day.

Although one or two sessions of aerobic exercise a week will improve your cardiovascular fitness somewhat, they won't be of much help in reducing body fat. If you do pounding, high-intensity exercise, such as running or high-impact aerobics, more than three times a week, you will increase your chance of injury. More than five such workouts a week are usually not recommended. Also, it's best to skip a day between high-intensity sessions to give your joints and muscles a chance to recover.

You can do lower-intensity exercises, such as walking at a speed that brings your heart rate into the low end of the target zone, every day if you want. That's especially true if you vary the muscle groups you use. Doing light activities that use muscles you don't exercise in your more intensive workouts helps with weight loss and maintaining flexibility and muscle tone.

Finding the Right Exercise

The right exercises are the ones you find enjoyable, comfortable, convenient, and safe—the ones you'll want to keep doing for years.

You can achieve aerobic conditioning with any activity that keeps your large muscles moving rhythmically and continuously. Walking, bicycling, swimming, skating, rowing, skiing, playing soccer, or doing something else—it's your choice. Try the activities that suit your fancy, your physical condition, and your schedule. Exercise makes muscles more efficient at using oxygen, but it primarily benefits the specific muscles you're working. Choose some activities that work both your arms and your legs. Keep in mind that arm activities are more likely to raise your blood pressure. This should be monitored.

The lists that follow will give you some ideas. And, remember, you don't have to do the same exercise every time.

Activities that provide aerobic conditioning:

- Aerobic dancing
- Badminton
- Bicycling
- Cross-country skiing
- Hiking
- Ice hockey
- Jogging
- Jumping rope
- Rowing
- Running
- Skating
- Stair climbing
- Stationary cycling
- Swimming
- Walking quickly (more than 4 miles per hour)

Activities that can provide aerobic conditioning if motion is continuous and brisk:

- Basketball
- Calisthenics
- Downhill skiing
- Fast ballroom dancing
- Field hockey
- Handball
- Racquetball
- Soccer
- Square dancing
- Squash
- Tennis
- Volleyball
- Walking moderately (3 to 4 miles per hour)

Gentler or less sustained activities that may not condition much:

- Baseball
- Bowling
- Croquet
- Gardening
- Golf (without using a golf cart)
- Housework
- Shuffleboard
- Slow ballroom dancing
- Softball
- Table tennis
- Walking leisurely (2 to 3 miles per hour)

If you are just starting out and are in poor physical shape, the activities in this third list may be vigorous enough to improve the conditioning of your heart and lungs.

Some of the most popular aerobic activities are walking, taking aerobics classes, biking, running or jogging, and swimming. The discussions that follow will give you details about them, including what you need to get started.

WALKING

For a wide range of people—all shapes, ages, and physical conditions—walking is the ideal aerobic exercise. For as long as you are able to walk, it can provide a fitness challenge that is perfect for any point in your life. This is true whether you are supported by a walker and are striving to reach the end of the hallway or are trying to qualify for the race-walking competition at the Olympics.

"When my wife and I started dating, she took me shopping for walking shoes. Now we walk almost every day, taking about thirty-five or forty minutes to walk a little over two miles. In the last eighteen months, I've lost forty pounds. I've also cut down on fatty foods, but I definitely feel like walking has made the difference."

Walking can condition your cardiovascular system and help you lose fat. It takes a little longer, but you can burn nearly as many calories by walking a mile as by running one.

Walking is safe for almost everyone. Compared with other aerobic exercise, it raises blood pressure only minimally. For that reason, it is often suggested for people with high blood pressure. Walking counters the pooling of blood in the legs and can often keep varicose veins from worsening. Because walking is a low-impact exercise, it puts less stress on the joints and feet than do running or jumping activities. This reduces the chance of injury, even if eventually you walk so fast you are leaving joggers behind.

When you walk for fitness, walk naturally. Keep an even stride and let your arms swing freely. Don't keep your feet stiff. Each foot should meet the ground at the heel and rock forward so you are pushing off at the toe. If you have good posture as you walk, you should be able to feel your abdominal and buttocks muscles working while your neck and shoulders stay relaxed.

The ideal place to walk is one where the scenery holds your interest and the path is clear enough that you don't have to watch the ground constantly. You may have been told to walk on level ground because of the condition of your heart or your joints. If so, try a treadmill, malls, or the track at a nearby school.

For cardiovascular conditioning, start your walk slowly and build up to a pace that increases your breathing and heart rate. Depending on your condition, that may mean a three-mile-an-hour pace or a vigorous twelve-minute mile. As you become more fit, you can increase your workout by walking longer, walking faster, or adding hills to your route.

"After my heart attack, I had been gradually increasing my walking house by house, block by block. I'll never forget getting to the corner one day and

SAMPLE WALKING PROGRAM

	Warm-up	Target Zone Exercising	Cooldown	Total Time
Week 1				
First Session	Walk 5 min.	Then walk briskly 5 min.	Then walk more slowly 5 min.	15 min.
Second Session	Repeat above pattern			
Third Session	Repeat above pattern			

Continue with at least three exercise sessions during each week of the program.

Week 2	Walk 5 min.	Walk briskly 7 min.	Walk 5 min.	17 min.
Week 3	Walk 5 min.	Walk briskly 9 min.	Walk 5 min.	19 min.
Week 4	Walk 5 min.	Walk briskly 11 min.	Walk 5 min.	21 min.
Week 5	Walk 5 min.	Walk briskly 13 min.	Walk 5 min.	23 min.
Week 6	Walk 5 min.	Walk briskly 15 min.	Walk 5 min.	25 min.
Week 7	Walk 5 min.	Walk briskly 18 min.	Walk 5 min.	28 min.
Week 8	Walk 5 min.	Walk briskly 20 min.	Walk 5 min.	30 min.
Week 9	Walk 5 min.	Walk briskly 23 min.	Walk 5 min.	33 min.
Week 10	Walk 5 min.	Walk briskly 26 min.	Walk 5 min.	36 min.
Week 11	Walk 5 min.	Walk briskly 28 min.	Walk 5 min.	38 min.
Week 12	Walk 5 min.	Walk briskly 30 min.	Walk 5 min.	40 min.

Week 13 on: Check your pulse periodically to see whether you are exercising within your target zone. As you become more fit, try exercising within the upper range of your target zone. Gradually increase your brisk walking time to 30 to 60 minutes, three or four times a week. Remember that your goal is to get the benefits you are seeking and enjoy your activity.

seeing a coffin being carried into a funeral home. Even though it was bad weather, I drove to the park and slowly walked a mile. It was the accomplishment of my life."

Essentials

Walking shoes that cushion your feet while letting them bend, providing support under the arches and the heels. Your shoes should give your toes plenty of room to wiggle and to keep from banging against the front when you're going downhill. Your shoes and socks should be made of breathable materials.

Options

A small, lightweight radio or cassette player with earphones to help you set the pace and pass the time. Either will make it hard to hear cars and other dangers, so stay alert.

AEROBIC DANCE

Aerobic dance lets dancers and nondancers alike experience the joy of moving to music. Aerobic dance combines rhythmic movements and simple dance steps into exercises that build cardiovascular fitness. You can use your current level of fitness and the type of music and movements you like as criteria for picking an enjoyable class or tape.

"Because the music and the dance steps are changing all the time, aerobics takes all my concentration. I never look at the clock, and I'm sorry when class ends. Going home, I think my walk is a little springier and a little more graceful."

Low-impact aerobics doesn't include jumping movements. Because you keep one foot on the floor at all times, you put less stress on your joints than you would in high-impact aerobics. Try to avoid doing your aerobics on concrete floors.

In *step* aerobics, movements include stepping on and off a stable step six to twelve inches high. The effort of getting on and off the step makes the cardiovascular workout more intense.

Each aerobic dance class or tape should include a warm-up period of five to ten minutes. Your movements during this time should bring you into your target heart rate zone. You'll also need a cooldown and stretching period. At first, you may be able to keep up with the class or tape for only the first five minutes or so of conditioning. Don't give up! Build up gradually until you can complete the full session.

In choosing a class, look for one where the instructor incorporates heart rate checks and helps dancers keep their bodies aligned correctly. He or she should also modify the movements for dancers who are out of shape, are pregnant, or have muscle or joint problems.

Essentials

Light, cushioned shoes that offer plenty of support and shock absorption, plus the right teacher or a tape geared to suit your particular needs.

Biking

"I take my bike whenever I need to run errands around town. For the weekend, I found a towpath along the canal where I can ride with no traffic."

Seventy-five million people bike for commuting, aerobic conditioning, or the sheer joy of watching the countryside fly by. Biking is excellent aerobic exercise. It also works the large muscles of the legs. Because it is a nonimpact activity, you can enjoy it even if running or aerobic dancing led to past injuries.

Biking has changed dramatically in the last few years. If you didn't enjoy biking in the past, try it again. No more dragging a heavy, single-speed bike up a hill. No more stretching out over downturned racing handlebars until you can't see the traffic without contorting your back and neck. Now, some bikes are even designed to tackle mountain trails. All-terrain bikes combine ease of peddling with the comfort and stability of fat tires and upright handlebars. Women can find bicycles specifically designed for their body proportions.

Before biking for aerobic conditioning, be sure to warm up by walking your bike or peddling slowly. Once you enjoy biking for twenty minutes or more in your target heart rate zone, you may want to add to the intensity of your workout. You can change speed, add hills to your route, or switch gears to increase the resistance. Using toe clips, which keep the feet securely on the pedals, you can work your leg muscles on the upstroke as well as the downstroke. Riding in too high a gear won't improve your workout, however. If resistance is too heavy, it invites knee injury. Too much resistance also slows down your pedaling cadence to a point where it compromises your aerobic conditioning. (Pedaling cadence usually is 70 to more than 100 rotations a minute.)

Stoplights and traffic are realities of city biking. Just don't count the time you spend waiting as part of your workout.

You may want to supplement biking with swimming or other exercises that build strength in the upper body.

Essentials

A sturdy bike and a hard-shell helmet. The right size bicycle is important to keep you from straining your back and knees.

Options

Toe clips and a water bottle you can attach to the bike frame.

STATIONARY BIKING

"After the car accident, my doctor said I might as well give away my regular bicycle. But I can still use a stationary bike because I can adjust it so it has no resistance."

If you enjoy biking but for some reason can't ride an outdoor bike, stationary biking might be an alternative. Also, when the weather keeps you inside, a stationary bike can keep you moving. Many stationary bicycles let you both see exactly how many rotations per minute you are traveling and set the precise resistance you want. This makes them ideal if you are a heart patient, have been sedentary, or have joint or muscle limitations. Some stationary bicycles offer movable handles that add upper body movement to the activity.

An adjustable seat and handlebars will let you share one stationary bike with family members or friends.

Listen to the radio or a tape, watch TV, read, or talk on the phone while you ride. It will make the time pass more quickly, while also letting you improve your mind or just enjoy some light entertainment.

RUNNING OR JOGGING

"I've been running for over twenty years, and I find it mentally and physically liberating. It allows my mind to not be caught up in mundane, everyday experiences. And it acts as a natural physical relaxer. If I don't sweat

and breathe hard and really put in a strenuous effort, I don't feel like I derive the same benefits. It's a personal thing, but I don't feel like walking lets me get to the same physical or mental place."

If you want a more intensive workout and enjoy the exhilaration of going fast, running may be the right aerobic exercise for you.

Running is one of the best calorie burners around. Here's an example that may surprise you. If you run at five and a half miles an hour, you will use far more calories than if you bike twice as far in the same amount of time.

However, jogging or running does put more stress on bones and joints than bike riding does. Also, you have a greater chance of injury with running than with lower-impact activities. When you jog or run, you are in the air for a moment of each step. Each time you hit the ground, you land with three or four times the force of your body weight.

SAMPLE JOGGING PROGRAM

	Warm-up	Target Zone Exercising	Cooldown	Total Time
Week 1				
First Session	Walk 5 min., then stretch and limber up	Then walk 10 min. Try not to stop	Then walk more slowly 3 min. and stretch 2 min.	20 min.
Second Session	Repeat above pattern			
Third Session	Repeat above pattern			
Continue with at least three exercise sessions during each week of the program.				
Week 2	Walk 5 min., then stretch and limber up	Walk 5 min., jog 1 min., walk 5 min., jog 1 min.	Walk 3 min., stretch 2 min.	22 min.
Week 3	Walk 5 min., then stretch and limber up	Walk 5 min., jog 3 min., walk 5 min., jog 3 min.	Walk 3 min., stretch 2 min.	26 min.
Week 4	Walk 5 min., then stretch and limber up	Walk 4 min., jog 5 min., walk 4 min., jog 5 min.	Walk 3 min., stretch 2 min.	28 min.

Week 5	Walk 5 min., then stretch and limber up	Walk 4 min., jog 5 min., walk 4 min., jog 5 min.	Walk 3 min., stretch 2 min.	28 min.
Week 6	Walk 5 min., then stretch and limber up	Walk 4 min., jog 6 min., walk 4 min., jog 6 min.	Walk 3 min., stretch 2 min.	30 min.
Week 7	Walk 5 min., then stretch and limber up	Walk 4 min., jog 7 min., walk 4 min., jog 7 min.	Walk 3 min., stretch 2 min.	32 min.
Week 8	Walk 5 min., then stretch and limber up	Walk 4 min., jog 8 min., walk 4 min., jog 8 min.	Walk 3 min., stretch 2 min.	34 min.
Week 9	Walk 5 min., then stretch and limber up	Walk 4 min., jog 9 min., walk 4 min., jog 9 min.	Walk 3 min., stretch 2 min.	36 min.
Week 10	Walk 5 min., then stretch and limber up	Walk 4 min., jog 13 min.	Walk 3 min., stretch 2 min.	27 min.
Week 11	Walk 5 min., then stretch and limber up	Walk 4 min., jog 15 min.	Walk 3 min., stretch 2 min.	29 min.
Week 12	Walk 5 min., then stretch and limber up	Walk 4 min., jog 17 min.	Walk 3 min., stretch 2 min.	31 min.
Week 13	Walk 5 min., then stretch and limber up	Walk 2 min., jog slowly 2 min., jog 17 min.	Walk 3 min., stretch 2 min.	31 min.
Week 14	Walk 5 min., then stretch and limber up	Walk 1 min., jog slowly 3 min., jog 17 min.	Walk 3 min., stretch 2 min.	31 min.
Week 15	Walk 5 min., then stretch and limber up	Jog slowly 3 min., jog 17 min.	Walk 3 min., stretch 2 min.	30 min.

Week 16 on: Check your pulse periodically to see whether you are exercising within your target zone. As you become more fit, try exercising within the upper range of your target zone. Gradually increase your jogging time from 20 to 30 minutes (or more, up to 60 minutes), three or four times a week. Remember that your goal is to get the benefits you are seeking and enjoy your activity.

If you are over forty and have not been active, you should build up your exercise capacity with walking or another less strenuous activity before starting to jog.

Although you don't have to have any special training, it takes time to build up stamina and strength to be able to run for a full workout. You may want to have a coach, exercise physiologist, or physical therapist observe your technique. Such a professional can see whether the way you move will place undue stress on any body part. To reduce the chance of foot, leg, and knee injuries, beginning joggers should follow certain guidelines. Don't run more than three times a week, and don't run two days in a row. Your muscles and bones need a chance to rest. Also, don't run longer than thirty minutes each time. Try to use a surface made for jogging, rather than a concrete surface.

Each time you run, be sure to include a warm-up and a cooldown period with stretching.

Essentials
Running shoes with shock-absorbing soles.

Options
A water bottle. A small, lightweight radio or cassette player with earphones. If you use the latter, be aware that you'll have a hard time hearing traffic and other dangers.

SWIMMING

"I have problems with my shoulder since my mastectomy years ago. When I swim, it's looser and more mobile. I also love how supported I feel by the water. It's comforting. I totally relax, and my body finds its natural alignment."

Swimming has all the benefits of other aerobic exercises, plus several advantages of its own. The buoyancy of water takes most of the weight off your bones and joints. That may make swimming and certain other water exercises enjoyable choices if you are overweight, are older, have arthritis, or can't walk.

Swimming uses all the large muscles of the upper and lower body. It also involves stretching your arms. Working against the resistance of the water provides overall toning and strengthening. If you are swimming at a pretty fast pace, you use more calories per minute than when walking.

If you don't know how to swim, you may need to choose another aerobic exercise while you learn and improve. Even with lessons, it may take quite a while for you to get a good aerobic workout through swimming. Meanwhile, a water aerobics class might be enjoyable.

A good warm-up is to swim a couple of laps slowly. That will get you used to the water temperature and gradually increase your circulation. Spend some time stretching your legs, arms, shoulders, and waist. During the conditioning part of your workout, you can alternate strokes to work different muscles. The breaststroke and the sidestroke, which require more gliding, are less aerobically vigorous than the crawl and the backstroke.

If you are worried about keeping your bones strong and preventing osteoporosis, you may want to supplement swimming. Walking or another weight-bearing exercise might be a good choice.

A special swimming caution: With cool water to keep you from feeling sweaty or overheated, you may not notice that you are overdoing. Build up slowly. If you are fatigued on the days you swim or have insomnia those nights, you may need to cut back or consult your physician. Of course, if you already know you tend to become dizzy with exercise, unsupervised swimming is not for you.

Essentials
A place to swim and a comfortable suit.

Options
Goggles, which can improve your vision and keep chlorinated water out of your eyes.

Pumping Up Aerobic Exercise with Strength Training

"In addition to walking, I go to an exercise class. A trained person leads us through strengthening exercises for the back and shoulders and arms and legs and all the things that give elderly people problems. The teacher is very strict about having us do the exercises properly so we won't hurt ourselves and we'll get all the benefit. Most people use one-pound weights, some three pounds, and some none at all."

Strength is the ability of muscles to apply force against resistance. You use resistance everyday. Doing a push-up, lifting a child or a suitcase, holding your posture erect, and unjamming the lid on a jar of jelly are examples.

As you age, you have a natural tendency to lose muscle strength. When that happens, you are more likely to feel achy and get injured during exercise and everyday activities.

Exercise that contracts a muscle against resistance—provided by weights, the floor, another part of the body, or water in a pool—builds muscle strength. Supplementing your favorite form of aerobic exercise with muscle-strengthening exercises can help you avoid injury and increase the ratio of muscle to fat in your body.

"My wife and I started using the weight machines along with the treadmill. I notice the fatty parts of my legs have turned to muscle. My abdominal muscles are stronger, and I don't have quite the protrusion I once had."

In exercise standards published in January 1995, the American Heart Association suggests that most people should supplement aerobic exercise with strength training two or three times a week. The training can be performed using a wide variety of equipment, including wall-mounted pulleys, exercise machines with various resistance settings, or free weights and dumbbells, which are convenient for use at home. What is right for you depends on your preferences and medical restrictions and on the availability of the equipment. If you have a medical condition such as a heart problem, high blood pressure, or a joint problem, ask your doctor whether strength training is advisable and what type is recommended.

A program to improve muscle strength should include exercises that work the major muscle groups of the body—arms, shoulders, chest, abdominals, back/trunk, hips, and legs. For many people, exercises that involve lower resistance but more repetitions are a safer choice.

Some health clubs and other facilities offer circuit training. This is a class that keeps your heart pumping fast while you alternate aerobics and strengthening exercises, such as bicep curls and sit-ups. Your local park may have a fitness trail, or parcours, dotted with strength-training stations that suggest various exercises.

Listening to Your Body

Every body is different, with a unique history and set of strengths and weaknesses. You may have an old sports injury, a particular sensitivity to humidity, or a tendency to work through pain instead of heeding it.

Learn to listen to your body as you exercise. With a little self-coaching, you can adjust your routine to accommodate it.

WHEN YOUR BODY SAYS: "PICK UP THE PACE"

Can you whistle or belt out an old show tune while you exercise? If your current routine is that easy—if it no longer makes you sweat a little or increase your breathing—you may be ready for a greater aerobic challenge. Your exercise diary may contain hints that it's time for a more strenuous workout. Maybe it shows that you're doing the same workout but your heart rate doesn't get as high, or your heart rate when you aren't exercising has become lower.

You can increase your total exercise by working out *longer, harder,* or *more often.*

It is usually considered safest to add more time to your workout first. You should probably wait awhile to make it more intense, particularly if you have problems with joints or muscles or have other health concerns.

To exercise harder, you can speed up, increase the setting on exercise equipment, or maintain the same speed but add some hills to your walking or running route. Have you been regularly exercising at the lower end of your target heart rate zone? If so, make some changes to boost the conditioning value. If you've been exercising and feeling good for several months, you can go to the 85 percent level on the target heart zone chart. But remember, you do not have to exercise that hard to stay in good condition.

WHEN YOUR BODY SAYS: "EASE UP"

Aches and Pains

"I pace myself on the treadmill by how I feel. If my calves begin to ache or I start breathing too rapidly, I slow down and then build back up again. And I recognize that after about thirty-five minutes, it's time to slow down."

As you use unfamiliar muscles, it's natural to have some aches and soreness. Try cutting back on your speed or intensity. Pay special attention to stretching the complaining muscles during your next warm-up. If you are just learning an activity, ask your teacher, an exercise professional, or someone with more experience than you have to watch your technique. Sometimes you can do something simple to help. For instance, alternately pointing and flexing stiff feet can help prevent cramping.

If the discomfort continues or if you have pain in your back or joints, don't ignore it. *Exercise should not hurt.* Look at your exercise schedule to see whether you might be doing too much. Are you skimping on your warm-up and cooldown periods? Are you wearing well-cushioned shoes that fit properly? If you have chosen a high-impact activity, do you give yourself a day of rest between sessions? Are you more comfortable swimming or doing a low-impact activity? Is your body more comfortable if you switch between activities that use different muscles?

If aches and pains continue, check with a physician.

General Fatigue

"My body is different every day. I can tell in the pool by the halfway mark whether I should do my whole workout or take it easy."

"I used to play tennis, and I didn't enjoy an easy game. But it took me longer and longer to recover after I played. Finally I decided tennis was a little too extreme for me. I switched to bicycling and walking."

Exercise should leave you refreshed, not worn out. If it takes more than ten minutes for your heart rate and breathing to return to normal after a workout, cut back on the intensity or length of your exercise. Do the same if you feel draggy instead of energized during the rest of the day.

Cramps and Nausea

"In the morning my joints feel stiff, and if I move around too quickly I get nauseous. So I never try to exercise then. I go ice skating on my lunch break or go walking after work."

If you feel nauseous or develop stomach cramps when exercising, you may need a change in the timing or intensity of your workout. If you aren't a morning person and need a slower routine when you first get up, try a different time of day for exercising.

If you will be exercising vigorously, wait at least two hours after eating. More blood is sent to your digestive organs after you eat. As your muscles start demanding extra blood for your workout, there may not be enough to keep all your organs well supplied. The result can be cramps, nausea, or faintness.

Insomnia

Exercise should improve your sleep, not disturb it. Do you feel tired but have trouble sleeping on exercise days? Try exercising earlier in the day. If the problem persists, tell your physician. Sleeplessness after exercise is sometimes a sign of heart problems.

Inability to Converse

If you pant and are unable to carry on a conversation while exercising, you may be working too intensely. Ease up and see whether you become more comfortable.

Postexercise Faintness or Nausea

If you feel faint or nauseous after exercising, your activity may have been too intense or you may have stopped too suddenly. Try decreasing the intensity of the workout and prolonging your cooldown period.

Asthma Symptoms

If you notice asthma symptoms when you exercise, talk to your health-care provider. You may be able to prevent symptoms by taking your medication before starting your workout.

WHEN YOUR BODY SAYS: "STOP NOW!!"

"I started sweating and feeling a pain in my chest, so I turned up the treadmill to check out what would happen. Then they took me to the hospital."

Surprisingly, trying to "test" heart attack symptoms by exercising harder is a pretty common mistake. *Don't do it!*

Ignoring the following signals and continuing to exercise may lead to serious heart problems. Stop exercising and call your physician if you experience any of these symptoms:

- Lingering pain or pressure on the left side or middle of your chest (The classic stitch-in-your-side pain is usually felt below rib cage level and goes away quickly. It is not heart related.)
- Pain or pressure in your left jaw, shoulder, or arm or the left side of your neck
- Sudden dizziness or fainting
- Breaking into a cold sweat
- Pallor

If you become dehydrated while exercising on a hot day, your body may show signs of heat exhaustion or heatstroke. Some symptoms of heat exhaustion are dizziness, headache, nausea, confusion, and a body temperature below normal. Dizziness, headache, and nausea are also symptoms of heatstroke, a more serious, life-threatening condition. Other heatstroke symptoms include thirst, muscle cramps, and sweating cessation. If these symptoms occur or if you feel that your body temperature is unusually high, stop exercising at once, get something to drink, and go to a cool environment. Ask for help if you feel woozy or confused. You may need medical assistance.

When Exercise Meets Real Life

Of all the well-meaning people who decide to exercise, more than half give up in less than a year.

An ideal exercise plan, no matter how carefully considered, may not always suit your less-than-ideal life. To help make exercise a lifelong habit, learn to adapt it to fit your changing mood, environment, and physical condition.

SCHEDULE CHANGES

Lack of Time

"I like to exercise first thing in the morning. It saves time because I don't have to take an extra shower, and I find that I'm much more alert and efficient when I get to work."

If you set aside specific times and days for your workouts, you'll be more likely to stick with your program than if you exercise on a catch-as-catch-can basis. But if exercise seems like just one more demand in an already overflowing schedule, it can become a source of anxiety rather than a healthful pleasure. A time crunch may spur a shift in when and where you exercise—or you might just need a shift in the way you think.

Move Your Workout Closer to Home

"Several years ago I joined a health club. It cost hundreds of dollars and I realized that the machine I used the most was the stationary bike. So I invested in my own. Now I can get up and ride for twenty minutes or so in

the morning. I don't have to clean up first. I don't have to wait for the club to open. And I don't have to wait in line to use the machine."

When you're under time pressure, the smallest demand on your schedule can feel like a burden. If it takes half an hour to get to a swimming pool or running track, no wonder you feel squeezed for time. Would it help if you took your bicycle for a spin right in your own neighborhood? Or maybe you can substitute an aerobics video for a class at the health club or buy some home exercise equipment?

If you are considering a health club membership, visit the facility at the hours you are likely to use it. Be sure to keep in mind how rushed you may be. How is the traffic getting there? Must you wait for room in the pool or at the machines you want to use? Is it more important for your club to be close to your home or to your office?

Double Up On Activities

"Instead of talking on the phone with my neighbor, we meet for a walk."

Exercise time may double as a visit with a friend, an outing with the kids, or newspaper- and mystery-reading time on the treadmill or stair machine.

Split the Difference

"When I'm going to be in court, I ride the stationary bike for fifteen minutes to rev myself up in the morning. When I get home, I ride for another fifteen minutes to relieve tension."

On days when you really can't squeeze in a half-hour workout, try sneaking in some ten- or fifteen-minute exercise refreshers. They do add up.

Change the Equation

"After a workout, my head is clear. I'm much more able to focus on a task and finish it instead of going from one thing to another."

"Since I started exercising, I have a whole different kind of energy. I walk at a different pace and I don't get tired in the way I used to. Even my dog has noticed the difference!"

Remember, regular exercise will increase your energy and stamina and help reduce tension. Rather than considering it time lost, try thinking of it as time invested. You reap the benefits daily in improved efficiency and productivity.

Prioritize

"My doctor got out a prescription pad and wrote 'Walking: a physiological activity.' He gave me a starting schedule and goals to work toward before our next visit. And he made it clear that it was just as important as taking my medicine."

If you feel like you're goofing off when you are exercising, maybe that's a positive sign. Exercise is beginning to be fun!

FITTING FITNESS IN

By spending little if any extra time, you can turn the fitness quotient up a notch in activities you already do.

- When driving, find a parking place several blocks from your destination and walk.
- When watching TV, sit up instead of lying on the sofa.
- At the beach, sit and watch the waves instead of lying flat.
- When bedridden, try to sit up for meals.
- At the bank, use the walk-up instead of the drive-through line.
- After dinner, take a stroll instead of watching TV.
- When shopping, walk between stores instead of driving.
- When golfing, don't use a cart.
- Play an instrument instead of listening to a recording.
- When walking, pick up the pace from leisurely to brisk.
- Hit the dance floor on fast numbers instead of slow.
- When cutting the lawn, choose a push mower instead of power.
- When walking, choose a hillier route.
- When gardening, also prune, dig, and pick up trash.
- When jogging, break into a run or fast jog now and then.
- Play singles tennis or racquetball instead of doubles.
- At a picnic, join in on badminton instead of croquet.
- At a lake, rent the rowboat instead of the canoe.
- Try cross-country skiing instead of downhill.
- Jump rope with your children instead of playing jacks.
- Go to the museum instead of a movie.
- Stand up while you talk on the phone.
- Take the stairs instead of the escalator or elevator.

But remember that as far as your health is concerned, exercise is serious and essential. If you need to, think of it as physical therapy: as deserving of a place in your appointment book as getting the car tuned up or catching up on work-related reading. If you had a busy spell, you probably wouldn't give up brushing your teeth. Don't give up exercising.

Travel

Maintaining fitness on the road takes a little forethought, but it's getting easier all the time.

Tuck your exercise clothes and your weights into your suitcase. When making hotel reservations, ask about fitness facilities, tracks, swimming pools, and guest access to health clubs. If your room has a VCR, pop in your favorite exercise video. Turn on the radio and dance around. Some motels will even let you reserve a stationary bike for private in-room use.

Ask about walking or biking paths in the area, or check out the local mall or high-school track. Just be sure to take safety precautions before exploring a city you don't know.

ATTITUDE ADJUSTMENTS

Dislikes

"Here's what I think about swimming: I hate getting cold, I hate having my face wet, I hate having my glasses off, and I hate redoing my hair in the middle of the day."

Do you loathe the routine that sounded like such a good idea? It's easy to switch to something more enjoyable. Exercise is available to suit all temperaments and lifestyles.

In making your new plan, try to evaluate honestly what didn't work out. Did you give your routine a fair chance? Did you dislike working out in front of other people? Did your shoes fit? Was the activity inconvenient? Did you have a hard time leaving work to make your class? Was there a run of nasty weather? Were you not physically flexible enough to do the activity without hurting yourself? Was the instructor right for you? Were you and your workout buddy starting from very different fitness levels? Did you hate being alone? Were you feeling down in the dumps?

Turn your dislikes into positive choices for the next activity you try.

Boredom

"If I had my druthers, there are lots of days I'd rather be doing something other than aerobics class. Almost anything sounds like it would be more fun. But I go anyway."

No single activity is likely to hold your interest day after day, year after year. If your workout has become a bore, there are many things you can do to make it more engaging.

Add Variety

"My advice? Vary the exercise, vary the location, vary the times. Otherwise it becomes mentally boring and you'll stop doing it."

If one activity provides all your exercise, look for alternatives. It can be something as simple as a minor change in your current choice. Or it can be a totally different way to exercise. Walk through the park instead of through your neighborhood. Change the music. Use a different machine at the health club.

"I like the variety of equipment I can use at the health club. And I'm more disciplined if I get away from home, where I always see something else that needs to be done."

Find a Friend

"At the pool, there is an interesting mix of people of all ages and abilities."

People who exercise alone have a higher dropout rate than those who join a group fitness program or find a walking companion or a health club buddy.

If you enjoy solitary exercise, fine. But if you're getting a little bored with your own company, consider joining a club or inviting someone along for your next workout. Exercising with a buddy is also a good safety precaution, especially if you're walking in an isolated area or have medical problems. Swimming alone is never recommended.

Increase Your Skill

"There was a special offer to have a coach videotape our swimming strokes and make suggestions. It was hilarious! Even though I'll never be a great swimmer, it gave me lots to think about."

To derive health benefits from exercise, you don't have to care a hoot about sports or even be good at the activity you choose. Sometimes, however, learning more about your exercise choice is a big help in rekindling your interest.

At your local library, you'll probably find magazines and books about walking, running, and fitness. You also might attend a workshop or take a class to improve your skills.

In many sports, you can increase the difficulty without changing your conditioning level. Try an aerobics class with more-complicated dance steps. Learn the technique racewalkers use. Master a flip-turn between swimming laps.

Chart Your Success

"To keep myself going, I fiddle with the electronic scanner on the treadmill. It's fun to see how far I'm going and how many calories I'm using."

Seeing a little success flashing before you can put a spark back in a humdrum workout session. Almost at the one-mile mark? You can keep

EXERCISE DIARY					
Week _____			Weekly Goal _____		
Day	Date	Activity	Exercise Heart Rate	Exercise Distance/ Duration	Comments
SUNDAY					
MONDAY					
TUESDAY					
WEDNESDAY					
THURSDAY					
FRIDAY					
SATURDAY					

going a few more minutes. Now almost at the 100-calorie mark? That's worth staying on the treadmill another few minutes.

You might find it very helpful to keep an exercise diary (see page 197; also available from your local American Heart Association affiliate or by calling 1-800-AHA-USA1) or a calendar. With either, you can keep track of goals, health data, calorie burnoff, physical reactions, or any other facts that are important to your exercise program. Make notes about each workout. How long did you exercise? How intensely? How far did you go? How did you feel during the workout and afterwards? Did you suffer any injuries?

If you are trying to lose weight or if you have diabetes, arthritis, high blood pressure, or another chronic illness or condition, your exercise diary is a good place to record health data. You can keep track of medications, weight, symptoms, and blood sugar or blood pressure readings. You can chart your progress and then review the diary with your physician to see whether your exercise routine needs any adjustments.

CALORIE USE CHART

The figures below show the approximate calories spent by a 75-, 100-, or 150-pound person doing a particular activity.

Activity	Calories used per hour for a person weighing		
	75 lb	100 lb	150 lb
Bicycling, 6 mph	135	160	240
Bicycling, 12 mph	225	270	410
Jogging, 5½ mph	365	440	660
Jogging, 7 mph	510	610	920
Jumping rope	415	500	750
Running in place	360	430	650
Running, 10 mph	710	850	1,280
Swimming, 25 yds./min.	155	185	275
Swimming, 50 yds./min.	270	325	500
Tennis singles	220	265	400
Walking, 2 mph	125	160	240
Walking, 3 mph	175	210	320
Walking, 4½ mph	245	295	440

DETERMINING CALORIE USE

Referring to your Exercise Diary (see page 197) and the Calorie Use Chart, determine how many calories you burn during exercise activity:

Example:
Activity: <u>Bicycling (100-lb person at 6 mph)</u>
Number of calories per hour <u>160</u> × number of hours <u>1/2</u> = <u>80</u> calories

A. Activity: _____
Number of calories per hour ___ × number of hours ___ = ___ calories

B. Activity: _____
Number of calories per hour ___ × number of hours ___ = ___ calories

C. Activity: _____
Number of calories per hour ___ × number of hours ___ = ___ calories

D. Activity: _____
Number of calories per hour ___ × number of hours ___ = ___ calories

E. Activity: _____
Number of calories per hour ___ × number of hours ___ = ___ calories

You may want to use the chart above to estimate how many calories you are using at each workout. Looking back at your diary, see whether your weekly total is as much as you planned.

Did you notice that certain workouts leave you feeling particularly tired or needing aspirin to ease muscle soreness? Think about what could account for this. Did you go farther or work out several days in a row, for example?

A diary can be a valuable document and a source of pride. If it sounds like piling drudgery on top of boredom, however, forget it.

Make Your Money Matter

"I spent $300 for the health club. On the first day, I told myself, 'If you never go back, this afternoon cost you $300.' The next time: 'If you never go back, this afternoon cost you $150.' I like how the membership became a bigger and bigger bargain, until I got too involved in the exercise to bother tracking anymore."

For some people, money can be a powerful motivator. For others, spending a lot on exercise equipment or clubs just adds to their guilt when they quit working out. The biggest profit makers for health clubs are all the people who pay large up-front fees and don't use the membership.

Sometimes, friends put money into an informal exercise pool. At the end of the week, the money is divided among those who kept to their exercise schedule. Another way is to be in a fitness program that creates financial incentives for groups of exercisers. In such an arrangement, if you don't keep moving, you and everyone else on your team will lose money.

Focus In

"Swimming could never be boring. Every few laps I switch my focus to what a different part of my body is doing—like the stretch in my shoulders or the way the whole body turns when I take a breath. By the time I've given a little attention to each part, it's time to get out."

Really focus on your body during your next workout. You may find that your inner experience is fascinating. It's likely that paying such close attention will even improve your form and comfort, since you will breathe more deeply and unclench tense areas.

"I find I go into a meditative state while I exercise. If I'm trying to solve a problem or make a decision, I think about it before I start. Then I put it out of my mind. Very often the decision will come to me when I'm exercising."

When you work your body, you may find it easier to relax your mind. Focus on the physical experience. Feel your feet touching the earth, concentrate on following a dance sequence, or enjoy the movement of sweet, fresh air on your face. You can give your mind a vacation.

WEATHER CHANGES

Heat

"We like to walk outside in the late afternoon. But in the summer, we switch to early morning or walk inside where it's air-conditioned."

When the temperature gets into the high seventies and beyond, your body's cooling mechanisms come into play. Blood vessels just under your skin open up to let heat dissipate. The same amount of exercise makes your heart beat faster. Humidity boosts your heart rate even more.

The following suggestions might help you keep from getting overheated as the temperature soars:

- Make your workout slower. When it's very hot, make your workout shorter also. It takes your body a week or two to adapt to warm temperatures. You may never adapt to extremely hot ones.
- If you have heart or lung problems, move your exercise routine into an air-conditioned space on hot days.
- Drink fluids before, during, and after exercise. Cool water is ideal.
- Try exercising in the cooler parts of the day. In high-pollution areas, these are also the times of day when ozone levels usually are lowest.
- Wear loose, breathable clothing. Never try to increase sweating by overdressing or wearing sauna suits and other nonbreathable clothing.
- Stay alert for signs of heatstroke and heat exhaustion (see page 192).
- Remember to apply sunscreen and wear a hat for skin cancer protection.

Cold

As autumn becomes winter, many people put away their walking shoes and their exercise program.

If you hate the cold and snow, find an indoor exercise to get you through the winter. If you are healthy and game to exercise in the elements, dress for comfort and safety. Think of what you would wear if you were going out for a nonexercise activity. Remove one layer and you should be dressed just about right. Remember to wear a hat and mittens or gloves.

When you're covered by extra clothing and are walking or running in snow, your heart will work harder. Check your pulse to be sure you are exercising within safe limits.

If you have heart or lung disease, your doctor may ask you to avoid prolonged exposure to air below twenty degrees Fahrenheit and to exercise indoors when the temperature is below ten degrees. Pay attention to the wind-chill factor as well as the temperature. A cold day will seem much colder if the wind is blowing.

BODY CHANGES

Infections

When you have an acute infection, your body needs rest more than exercise. Wait until you feel better and your fever has been gone for two days. Then start exercising again at a lower intensity.

If you have a cold but aren't feverish or really feeling ill, try some gentle exercise if you want to.

If you have an infection involving the heart—*myocarditis, endocarditis,* or *pericarditis*—you need rest and careful medical monitoring. Talk to your doctor before beginning or resuming an exercise program after having such an infection.

If you have a chronic infection, ask your physician how much exercise he or she recommends.

Neuromuscular Diseases

Redness or swelling of muscles or joints, whether from an injury or a chronic disease, such as arthritis, should be evaluated by a qualified health-care professional. That person will advise you whether it is safe to exercise and can help you select a suitable activity.

Pregnancy

Unless you have specific pregnancy problems, you can exercise throughout pregnancy. During the hard work of labor and delivery, your cardiovascular conditioning will serve you well.

If you'd like to start an exercise program during your pregnancy, discuss it with your obstetrician. If you already work out regularly and have your obstetrician's blessing, by all means keep doing the activities you enjoy. Just be mindful of your changing body. Pregnancy hormones cause ligaments to become softer and stretchier. That's perfect for delivery but not so good for your ankles and other joints, which become more easily injured. As you gain weight, it will take more effort to do the same amount of exercise. Take care not to become dehydrated and overheated. As your center of gravity shifts, you may find it difficult and precarious to continue exercises that rely on balance. Ice skating, skiing, and even bicycling in the later months are among these exercises. Avoid sports likely to result in a collision or fall, such as football, downhill skiing, and waterskiing.

Whatever exercise you enjoy, it's time to cut back if it leaves you feeling worn out or irritates your lower back. Many women find that swimming is a perfect pregnancy exercise. The water eliminates concerns about balance, body weight, and overheating.

Heart and Circulatory Problems

Are you reluctant to exercise because you have a heart or circulatory problem? In fact, you probably can benefit from exercising. It may even be just what your doctor recommends.

Walking is one of the major treatments doctors prescribe for peripheral vascular disease. That disease causes blockages in the arteries feeding the legs. When you exert yourself, peripheral vascular disease may cause cramps in your calf muscles or make them tired and painful. By walking twenty to thirty minutes at least three times a week, you will help your blood vessels. You'll also gradually increase your capacity to move with ease. Just be sure to stop when you feel pain, then wait for it to subside. After the pain eases, it is fine for you to continue exercising.

Thromboembolic disease, such as phlebitis or embolisms, is usually treated with rest until the symptoms have subsided and you are in a stable treatment program. At that time, your physician may suggest walking or gentle exercises to maintain flexibility. He or she may approve your return to a moderate exercise program six weeks after your last symptoms or the last dose of your anticoagulant medication.

If you have an arrhythmia, it needs to be evaluated to determine how you should exercise. Regular physical activity helps some people with arrhythmias. Other people need to avoid vigorous exercise altogether and may be closely monitored while decisions are made about the proper medication and exercise.

After a stroke, people's abilities vary widely. However, almost every stroke survivor will benefit from some type of regular activity to help prevent complications and increase independence.

"Whatever can go wrong with a heart, I've got it: arrhythmia, congestive heart failure, enlarged heart, mitral valve prolapse, a kink in the main vessel. My new cardiologist sent me to an exercise program. At first, they let me ride a bike for two minutes. Now I can walk two miles and bike five miles, and I have two fewer prescriptions to take."

According to the 1990 findings of an expert advisory committee of the AHA, even if you have a pacemaker, a heart transplant, or another of the heart conditions listed on the next page, the chances are good that you can benefit from exercise. Your heart condition must be stable and the exercise must be carefully planned and monitored, though. That's because these are the conditions associated with higher than normal risk for heart attack during exercise. As you build a stronger heart, you will be able to enjoy more activities. You may even prevent these complications in the future:

+ Too little oxygen supply to the heart muscle, shown by an exercise test;
+ Angina;
+ Myocardial infarction;
+ Coronary bypass surgery;
+ Heart transplant;
+ Angioplasty;
+ Cardiomyopathies (including heart failure);
+ Valve disease;
+ High blood pressure;
+ Having a pacemaker.

For most significant heart problems, an exercise tolerance test (see page 170) will help in planning a safe exercise program. You will start out with close monitoring and plenty of supervision. If you are released to exercise independently, you may feel more confident if you use an electronic pulse monitor to keep close tabs on your heart rate.

Hospitalization

When you are hospitalized for surgery, cancer treatment, or treatment of another illness, you will almost certainly lose some of your conditioning and muscle strength. During this time, exercise means trying to move and do as much for yourself as possible, within the limits of your physical condition and the restrictions your doctor sets.

You have no choice about coping with the symptoms of your illness and the rigors of treatment. However, exercise can help prevent some unpleasant side effects that you might have if you're immobile. Those side effects are:

+ Breathing problems;
+ Poor appetite;
+ Constipation;
+ Bedsores;
+ Stiff joints;
+ Confusion.

Ask your nurse or physician how much you can move around. If you are supposed to take pain medications, take them as prescribed. It is more healthful to use proper medication and move around than to go without it and stay in bed.

Depending on your physical condition, your hospital exercise may include any or all of the following:

- Sitting up for your meals;
- Combing your hair and brushing your teeth;
- Turning over in bed every few hours;
- Walking to the bathroom;
- Walking the halls with your IV pole or with the help of a walker, a cane, or a friend;
- Slowly taking your joints through their full range of motion, however limited that may be;
- Going to physical therapy.

Raising Active Children

"My nine-year-old son has always been a big child, but I'm starting to notice more and more flesh around his stomach and chest."

In the United States, children today are fatter and less fit than they were even a generation ago. With today's concerns about safety, many children aren't allowed to roam, even in their own neighborhoods. Instead, they spend an average of seventeen hours a week watching TV. And that's in addition to the time they spend on video and computer games. Those games may promote hand-eye coordination, but they do nothing for the children's hearts and other muscles.

When examining early signposts on the road to heart problems, experts have documented some worrisome things about inactive kids. Compared with more-active children, they weigh more. They also have higher blood pressure and lower levels of heart-protective high-density lipoproteins. Add to that the fact that inactive children are probably more likely to become inactive adults. Now you have a foundation for adults who will be facing the challenge of staying healthy while having several heart disease risk factors.

Making sure your children get plenty of exercise can prevent the early onset of these adult risk factors. Any activities that get the heart beating faster than when the children sit still is acceptable. If they are obese or have high blood pressure, increasing exercise is sometimes all the treatment that's needed to reverse the problem.

"On some days I use exercise videos, and on other days I go running. Our kids see my husband and me exercise, and I think they get the idea that it's important."

Do your children get the message from you that physical activity is a normal, fun part of life? You can set a good example by showing them that exercise is important to you. You can also use the following tips to help lower the couch-potato quotient at your house.

♦ Limit television, movies, and video and computer games to a maximum of two hours a day. Studies show that every hour in front of the television increases the risk of obesity in children. In many cases, rationing TV is enough to make them find something more active to do.
♦ On family outings and vacations, hike, cycle, ski, swim, and do other vigorous activities.
♦ Give your children some chores that require physical exertion. Be sure to keep in mind their levels of strength, coordination, and maturity. Mowing lawns, raking leaves, scrubbing floors, and taking out the garbage not only teach responsibility but also can be good exercise.

"I see our job as giving our son plenty of activity options and letting him pick what's right for him. We let him know we'd like him to do something active this summer. It can be whatever he wants. He likes the idea of individual activities like swimming, golf, and tennis. He's never going to be one of the boys who like baseball."

♦ See what sports and activities appeal to your children. Then find out about lessons and clubs. Some children thrive on team sports; others hate them. The main thing is to help them explore vigorous options. Some activities, such as swimming and tennis, can be enjoyed for a lifetime and are much easier to learn during childhood.
♦ Notice whether you're chauffeuring your children to school or other places where walking or biking is safe. Try biking with your children. When you go somewhere together, use stairs instead of elevators, and increase the distances you walk.
♦ If you live in an area where kids can't play and explore outside, schedule more trips to playgrounds or other nearby play facilities.
♦ Check on your children's schools or day care. Do the kids exercise at least twenty minutes each day? Are less-coordinated or less-sports-minded youngsters urged to take part in energetic activities?

♦ When your children are bored, suggest something that gets them moving. What about playing catch or building a snowman in the yard?

Moving for Life

Whether you come to exercise as a child or after retirement, make it a habit to last forever. You will be rewarded with a more buoyant spirit and a stronger and smoother-running body. Enjoy it now and for the rest of your life!

CHAPTER 5

Working with Your Health-Care Providers

Forming a Preventive Partnership

YOUR LIFESTYLE IS LARGELY UNDER YOUR CONTROL. AS YOU MAKE choices about what you eat and how you work and play, you can reduce the chance of developing cancer and heart disease.

You may feel completely confident about your health habits. Even so, health-care providers are important partners in helping you reduce your risk for these diseases. Some cancers, such as cervical cancer, can be avoided if precancerous tissue is detected and treated. Other cancers are quite treatable if they are discovered early. Cholesterol and high blood pressure don't cause symptoms until a lot of damage has been done. Detected early, these health concerns can be handled with a modified lifestyle or a combination of lifestyle changes and medical treatment.

A successful prevention partnership has four parts:

- Getting prevention-oriented medical checkups;
- Noticing suspicious changes in your body and having a health-care provider evaluate them;
- Being conscientious about following directions for medical and lifestyle treatment;
- Asking for the support you need so you can take an active and positive role in prevention.

THE PARTNERSHIP AGREEMENT

In our diverse and complex health-care system, you as a consumer must often take the initiative to get the preventive health care you need. You and your health-care providers share the responsibility for ensuring that you get good preventive care. The general guidelines that follow may help you discuss and encourage the partnership.

Your Health-Care Providers Need to Know What You Expect

If you consider your primary-care physician or other physician to be the major professional involved in your preventive care, say so. Be sure that both you and your doctor are clear about who is taking what responsibilities. Unless the two of you discuss this in advance, a generalist physician may think your gynecologist or dermatologist is doing specific cancer screening. Unless you let your gynecologist know otherwise, he or she is likely to assume that you will have someone else monitor your cholesterol and conduct a complete skin examination.

Your Health-Care Providers Need Accurate Information from You

"My father saw several different doctors and only listened to what he wanted to hear. One gave him medicine for his high blood pressure. The next checked his blood pressure and pronounced it normal, not knowing he was taking medication. My father died of a heart attack in his forties."

Honest and open communication in both directions is crucial to a good doctor-patient relationship. For instance, let your physician know if you have not completely followed instructions on how to prepare for a test. If your doctor thinks you fasted but you didn't, you may get a false-positive reading. That, in turn, can cause your doctor to order expensive and invasive follow-up tests that you don't need.

That medical history form you fill out each time you see a new doctor will help him or her plan your preventive care. When filling out and discussing those forms, be sure to include pertinent information on your family medical history as well. If your doctor knows that one or more of your relatives have high cholesterol, certain cancers, or heart disease, he or she may suggest a different schedule of screening tests. Perhaps the doctor also will suggest that you should devote extra attention to certain lifestyle factors.

If you haven't been adhering to a recommended diet or exercise plan, let your physician know. The two of you can then talk about possible problems with the plan. This can make all the difference in what you and your physician decide to do next. For example, if you have elevated cholesterol and your agreed-on diet plan isn't lowering it, that may mean the beginning of a long-term regimen of prescription drugs. If, on the other hand, you are having trouble getting started on your new way of eating, the next step may be a referral to a nutritionist.

Not everyone responds to medications in the same way. Don't be silent and stoic about any side effects you experience. Physicians can choose from a variety of medications to lower high blood pressure and high cholesterol. Since you may be taking them for a long time, it is worth a little trial and error to find the drug or drug combination that will be the easiest for you to live with.

Your Health-Care Providers Need to Know What Support You Want and Need

"I have a degree in nutrition, so my physician says he's not going to spend time telling me what I need to do to get my cholesterol down. He says I know better than he does. But the truth is, I've had trouble getting motivated and making changes on my own."

Ask to have instructions written down, with specific follow-up plans. You may feel overwhelmed by the information you are given or believe your family will react poorly to the changes in your routine. Or for some other reason, you may think you will have trouble following the advice. If so, ask where you can get more information. A book, class, health educator, nutritionist, counselor, or video may provide just what you need.

Your doctor may be an excellent source of help if you're trying to stop smoking. That help could be in the form of finding a support group for you or prescribing nicotine gum or a nicotine patch (see pages 49–50).

Your Health-Care Providers Should Provide You with Your Test Results

It can be reassuring to hear that your cholesterol is "okay," your blood pressure is "normal," or your Pap smear was "fine." However, as you learn more about prevention, test results may not tell you all you need to know. For example, cholesterol that is steadily creeping up from year to year is a sign that you may need to change the way you eat. A rising cholesterol level can be tackled more easily *before* it crosses the border into a definitively high reading.

Keep your own records of the results of your major preventive tests (with dates) and of trends in your health for later reference. They serve as a reminder of when to be retested and are useful if you switch physicians, see different specialists, or see different physicians at different visits.

You Need to Have Preventive Care Taken Seriously

If your physician has never discussed screening tests or your family medical history, doesn't know whether you smoke, or seems uninterested in whether you exercise and what you eat, ask why. Your physician may assume you are getting preventive advice elsewhere. He or she may perceive you as so well informed and health conscious that you will take the initiative in leading a healthful lifestyle. Alternatively, your doctor may think you aren't very interested in the preventive aspects of health care. Discuss the kind of partnership you are looking for. Then determine whether your doctor can provide, and is interested in providing, the kind of care you want. If not, you may need to see someone else.

You Need to Be Able to Discuss Costs and Reimbursement Issues Frankly

When a health-care provider suggests a course of action, ask about cost. "If money were no object, is this the plan you would recommend?" "Are there other medications that might be less expensive?" "Are there any disadvantages to trying the less-expensive medication first?" "Why do you think the cheaper drugs aren't right for me?" "How long do you think I will need to take this medication?"

With so many health plans, each with its own rules about reimbursement, your physician may not realize that one course of action will cost you more out of pocket than another. Ask whether you can check on reimbursement before making a final decision. Your health plan may pay 80 percent of some medications but only 50 percent of others. The amount you pay may be even less if you can plan long-term care in advance and take advantage of a discount mail order plan. One hospital may have easier terms than another for paying for exercise rehabilitation. Payment terms may depend on what kind of professional is supervising you. You may be reimbursed for certain types of nutritional advice, depending on who is providing it and how the prescription is written. Your plan may offer discounts on specific programs to help you stop smoking or lose weight. Once you provide the needed insurance information, your doctor should help guide you toward choices that are both medically and financially sound.

Cancer Screening Tests

Screening tests and checkups are designed to detect cancer as early as possible—usually long before you feel pain or have any other symptoms. The tests described here are usually used for people without any particular risk factors or cancer history. Knowing your medical and family history, your physician can help you determine which tests are most appropriate. He or she can also recommend how often you should have them.

Technology keeps improving, and ongoing research offers more information about the comparative value and efficiency of tests in helping to preserve health and save lives. Therefore, the American Cancer Society and the American Heart Association from time to time alter their guidelines on screening. For the latest recommendations about these or other tests, contact the local office of the organizations, call 1-800-ACS-2345 or 1-800-AHA-USA1, or ask your doctor for advice.

BREAST CANCER

More than 180,000 women were diagnosed with breast cancer in 1994. So were about 1,000 men. Since relatively few men are diagnosed with the disease, this section will primarily address women. However, men should be vigilant about noticing any change in their breasts.

When breast cancer is diagnosed and treated early, the five-year survival rate is high—about 93 percent. If breast cancer is not diagnosed until it has begun to spread, the chance that treatment will be effective goes down. You owe it to yourself to detect breast cancer as early as possible. That will give you the widest range of treatment choices.

Breast Self-Examination

"I examine my breasts while I'm lying in bed. I feel around in concentric circles. Then I pay special attention to the lymph areas under my arms. Only once did I find something, and at first I was panicked. But a mammogram

and exam by the doctor showed it was a blocked duct. It's harmless and will be there forever. Now I just check to make sure it feels the same."

What's Being Looked For?
Changes in the breasts that may indicate early cancer.

Do You Need to Examine Yourself?
The American Cancer Society recommends that *all* women twenty years and over should get in the habit of examining their breasts each month.

When your doctor asks whether you do breast self-exams (BSEs), resist the temptation to lie if you don't. Ask to be shown the technique to use. If your breasts are very lumpy and fibrous, self-exams may seem overwhelmingly difficult. In that case, your physician may want to schedule more-frequent exams in the office so you'll still be regularly monitored.

How Do You Get the Best Test?
Choose a time a few days after your menstrual period ends. Your breasts shouldn't be tender or swollen then. If you don't have regular periods or have gone through menopause, do the breast self-exam on the same date every month.

You can do breast self-exams during pregnancy, but your breasts may be swollen and feel tender. If you are nursing your baby, just after a feeding may be the easiest time. During breast-feeding, your breasts will feel different. They'll be filled with fluid and have an overall soft, lumpy texture.

If you have had a lumpectomy or mastectomy, ask your physician how to examine your breast tissue. After your surgical scar has healed, tell your physician if the scar seems to get thicker or becomes red and hard.

How Is the Test Done?
Examining your breasts may seem daunting, sort of like probing for a single grain of sand in a bowl of gelatin. To make it less intimidating, breast experts advise that you flip your thinking: Don't seek the tiniest lump, and don't expect to find *anything* amiss. Just become very familiar with the way your breasts normally look and feel.

After months of the routine, you *will* notice a change if it occurs. If you or your doctor ever does feel anything, it is likely to be closer to the size of a pea than to that grain of sand.

Steps for Performing a BSE

Your doctor or other health-care provider can guide you in the specifics of examining your breasts. (See the illustration on page 215.) The ACS recommends the order of steps outlined below.

First, lie on your back and place a pillow under your right shoulder area. Raise your right arm over your head.

Using the pads of your left-hand fingers, pick a spot on your right breast. Press firmly enough to feel through the breast tissue. Then move to an adjacent spot, tracing a set pattern. You may choose a circular pattern, vertical rows, or a series of wedges moving from the nipple outward. The point is to cover the entire breast area and the armpit.

In the lower curve of your breast, you may feel a firm ridge of supportive tissue. If you feel a lump or thickening, check the same spot on the other breast to see whether it matches.

Repeat the procedure on your left breast.

After you have checked both breasts, stand in front of a mirror and raise your arms. Notice whether there are any changes in the way your breasts look. Are there any depressions or bulges? Dimples or puckering of the skin? Moles? Dark or reddened areas? Rough areas or prominent veins? Changes in the nipple area? Does the nipple look crusty? Does it seem to pull to one side? Is there any discharge?

You may also want to do an extra breast self-exam while in the shower. Soapy hands easily slide over the wet skin, making it simple to check how the tissue underneath feels.

Tell your physician if you find any changes in your breasts or notice anything unusual. You may find structures that worry or confuse you but do not seem remarkable to your physician. Ask what they are and how they should feel.

What's Next?

Don't be afraid to report any lumps or suspicious changes to your physician. They usually *do not* indicate cancer, but they should be checked.

If your physician's breast check detects the same suspicious area, you may need a *mammogram* and perhaps a *biopsy* to determine whether it is cancerous. If it is, you'll know that your conscientious self-exam helped you get medical attention at the earliest stage possible.

Clinical Breast Exam

What's Being Looked For?

Changes in the breast that may indicate early cancer.

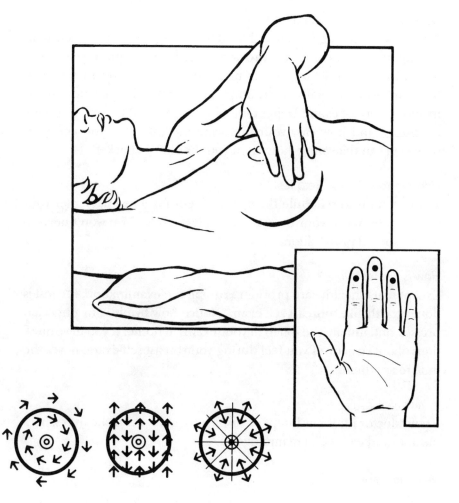

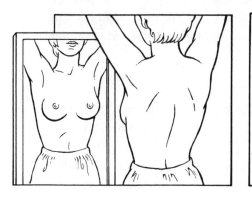

Do You Need to Be Tested?

All women over age twenty should have regular breast exams by an experienced health-care provider at least every three years. The American Cancer Society recommends that women over forty should have an annual exam. A routine gynecological checkup usually includes a breast exam. Depending on your medical history, your family history, and how easy your breasts are to examine, you and your physician can determine how often you should be checked.

How Do You Get the Best Test?

You may want to schedule the appointment for a few days after your period ends, when your breasts may be less tender. You won't need to do any special preparation.

How Is the Test Done?

Except that a health-care provider is doing the examination, the test is done exactly like a breast self-exam. Notice how firmly your physician presses, and imitate the touch in your exams at home. If you have questions about structures you feel during your breast self-exam, now's the time to ask them.

What's Next?

If your doctor finds any lumps or suspicious areas, he or she may schedule a second exam or a mammogram.

Mammography

"My mother was afraid of mammograms, and she died of breast cancer. I don't want to take the route of avoidance that she took. If I get breast cancer, at least I want it caught early. Even so, I carried around the prescription for my first mammogram for three years. Then one night I had a nightmare that I had a lump in my breast. I woke up in a cold sweat and then I made an appointment."

What's Being Looked For?

Tumors inside the breast as small as one-fifth of an inch in diameter. These are too small to be felt in a breast self-exam or a breast check by a health-care provider.

A screening mammogram is performed at regular intervals to detect a lump as early as possible. A diagnostic mammogram is performed after a lump is found and may consist of more images.

How Do You Get the Best Test?

In October 1994 it became easier for you to be sure that mammography is safe and delivers a high-quality picture. Now all facilities offering mammography—whether in a hospital, a mobile van, or your physician's office—must be certified by the Food and Drug Administration. Certification means that a facility is inspected each year. Its mammograms must be as clear as possible, personnel must be well trained and experienced, and the amount of radiation must be monitored. If a facility is "provisionally certified," that means it has applied for certification but the application is still under review.

Before scheduling a mammogram, ask about the equipment the facility uses. Is it a "dedicated" machine? If the answer is yes, that means that the unit is made especially for mammography and will expose you to an extremely low amount of radiation. If the answer is no, ask how much radiation you will be exposed to. Check out alternative sites if the exposure is more than one rad.

As you'll want to do for clinical and at-home breast exams, try to schedule your mammogram for a few days after your period ends. Your breasts are less likely to be tender then.

Some sources recommend that on the day of your mammogram, you do not use deodorant, talcum powder, or body lotion. That's because these innocuous products may show up as suspicious-looking areas on the mammogram. Check with your health-care provider about this before your mammogram.

How Is the Test Done?

"I have large breasts, and I really expected it to hurt. It didn't, though. It was just a feeling of pressure and the weird feeling of standing like a statue while someone moves your breast into different positions."

First, you will change into a hospital gown or remove all clothing above your waist. Guided by a technician, you will place one breast on a flat shelf. The technician will use a flat plate to compress the breast tissue briefly. For each breast, you'll usually have one side view and one view from the top.

The entire procedure for both breasts will take only five to fifteen minutes. You may find the procedure a little uncomfortable or even a little painful. The discomfort lasts only while the breast is compressed, however.

What's Next?

The X-ray picture provided by mammography should highlight cysts, solid tumors, spots where calcium has collected, and dense breast tissue.

At centers with a radiologist on-site, you'll get an immediate initial assessment of your mammogram. The physician you specify will soon get a more detailed report.

If a suspicious area is noted, you may need further tests to see whether cancer is present. Such tests might include a biopsy, where a piece of tissue is removed for evaluation, or an *ultrasound,* another imaging device. Even if an area looks highly suspicious on a mammogram, a definitive diagnosis of cancer cannot be made until cells are examined under a microscope. Most suspicious areas turn out *not* to be cancer.

A reassuring mammogram is definitely good news, but it is not a guarantee that no cancer is present. Dense breast tissue can sometimes obscure a tumor. However, as women get older and their breasts have more fatty tissue, a dense tumor is easier to spot on a mammogram. A mammogram can picture only the portion of your breast that extends out. Other breast tissue reaches up to the collarbone and around to the armpit. That's why it's important to practice BSE and to have a clinical breast exam and mammogram regularly.

COLORECTAL CANCER

Nearly 150,000 people are diagnosed each year with cancer in the colon (large intestine) or rectum (the last four inches of the colon, near the anus). Over the last thirty years, the death rate from colorectal cancer has fallen 30 percent for women and 7 percent for men. Improvements in detection and treatment get part of the credit.

Growths in the rectum and the colon don't start out as cancer. Most appear first as small benign *polyps* sticking out from the wall of the colon into the channel where food passes. Some are so small they are almost invisible; others grow quite large. Eventually, cancer cells may form within a polyp. (The larger the polyp, the more likely this will occur.)

Symptoms

Most colon cancers ooze small amounts of blood. Later they cause pain and noticeable disturbances in digestion. Tell your physician if you notice blood in your stool or develop persistent diarrhea or constipation. Report it if your bowels always feel full or if you feel pain or cramping in your lower abdomen or your anus. Do *not* wait for your next screening test.

The trio of tests described next helps diagnose as many colorectal growths as possible while they are benign or treatable.

Digital Rectal Examination
What's Being Looked For?
Polyps or growths in the rectum that may be benign or cancerous. About 30 percent of colorectal cancers occur in the rectum.

Do You Need to Be Tested?
Regular digital rectal examinations (DREs) are recommended for both men and women after the age of forty. Ask your physician how often to be tested. A combination of tests for colorectal cancer may be scheduled for various reasons. They include a personal history of colon cancer, benign growths in the colon, or *ulcerative colitis,* a close relative with colon cancer, or a family history of *familial polyposis* (Gardner's syndrome).

How Do You Get the Best Test?
No special preparation is needed for a digital rectal exam.

How Is the Test Done?
Using a glove, the doctor inserts one finger into your rectum. It may be a little disconcerting the first time, but it's usually painless and quick. The doctor will feel for any growths or imperfections in the wall of the rectum. During the exam, he or she takes a small stool sample to check for hidden blood.

What's Next?
If the exam reveals a possible problem, the doctor may inspect the rectum and the colon visually, using a lighted scope. He or she can surgically remove any cancer or precancerous growth.

Stool Blood Test

> *"I'm a little squeamish, but I like the new system. All I had to do was throw a special tissue into the toilet bowl and see what color it turned."*

What's Being Looked For?
Tumors in the colon or rectum. These often bleed, and the stool blood test detects blood in the stool that you may not have noticed. This test is also called the fecal occult blood test.

Do You Need to Be Tested?
Both men and women over age fifty are advised to have a stool blood test annually. Your doctor will suggest a combination of tests if you have had colon cancer or benign growths in the colon, if a close relative has colon cancer, if you have a family history of familial polyposis, or if you have had ulcerative colitis.

How Do You Get the Best Test?
The test works by detecting hemoglobin, a component of blood. To prepare, you'll need to skip red meat and eat a diet high in fiber for a few days. You may be asked to avoid taking aspirin, vitamin C, and iron. Red meat and iron supplements can give false-positive results. Aspirin or large amounts of vitamin C can result in bleeding from normal tissue, also giving a false-positive result. The high-fiber eating plan may encourage any existing polyps to bleed.

If you are having problems with bleeding hemorrhoids, ask whether to postpone the test.

How Is the Test Done?
Your health-care provider will give you instructions and supplies so you can smear small samples from your stools onto specially treated slides. Alternatively, you may be asked to throw a chemically treated paper into the toilet bowl after a bowel movement or to use a special wipe and report its color changes to your physician.

What's Next?
A positive test means that blood has been detected. It might mean cancer, or it might mean a bleeding ulcer, bleeding hemorrhoids, or a false-positive reading.

If the test is positive, your doctor will suggest additional tests to locate where the bleeding is from and its cause.

A negative test does not completely rule out cancer. Not all cancers bleed, and bleeding cancers don't bleed all the time. That's why doctors also use a digital rectal exam and *proctosigmoidoscopy* (discussed below).

Proctosigmoidoscopy Exam

"The tube is little and flexible. But when they snake that thing up inside of you and go around the corners, you definitely feel places in your body where you didn't know you had nerves. I'll do it again, but I'm glad it's over with for another five years."

What's Being Looked For?
Polyps or growths in the *sigmoid colon,* which curves from the rectum up the left side of the abdomen. Many colon cancers occur in this part of the colon.

Do You Need to Be Tested?
If you're over fifty, you should have a proctosigmoidoscopy, preferably flexible, every three to five years.

How Do You Get the Best Test?
To clean out the colon before your proctosigmoidoscopy (also called a procto), you will be asked to use a laxative, an enema, or both.

How Is the Test Done?
If you've heard of, or experienced, practically standing on your head while a hard proctoscope was inserted up your rectum, you'll be glad to learn about today's improved technology. A far preferable alternative, the flexible sigmoidoscope, is now available.

The old instrument, the rigid proctoscope, was as wide as a garden hose. It allowed a doctor to see only the first six or seven inches above the anus. The supple sigmoidoscope is about as wide as a pencil. The doctor can see two feet into the colon, and do so with less discomfort to you.

For the exam, you will lie down on your side with your knees bent (no more bottoms-up embarrassment!). The physician slowly inserts the tube and, using its lighted tip, sees a magnified inside view. Air or water will be squirted in to improve visibility and help with navigation around corners. The examination usually takes between five and fifteen minutes.

Rigid proctoscopes are still in use. When your doctor suggests a procto, ask what kind of instrument he or she will use. If it is rigid, ask why it is being used. Also ask whether you can go to a facility where a flexible scope is used.

If the instrument is flexible, ask how often the doctor performs the procedure. It takes training and experience to use the new equipment well.

What's Next?
If the proctosigmoidoscopy reveals a benign growth or possible tumor, the doctor may remove it with instruments that are passed right through the tube.

"At one point the gastroenterologist handed me a scope and said, 'Here, look.' It's quite a bizarre sensation to be looking inside yourself."

If your doctor sees polyps in the sigmoid colon or you have a family history of colon cancer, other polyps may exist higher up. Your doctor may suggest a *colonoscopy* (a more intensive examination of the entire colon, using a similar scope) and a barium enema to provide an X-ray view of the intestines.

Many polyps can be removed through the colonoscope, reducing the need for major abdominal surgery. If you had previous medical problems or have a family history of colon cancer, cancer experts may suggest that you get routine colonoscopy instead of using the other screening tests first. If you are considered at high risk for colon cancer, you should review your eating habits with a nutritionist or physician. Such professionals can help you make sure you are taking advantage of dietary means to reduce risk.

MELANOMA AND OTHER SKIN CANCERS

So many people develop basal cell or squamous cell cancers—and these common skin cancers are so readily curable—that they are not even counted in the overall cancer statistics. Each year, physicians diagnose more than 700,000 cases of basal cell or squamous cell cancers. About 2,300 people will die as a result. In contrast, the most serious skin cancer, melanoma, is often fatal. About 32,000 people are diagnosed with melanoma each year. Of those, about 6,900 will die.

Of course, the best protection is to prevent skin cancer by reducing your exposure to damaging rays from the sun (see pages 258–64). However, it is also important to examine your own skin once a month and alert your physician to any suspicious areas. That will greatly increase the chance that a skin cancer will be detected early, when it is most treatable.

Symptoms

"Every once in a while, Grandpa would say, 'Who hit you in the eye?' I had what looked like a little broken blood vessel, but it was my first skin cancer."

Tell your physician about any unusual skin condition, especially if you find a new mole or if any mole or dark spot seems to be growing or changing color. Report any spots that are scaly, ooze, or bleed. If a familiar bump or nodule on your skin changes, it is a warning sign of melanoma. You should report it to your physician. Commonly the affected area may itch, feel tender or painful, or soften in texture. Also, dark pigment may move beyond the edge of the mole and into the surrounding skin.

Skin Self-Exam

"I told the doctor I'd just gotten married and he said, 'Great! When you're in the shower, let your husband examine your back.' Is that romantic, or what?"

What's Being Looked For?
Early signs of skin cancer.

Basal and squamous cell skin cancers may look like pale, waxlike, pearly nodules or sharply outlined patches of red, scaly skin. You may notice that the redness will seem to improve and then return.

A melanoma is more likely to appear as a new growth than as a change in a mole you've had for years. Almost everyone has at least a few darkly pigmented moles, and most moles are not dangerous. Learning to recognize the danger signs can help keep them that way.

Use the following ABCD rule to look at your moles for the warning signs of melanoma:

A is for Asymmetry. One half of the mole does not match the other half.

B is for Border irregularity. The mole's edges are ragged, notched, or blurred.

C is for Color. The mole is speckled, with color variations.

D is for Diameter. The mole is greater than six millimeters (just under one-quarter inch) across or has grown in size.

Do You Need to Be Tested?
Everyone needs to stay alert for early signs of skin cancer. For most people, a self-exam once a month and a physician skin exam once a year

are recommended. You may need to be extra vigilant if you have had skin cancers, have fair skin, or have had excessive exposure to sunlight or other ultraviolet radiation. You also may need to be very careful if you've been treated for psoriasis with medications that increase sun sensitivity or if you often come in contact with coal tar, pitch, creosote, arsenic compounds, or radium.

If you have been designated as high risk for skin cancer because of your family history or exposures, your physician may set up a schedule with more than one exam a year.

How Do You Get the Best Test?

You know the skin you live in better than anyone else does. Get to know it even better by performing a self-exam.

How Is the Test Done?

Examining your skin takes only a few minutes. The best time to do this simple monthly exam is after a bath or shower. Use a full-length mirror and a hand mirror so you can check any moles, blemishes, or birthmarks from the top of your head to your toes. Note anything new—a sore that doesn't heal or a change in size, shape, or color.

To make sure you don't miss an inch, follow these four easy steps:

1. Examine your body front and back, then right and left sides, arms raised.

2. Bend your elbows and look carefully at forearms and upper underarms and palms.

3. Sit, if that is more comfortable, to look at the backs of your legs and to examine your feet. Don't forget the soles of your feet and the spaces between your toes.

4. Use a hand mirror to examine the back of your neck and your scalp. Part your hair or use a blow dryer to lift your hair and give you a close look at your scalp.

If you have lots of moles and spots, you may want to note them on a chart. Just draw or trace a simple body outline and mark the location of the moles and spots and what you observed during the last check. That may be easier than remembering how they look from month to month and may simplify recognizing new moles or subtle changes.

Report any suspicious areas to your doctor.

What's Next?

To diagnose a skin cancer, your doctor will send a sample to a pathologist to be examined under a microscope. Usually, the entire suspicious area is removed. For malignant melanoma, it is important to remove plenty of tissue surrounding the growth.

Physician Skin Exams

"My doctor is so thorough I told him he could get a job doing body searches at the prison."

Besides checking your own skin, you should probably have a thorough skin examination by a dermatologist or other physician every year or so. If you have a skin cancer removed, however, you'll need follow-up examinations more frequently for a while.

ORAL CANCER

Each year, almost 30,000 people are diagnosed with oral cancer. When diagnosed early, it is usually curable.

Symptoms

Tell your doctor or dentist if any sores in your mouth bleed easily, are recurrent, or don't heal in a few weeks. Report any white or red patches that persist. Point out any lumps or thickenings, particularly if you notice them on only one side.

If you ever have trouble moving your tongue, chewing, or swallowing, be sure to tell your physician. These also can be signs of oral cancer but usually occur later.

Oral Examinations

"I was sure that pesky sore in my mouth was because my crown never fit right. But eventually I had my doctor look at it—and I'm glad I did."

What's Being Looked For?

Lumps, sore spots, and red or white patches that may become cancerous. Cancer in the mouth can occur on any surface—your lips, the linings of your cheeks, your tongue, your gums, or the roof or floor of your mouth.

When your mouth is irritated, perhaps because you use tobacco or wear dentures that don't fit, a hardened whitish patch called *leukoplakia* may form. Usually it is not particularly sensitive. It may look like a thin film right on the surface, or it may become thick and rough, with cracks and crevices.

Velvety red patches are of greater concern in cancer detection. You should report them to your dentist or physician.

Do You Need to Be Tested?

Every year or so, your physician or dentist should examine your mouth for signs of cancer. Oral cancer is most common in men over the age of forty. Heavy smoking, the use of chewing tobacco, heavy drinking, and malnutrition (especially vitamin A and B-complex deficiencies that are seen in heavy drinkers) dramatically increase the risk.

How Is the Test Done?

When you visit your dentist for any reason, he or she should quickly inspect for any abnormal tissue changes that might indicate early oral cancer.

Because the mouth is so sensitive and you look at it so regularly as you insert dentures or brush and floss your teeth, you are unlikely to miss any sore or suspicious areas. For that reason, you probably don't need to do any specific regular self-examination. Instead, just be certain to tell your physician or dentist if you notice any worrisome changes—especially if they persist.

If you notice a velvety red patch or an area that looks like leukoplakia, check for possible sources of irritation and try to correct them. If the spot hasn't disappeared in a few weeks or if it is quite thick and raised, you may need a biopsy. Occasionally but not often, patches of leukoplakia are early signs of a tumor in the mouth.

OVARIAN CANCER

Ovarian cancer strikes about 24,000 women a year. It causes more deaths than any other cancer of the reproductive system in women, killing about 13,600 a year.

When ovarian cancer is diagnosed and treated early, the five-year survival rate is 88 percent. Unfortunately, an ovarian tumor often grows "silently," not causing noticeable symptoms until late in its development. Currently, only about 23 percent of all cases are detected early. The overall survival rate is 41 percent.

Symptoms

It might seem odd to discuss digestion with your gynecologist, but you should. Sometimes persistent stomach discomfort, nausea, bloating, and gas can be signs of ovarian cancer. Also mention if you seem to be retaining water around your abdomen, if you notice any abnormal vaginal bleeding, or if you need to urinate frequently.

Pelvic Examination

"I was never pregnant, so I never saw any reason to see a gynecologist after my wedding. Then I got cancer and saw about twenty gynecologists in one year."

What's Being Looked For?

Growths on the ovaries or a change in their size or shape that may indicate ovarian cancer.

Do You Need to Be Tested?

Regular pelvic examinations by a health-care provider, every one to three years depending on your age and medical history, are suggested for all women over eighteen.

The risk for ovarian cancer increases with age. Women who haven't had children are more likely to develop ovarian cancer than those who have.

If you have had breast cancer or if you have a family history of ovarian cancer, you are at increased risk. Your physician may suggest an alternative schedule of screening tests for you.

How Do You Get the Best Test?

Urinate just before your exam. Overall, being relaxed is the best preparation. Clenched abdominal muscles make a pelvic exam more difficult for the physician.

How Is the Test Done?

You will lie on an examining table and rest your feet in metal stirrups, sliding your hips down as close to the bottom edge of the table as possible. Your knees will be spread apart.

The check of your ovaries is called a bimanual exam. The practitioner will put on rubber gloves and insert two fingers of one hand into your vagina. The other hand will press on your lower abdomen. Between the two hands the physician will feel the shape, size, and consistency of your uterus and ovaries. The ovaries are likely to be a little sensitive to the pressure applied during the exam, which only takes a minute or two.

After that is complete, the practitioner will move so that two fingers remain in your vagina and one finger on the other hand is inserted into your rectum. Again, he or she will feel the structures between the two hands. This position usually allows a more thorough exam of the ovaries.

In a typical pelvic examination, you get several important cancer screening tests done at once. Before the bimanual exam, a speculum is inserted so that a Pap smear can be taken and the inside of the vagina examined (see "Uterine Cancer—Cervix" on page 232). With a finger inserted in your rectum, your doctor will perform a digital rectal exam to screen for colorectal cancer (see page 219).

What's Next?

If a growth is on one of your ovaries or an ovary seems to be enlarged, your doctor may use other tests to learn what the problem is. It could be ovarian cancer, a fluid-filled cyst, or a noncancerous growth. The tests may include ultrasound, other visualizing techniques, biopsy, and blood tests. Your pelvic exam may be repeated while you are under anesthesia so your muscles will be totally relaxed.

Four out of five growths on the ovaries are *not* cancer.

CA 125 Blood Test

After women are treated for ovarian cancer, part of their follow-up care includes a blood test called CA 125. This test detects antibodies to a foreign substance often found in the blood of women with ovarian cancer. It has been very useful in determining whether an ovarian tumor has recurred or has responded well to treatment.

The CA 125 blood test has been used as a screening test for ovarian cancer. Unfortunately, it is not specific enough to be very helpful. If you have endometriosis, hepatitis, or pelvic inflammatory disease, you may have a positive CA 125 test. The same result can happen if you are pregnant. Therefore, many women will undergo unnecessary biopsies for every one case of ovarian cancer that is detected. (In one study, for every sixty-five women who underwent surgery following a positive CA 125 test, only one cancer was detected.) The American Cancer Society does not recommend the CA 125 test as a general screening test for ovarian cancer. If your doctor suggests this test to you, get more information before saying yes.

PROSTATE CANCER

Each year, about 200,000 men are diagnosed with prostate cancer. About 38,000 die, making it the second-leading cancer killer of men.

Symptoms
The first symptoms of an enlarged prostate—whether caused by cancer or not—are urinary problems. The symptoms run the gamut from trouble starting to trouble stopping urine flow. They include weak or interrupted flow of urine, needing to urinate frequently or urgently, pain or burning while urinating, blood in the urine, or inability to urinate at all. Another is continuing pain in the lower back, the pelvis, or the upper thighs. You need to report all such symptoms to your physician.

Most urinary symptoms are not caused by prostate cancer, but they need to be checked out.

Digital Rectal Examination
What's Being Looked For?
An enlarged or hardened prostate gland, or a nodule on the gland, that may indicate prostate cancer.

Do You Need to Be Tested?
A regular digital rectal examination (DRE) is suggested for all men age fifty and over to check for prostate cancer. (Men over forty should have the DRE to check for colon cancer.) Prostate cancer occurs more frequently in African-American men. If you're in this category, you may decide with your physician that it makes sense to start screening earlier. If you have a strong family history of prostate cancer, your physician may suggest a different screening schedule. If you're exposed to cadmium in the workplace, you may be at increased risk and should get regular checkups. Ask about your exposure to cadmium if you are a rubber worker or welder or if you make alkaline batteries. Additionally, some research indicates that a high-fat diet may play a role in prostate cancer.

How Do You Get the Best Test?
No special preparation is needed. You can have two cancer screening tests at once if your exam also checks the walls of the rectum for signs of colorectal cancer.

How Is the Test Done?
Using a glove, the physician inserts one finger into your rectum. Through the rectal wall, he or she can feel the size and consistency of the prostate.

What's Next?
A doctor who suspects that a nodule in the prostate is cancerous may do an ultrasound examination and a biopsy to further evaluate the prostate. About 50 percent of nodules that rectal exams detect are cancerous.

More than half of all prostate cancers are diagnosed before they have spread. In such cases, the five-year survival rate is more than 90 percent.

Prostate-Specific Antigen

What's Being Looked For?
A substance in the blood that is found in higher levels when the prostate is enlarged, cancerous, or infected. That substance is known as *prostate-specific antigen* (*PSA*).

Do You Need to Be Tested?
PSA measurements, along with digital rectal examination, are valuable in detecting prostate cancer, according to the American Cancer Society. Men should have an annual PSA blood test after age fifty.

How Do You Get the Best Test?
Some medications reduce the size of the prostate gland, which may affect how the antigen levels are interpreted. Tell the physician who will evaluate the test results about medications you are taking.

How Is the Test Done?
A physician, nurse, or technician will draw a blood sample. The antigen level can be determined from it.

What Do the Results Mean?

The PSA requires a physician's interpretation. Elevated PSA alone does not diagnose prostate cancer. If your PSA is raised, your physician will use a digital rectal exam and ultrasound to help determine why. Age, an enlarged prostate gland, or a prostate infection can boost the PSA levels. The PSA test cannot tell whether cancer is definitely present or whether a cancer is an aggressive or slow-growing form. If the combination of tests makes your doctor highly suspicious of cancer, a biopsy may be recommended. The same may be suggested if your PSA level is extremely high.

TESTICULAR CANCER

Cancer of the testes, the male reproductive glands, is one of the most common cancers in young adult men. If detected and treated early, testicular cancer is highly curable. The survival rate is close to 100 percent for the most common type of testicular cancer and is about 87 percent overall.

Symptoms

Lumps, swellings, or changes in size or consistency of the testes may be signs of testicular cancer. So may a feeling of heaviness or a dull ache in the groin or lower abdomen.

Testicular Self-Exam

"What are you talking about? I'm fifty years old and no one has ever, ever mentioned doing this."

What's Being Looked For?

Lumps that may represent early testicular cancer. When found and treated before the cancer affects the lymph nodes, cancer of the testes is one of the most easily curable cancers.

Do You Need to Examine Yourself?

All men are advised to perform a testicular self-exam once a month. Testicular cancer is most common in men between the ages of eighteen and thirty-two and men over age sixty. If you were born with an undescended testicle, you are also at higher risk and should be sure to examine yourself regularly.

How Do You Get the Best Test?
Examine your testicles just after a shower or bath. The skin of your scrotum is at its most relaxed then.

How Do You Do the Test?
Gently roll one testicle between the thumbs and fingers of both hands. You will feel the testes inside the scrotal sac. The cordlike structure you feel along the back of the testicle is the epididymis, the area where sperm mature. Massaging the surface of the entire testicle, notice whether you feel any lumps, nodules, swellings, or different consistencies. Repeat this procedure for the other testicle.

The typical testicular tumor is a hard, painless lump about the size of a pea. Often it is located on the front part of the testicle. Report any lumps or suspicious areas to your doctor.

What's Next?
If you find a lump or suspicious area, a physical exam and other diagnostic tests (such as ultrasound) may be used to determine whether you have cancer or a benign condition. Most lumps are *not* cancerous.

If you do have cancer, how widespread it is will determine the treatment.

Physician Testicular Exam
A cancer-related checkup for a man of any age should always include an examination of the testes. Except that a health-care provider is doing the examination, it is performed exactly like a self-exam. If you have questions about structures you feel during a self-exam, this is a good time to ask them.

UTERINE CANCER—CERVIX

About 70,000 women a year are diagnosed with cancer of the cervix, the neck of the womb. About 4,600 women die annually from this cancer, which is usually fatal only if diagnosed at a late stage.

Symptoms
Abnormal bleeding, such as spotting between your menstrual periods, after intercourse, after douching, or after you have gone through menopause, can be symptoms of cervical cancer.

Pap Test

"I got a Class III Pap smear, but I wasn't really concerned. I was sure it was a mistake. But the repeat was definitely abnormal and the follow-up tests showed I had a small area of cancer."

The Pap smear, or Pap test, is one of the great success stories of screening tests. Because so many women receive regular Pap smears, most cervical cancer is diagnosed when it affects only the cells on the surface. With early diagnosis, cancer of the cervix is quickly and easily treated in most cases.

What's Being Tested?
Using a microscope, a technician examines cells collected from the surface of the cervix and vagina to identify cells that look abnormal.

Do You Need to Be Tested?
Regular Pap tests are recommended for adult women and for younger women who have been sexually active. Even after menopause or a hysterectomy, you should continue to have Pap tests. There is no upper age limit.

Depending on your medical history and the results of previous Pap tests, your health-care provider can recommend a test schedule. Regular screening is particularly important if you have had vaginal herpes or warts, had intercourse early in your teens, have more than one sex partner, or have been pregnant many times. Women who were exposed before birth to DES (diethylstilbestrol, a synthetic estrogen given to many women in the belief it could prevent miscarriage) often need more-frequent Pap tests and specialized pelvic examinations.

How Do You Get the Best Test?
Before you have a Pap test, you should leave the cells of the cervix undisturbed for a few days. Don't douche for at least three days before the test. Don't use birth control foams, creams, or jellies for five days. You can have an accurate Pap smear during your period, but don't use a tampon for five days before the test. Use the shower instead of taking a tub bath for the last two days.

If you have symptoms of a vaginal infection, ask whether you should reschedule your Pap test until after it has been treated.

2342

LIVING WELL, STAYING WELL

How Is the Test Done?

A Pap smear can be done quickly in a doctor's office, a clinic, or a hospital.

While you lie on an exam table, the clinician inserts a speculum into your vagina. That will widen the opening. With a wooden scraper, a cotton swab, or a small special brush, the clinician takes a sample of cells from in and around the cervix.

The Pap smear is usually performed as part of a complete pelvic exam (see page 227).

What Do the Results Mean?

Different systems may be used to rate and report your Pap test results.

If the results are rated on a scale from Class I to Class V, it means the following:

Class I. All the cells examined were normal.

Class II. A catchall category, this includes infection, inflammation, abnormally shaped cells, or actively changing cells, called metaplasia. Your Pap smear may be rated Class II whether you have an infection or beginning cell changes that may eventually become cancerous. Ask for details about a Class II Pap.

If your smear identified a specific infection, you may need a repeat Pap after the condition is treated. Repeat testing in less than a year is suggested for most Class II ratings to see whether the condition has returned to normal or whether any precancerous cells are detected.

Class III. Dysplastic cells were seen. Large and irregular in shape, they are precancerous and need to be removed. Dysplasia is not cancer.

Class IV. Early cancer cells confined to the surface of the cervix were seen. Many experts consider this condition, called *carcinoma in situ,* a precancerous condition. It should not be ignored. Several types of treatment are available.

Class V. Cancer cells have spread beyond the surface of the cervix. Treatment is needed.

The Bethesda system is an alternative method of reporting Pap results. If the laboratory uses this newer, more descriptive way of delivering results, your report will first confirm whether the lab had plenty of cells to examine. That reduces the likelihood of a false negative resulting from too few cells in the sample. The report should also note any inflammation or other hints of infection.

If dysplasia is detected, the report rates the cells as CIN (*cervical intraepithelial neoplasia,* or new growth on the surface of the cervix) I, II, and III. CIN I means mild dysplasia, II is moderate dysplasia, and III includes severe dysplasia and carcinoma in situ. Moderate or severe dysplasia, unless treated, often will proceed to cervical cancer.

What's Next?
No diagnosis of a problem should be made—and no treatment given— on the basis of a single Pap smear. If your Pap test is abnormal, your physician may suggest a repeat test or a more specific diagnostic test to find out what is wrong.

You may be reexamined using a colposcope, a viewing scope that lets the physician look at the cervix under magnification. First, the physician dabs weak acetic acid on the cervix to highlight the dysplastic cells. He or she will snip off a few cells from any abnormal areas and send the cells to the laboratory for definitive analysis.

If the tests confirm cancer or a precancerous condition, treatment can be planned from among the many options available.

UTERINE CANCER—ENDOMETRIUM

Cancer in the main portion of the uterus, usually in the lining (called the *endometrium*), is diagnosed in about 31,000 women each year. And each year almost 6,000 women die of it.

Symptoms
If you notice bleeding or staining after you have gone through menopause or between your periods, tell your physician. Bleeding due to uterine cancer is likely to be unpredictable, following no set pattern in how frequent or heavy it is. Sometimes a watery discharge can be the first sign of uterine cancer.

Pelvic Exam
During a pelvic exam (see page 227), your health-care provider will feel the size and shape of your uterus for any indications of abnormal growth.

Endometrial Tissue Sample or Endometrial Biopsy

> *"I went home and taught a yoga class a few hours after the test. I had cramps for about twenty minutes, but they weren't any worse than the menstrual cramps I'm used to."*

An endometrial biopsy is a screening test most often suggested for women who have entered menopause and who have one of the risk factors associated with uterine cancer.

What's Being Looked For?
Precancerous changes in the tissue lining the uterus.

Do You Need to Be Tested?
Not every woman needs to have a biopsy so endometrial tissue can be examined. These risk factors indicate a need for one:

- A history of infertility;
- Obesity;
- Failure to ovulate;
- Abnormal uterine bleeding;
- Taking estrogen without progestin;
- Taking *tamoxifen.*

The common link in these risk factors is they all increase the amount of the hormone estrogen your uterus is exposed to. Estrogen stimulates growth of the lining of the uterus.

How Do You Get the Best Test?
You don't need to do anything special to prepare for an endometrial biopsy. If you have not gone through menopause, ask whether your physician prefers a particular time of your cycle.

How Is the Test Done?
An endometrial biopsy can be done in the physician's office. While you are in position for a pelvic exam, your cervix is cleansed with an antiseptic. Then the doctor inserts a slim tube through the cervix into your uterus, removes a sample of tissue, and sends it to the lab for analysis.

When the doctor takes the sample, you will feel a quick pinch. Afterwards, you will have cramps for a while and may need to use a tampon or sanitary napkin for a few hours to absorb any bleeding.

What Do the Results Mean?

A laboratory technician measures the thickness of the lining and examines the cells for precancerous changes. A lab report of *endometrial hyperplasia* means there is excess growth of the uterine lining. It is not cancer and may be expected if you are taking estrogen or estrogenlike medications. A report of *atypical* or *adenomatous* tissue indicates that precancerous changes have occurred in the cells.

What's Next?

If you are taking estrogen and abnormal cells have been found, your doctor may want to alter your hormone prescription and repeat the test later.

If the tissue sample is suspicious, your doctor may want to do a D&C (dilatation and curettage). In that procedure, the doctor removes the entire thickened uterine lining and sends the tissue to the laboratory. If uterine cancer is discovered at an early stage, the five-year survival rate is 94 percent.

Heart Disease Screening Tests

HYPERTENSION (HIGH BLOOD PRESSURE)

Fifty million Americans may have high blood pressure. Unfortunately, about 30 percent of them don't know it.

High blood pressure can injure artery walls, so it's important to monitor blood pressure. This condition is especially likely when excess pressure continues for many years because it has not been detected or properly treated. Over time the arteries become scarred, hardened, and less elastic. That leaves the unsuspecting person at elevated risk for heart attack and stroke. High blood pressure also makes the heart work harder, setting the stage for heart failure from weakness of the muscle later in life.

Symptoms

High blood pressure is usually a "silent" condition. As a rule, it causes no noticeable symptoms, even though it is causing damage. Serious, out-of-control blood pressure can cause headaches, vision problems, breathing difficulty, or temporary weakness or paralysis from a mini-stroke.

Blood Pressure Monitoring

"At first, I resisted treatment. I told myself my pressure only got high when I was nervous in the doctor's office. Then I started checking the pressure at home and found out that almost anything could send it up."

What's Being Looked For?

High blood pressure. Blood pressure is the force created as the heart pushes blood into the arteries and through the circulatory system.

Do You Need to Be Tested?

Because high blood pressure is so common—and can cause serious damage long before it causes any symptoms—routine blood pressure checks are valuable for everyone. No matter why you see a physician, each visit should include a blood pressure check.

Certain people and circumstances warrant particular attention to blood pressure. If the characteristics below apply to you, make sure that a health-care provider is monitoring your blood pressure carefully.

IF YOU ARE OVERWEIGHT

Gaining a lot of weight or being overweight makes it more likely you will develop high blood pressure.

IF YOU ARE AFRICAN-AMERICAN

One in every three African-Americans over the age of eighteen has high blood pressure. High blood pressure tends to occur earlier and to be more serious among African-Americans.

IF YOUR PARENTS OR OTHER RELATIVES HAVE OR HAD HIGH BLOOD PRESSURE

If you have a family history of high blood pressure, there is a good chance that you and your children may also develop it.

IF YOU TAKE BIRTH CONTROL PILLS

Some women who take oral contraceptives develop a rise in blood pressure. Even so, their blood pressure usually remains in the normal range. If you plan to take the Pill, have your blood pressure measured before the Pill is prescribed. Then have it checked every six months or so. Pill-induced high blood pressure is more likely if you are overweight, if you developed high blood pressure during any pregnancies, or if you have a family history of high blood pressure.

Smoking cigarettes and taking the Pill greatly increases the risk of cardiovascular problems, especially in women over the age of thirty-five.

You should exert every effort to avoid smoking. Consider not taking the Pill if you continue to smoke. If you just can't avoid this dangerous combination, get regular blood pressure checks.

If You Are Pregnant

High blood pressure occurs in one out of ten pregnancies. It can develop rapidly during the last three or four months. Uncontrolled, it can be dangerous to both mother and fetus. Blood pressure should be measured at all prenatal visits.

How Do You Get the Best Test?

Do not smoke and do not drink any beverage with caffeine for at least a half-hour before the measurement.

You don't need to stop taking a medicine you use routinely, but be sure to report all medications you have taken recently. Many common types of medication can raise blood pressure. These include steroids; nonsteroidal antiinflammatory medicines, such as ibuprofen; and decongestants containing pseudoephedrine, phenylephrine, or phenylpropanolamine. Others are Ritalin and certain antidepressants and drugs to treat Parkinson's disease. Cocaine and PCP can raise blood pressure dramatically.

Don't have your blood pressure taken where it's noisy or hectic. To help ensure accuracy, rest comfortably for at least five minutes before having your blood pressure measured. You should be seated with your arm supported at about heart level. Blood pressure should not be measured through clothing.

How Is the Test Done?

Having your blood pressure measured is quick and painless. An adjustable padded cuff momentarily constricts the blood flow through your arm. As the squeezing is gradually eased, the pressure is measured.

What Do the Results Mean?

The blood pressure measurement is divided into two parts. The systolic blood pressure (top number) indicates how hard the blood pushes against the inside of the arteries during a heartbeat. The diastolic blood pressure (bottom number) indicates the amount of force during the brief relaxation period between heartbeats. The traditional device for measuring blood pressure (a *sphygmomanometer*) uses a long glass measurement column filled with mercury. Your blood pressure measurement will be expressed as millimeters of mercury.

Younger and more active people usually have lower blood pressure. In general, the lower your blood pressure, the better—unless the low pressure results from a medical problem.

BLOOD PRESSURE RESULTS

Systolic (mm Hg)	Diastolic (mm Hg)	Category
Below 120	Below 80	Optimal for cardiovascular system
Below 130	Below 85	Normal
130–139	85–89	High normal
		Hypertension
140–159	90–99	Stage 1 (formerly called mild)
160–179	100–109	Stage 2 (formerly called moderate)
180–209	110–119	Stage 3 (formerly called severe)
210 or higher	120 or higher	Stage 4 (formerly called very severe)

This chart is based on one from the Joint National Committee on Detection, Evaluation, and Treatment of High Blood Pressure, 1992.

What's Next?

Because various circumstances can influence blood pressure, high blood pressure is not diagnosed or treated after a single reading. For instance, your blood pressure can rise momentarily when you are nervous or excited, but it should quickly return to normal.

If your blood pressure is high at one visit, you should have two more readings taken at different times over the next several weeks. The exception is blood pressure so high that it constitutes a medical emergency.

So-called white-coat hypertension causes you to have high blood pressure at the doctor's office but not at home. It is a real phenomenon—but it doesn't mean that you can ignore the high readings. Blood pressure that goes up when you're stressed is still a concern regarding heart disease.

If your blood pressure is consistently in the high-normal or borderline range, your physician may want to discuss lifestyle changes you can make to lower your blood pressure or keep it from edging higher.

Losing weight (if you need to), exercising regularly, eating less salt, and drinking less alcohol may reduce your blood pressure enough to put it back in the normal range.

A physician who finds that you have high blood pressure will want to answer three questions before deciding what to do:

1. *Is your high blood pressure an isolated condition or a symptom of an underlying medical problem that needs attention?* For most cases of high blood pressure, the cause is not known. That condition is called *essential,* or *primary, hypertension.* In 5 to 10 percent of high blood pressure cases, physicians can find a specific medical problem causing the elevated pressure. Such a condition is called *secondary hypertension.* Causes include a kidney problem, a tumor in the adrenal gland, or a heart defect. When the problem is corrected, blood pressure usually returns to normal. A blood test, urinalysis, and physical examination can usually rule out that you have one of these relatively rare conditions. If high blood pressure doesn't respond to standard medication, that also may indicate secondary hypertension.

2. *Has your high blood pressure already caused damage?* If the damage is to your eyes, kidneys, or heart and blood vessels, prompt treatment is important.

3. *Do you have other risk factors for heart disease?* If you smoke, have high cholesterol or diabetes, or have already shown signs of heart problems, your doctor may take a more vigorous approach to treatment to get the problem under control quickly. The measures described above may be enough to regulate your blood pressure. If not, you will need medication. Some people in this category need the medication only temporarily, and some must take it for the rest of their lives.

The following list shows types of medication available to treat high blood pressure:

- *Diuretics* work by helping the body get rid of excess fluids and sodium.
- *Beta blockers* cause the heart to beat more slowly and push out a smaller amount of blood with each beat.
- *Alpha blockers* keep nerve impulses from constricting blood vessels. That lets arteries stay open wider.
- *Vasodilators* relax the muscles in the walls of blood vessels, also keeping arteries open wider.

- *Angiotensin-converting-enzyme (ACE) inhibitors* interfere with the body's production of *angiotensin*. That's a chemical that causes arteries to constrict.
- *Calcium channel blockers* reduce the heart rate and relax blood vessels.

All blood pressure medications can have side effects. If you are not happy with how you feel when taking a certain blood pressure medication, tell your doctor. Many types are available. Your doctor can work with you to find the right one. Taking lower doses of two different medications may even be the best way to control your blood pressure with a minimum of side effects.

Regular monitoring is important if you have borderline or high blood pressure. Several types of machine let you measure blood pressure at home. They differ widely in cost, accuracy, necessary upkeep, and ease of use. Before making a purchase, consult your physician to see whether he or she recommends home monitoring. If you use home equipment, bring it to your doctor's office at least once a year to have the measurements compared with your readings on the office equipment. Home monitoring does not replace the need for regular professional blood pressure checks.

HIGH CHOLESTEROL AND OTHER LIPID ABNORMALITIES

We've come a long way since first discovering the link between cholesterol levels and heart disease risk. In recent years, heart disease experts have learned more about the metabolism of cholesterol in the body. They've also determined the various proteins that carry it through the body.

Cholesterol

A fatlike substance that is produced in your liver, cholesterol is part of the membrane around every body cell. It is essential in making some hormones. However, most people have much more cholesterol than they need. That's either because their bodies are not very efficient at metabolizing it or because much of what they eat is high in fat and cholesterol. A high level of cholesterol in the blood is a major risk factor for heart disease.

Cholesterol doesn't dissolve in blood. It travels through the bloodstream in tiny particles made up of lipid (a general name for any fatty substance) and protein.

Low-Density Lipoproteins

Usually called LDLs, or bad cholesterol, low-density lipoproteins are the major carrier of cholesterol in the blood. High levels of LDLs circulating in the bloodstream can slowly build up within the walls of arteries. That increases the risk of heart disease.

High-Density Lipoproteins

One-third to one-fourth of the cholesterol in the bloodstream is carried by high-density lipoproteins (HDLs). HDL cholesterol is often called the good cholesterol because a high level seems to protect against heart attack. Medical experts think that HDL tends to carry excess cholesterol away from the arteries and back to the liver. There it's metabolized and passed from the body.

Triglycerides

Triglycerides are made from excess calories in your diet. Shortly after you eat, the level of triglycerides in your bloodstream gets higher. When you eat more food than your body tissues can use right away, the extra calories are converted to triglycerides. They are stored in your fat cells until needed to provide energy between meals. Excess triglycerides may be an indicator of risk for heart disease.

What's Being Looked For?

The concentration of total cholesterol, or its various forms, in a blood sample.

Do You Need to Be Tested?

All adults should have their total cholesterol and HDL cholesterol measured at least every five years. If you have other risk factors for heart disease, have the testing more often.

How Do You Get the Best Test?

A blood test for total cholesterol and for HDLs does not require any special preparation. However, if triglycerides and LDLs will also be measured, don't drink alcohol or eat anything for nine to twelve hours prior to the test. It may be easiest to schedule the test for early in the morning.

If you are sick, have an infection, or recently had surgery or were injured, ask whether your cholesterol test should be scheduled for another time. Let the practitioner know if you recently changed your eating plan or lost weight. Any of these things may influence your cholesterol measurement.

"My cholesterol was over 300, but I didn't worry because I was pregnant and they said it might be high. Now my daughter is four years old and it's still over 300. I shouldn't have waited so long to find out and start changing how I eat."

If you are pregnant, it is normal for your lipids to go up temporarily. Your cholesterol test should be scheduled for some time after you deliver.

If blood lipids are measured while you are hospitalized or after an invasive test, the results may be altered. The test should be repeated after your hospital stay and when you're back on a normal eating plan.

Mention whether you are taking any medications. Some medicines, such as progesterone, certain diuretics, and steroids, can raise LDL levels. In some women, estrogen taken by mouth dramatically increases triglyceride levels. (The estrogen patch doesn't affect triglycerides significantly.)

Before your blood is taken for a cholesterol test, sit quietly for at least five minutes.

Home-based tests are available for measuring total cholesterol. The American Heart Association has not taken a position on these test devices. However, the AHA cautions that home-based tests do not measure HDLs. This measurement is important in assessing heart disease risk and selecting preventive strategies.

How Is the Test Done?

One method is for a technician to use a syringe to withdraw a small amount of blood from a vein in your arm. A second method is for a drop or two of blood to be drawn into a narrow tube from a finger prick. For the latter way to work, the blood must flow freely. If the technician has to milk your finger to get the blood, the results will not be reliable.

What Do the Results Mean?

A total blood cholesterol test has two purposes. It is used in a preliminary assessment of cardiovascular risk and to determine whether you need further tests.

All cholesterol measurements are reported as milligrams (mg) per deciliter (dL) of blood.

TOTAL BLOOD CHOLESTEROL

This is the most common measurement of blood cholesterol. If you hear someone say he or she has a cholesterol level of, for example, 194, that person is referring to total cholesterol. Your HDL level may be measured at the same time. That measurement can be used to help interpret your total cholesterol level.

TOTAL CHOLESTEROL RESULTS	
Less than 200 mg/dL	Desirable
200 to 239 mg/dL	Borderline high risk
240 mg/dL and over	High risk
Less than 35 mg/dL HDL cholesterol	Low HDL cholesterol

If your cholesterol level is less than 200 and your HDL is 35 mg/dL or higher, your chance of heart attack is relatively low unless you have other risk factors for heart disease. It still is a good idea to eat foods low in fat, saturated fat, and cholesterol and become physically active. Doing so will help you keep your desirable cholesterol level. If you're in the desirable range, have your cholesterol checked again within five years.

If your cholesterol level is between 200 and 239 mg/dL and your HDL is less than 35 mg/dL, you may be at increased risk for heart disease. This is especially true if you have other risk factors. Medical treatment is *not* based on total cholesterol, but on HDL, LDL, and triglyceride levels. If treatment seems to be indicated, your doctor will probably have your LDL and triglycerides measured. Depending on the results, you and your doctor will need to discuss making lifestyle changes and/or using medication to lower your cholesterol. Your cholesterol should be tested again within a year or two.

If your cholesterol level is 240 mg/dL or higher, you are definitely at increased risk for heart disease. Your doctor will probably further evaluate your lipid levels. Depending on those results, the doctor will recommend lifestyle changes and, possibly, the use of medication. Your cholesterol should be retested as often as your doctor suggests.

HDLs

Levels of HDL vary with a person's age and gender, averaging about 47 mg/dL for men and about 56 mg/dL for women. Levels above 60 mg/dL are considered a strong protective factor against heart disease. A level below 35 mg/dL is defined as low HDL cholesterol and is a major risk factor for heart disease.

If your HDL level is below 35—no matter how low your total cholesterol—your doctor may recommend a lipid test that gives the exact figures for LDLs and triglycerides. With those results, the doctor can better determine your risk and suggest measures to protect your heart.

Total cholesterol includes both good HDLs and bad LDLs. That's why heart experts want your lab results to give numbers for both if you have borderline cholesterol levels with other risk factors or if you have high cholesterol.

LDLs

When heart disease rates and lipid levels of different groups of people are compared, LDLs are the measurements most linked with the risk of heart disease and of death. If you are being monitored for heart disease risk, your doctor will pay closest attention to LDLs.

LDL CHOLESTEROL	
Below 130 mg/dL	Desirable
130–159 mg/dL	
with one or no other risk factors	Borderline high risk
with two or more other risk factors	High risk
160 mg/dL or higher	High risk

The risk factors referred to in the LDL cholesterol chart above include being a man at least forty-five years old, being a woman at least fifty-five years old, or being a postmenopausal woman (regardless of age) who is not taking hormone replacement therapy. Younger men and women with high LDL levels will be watched carefully by their doctors. The doctors will encourage them to avoid smoking, follow a low-fat eating plan, and be physically active. Other risk factors are having a family history of heart disease at an early age, smoking, having high blood pressure, having an HDL cholesterol level below 35 mg/dL, or having diabetes.

If your LDL level is in the desirable category, you should discuss how to minimize any heart disease risk factors you have. Recheck your cholesterol within five years.

If your LDL level is borderline high risk, you and your physician should discuss ways to use proper nutrition and exercise to lower your cholesterol. Have your LDLs measured again within a year.

If you are in either of the high-risk categories, you'll need further evaluation right away. Then you and your physician can plan your care (see "What's Next?" on page 240).

Triglycerides
The relationship between triglyceride levels and heart disease is complex. The amount of concern that a high reading generates will depend on your medical and family history and other risks. High triglycerides often occur in people with high LDL cholesterol or low HDL cholesterol. These numbers (LDL and HDL) define the risk. Triglycerides add little to the risk.

TRIGLYCERIDE LEVELS	
Less than 200 mg/dL	Normal
200–399 mg/dL	Borderline high
400–999 mg/dL	High
1,000 or higher	Very high

What's Next?
You should not be told you have high cholesterol or triglycerides based on a single test. If the levels seem high, the test needs to be repeated.

The bad news in treating high cholesterol is that it cannot be cured. You will need to pay attention to your cholesterol for the rest of your life. The good news is that high cholesterol *can* be lowered through lifestyle changes and medication, if needed. That control can save your life.

HIGH TOTAL CHOLESTEROL OR HIGH LDLs
If you have elevated LDLs or total cholesterol, your physician will want to answer the five questions below before working with you to plan your care.

1. *Do you have a disease that is raising your cholesterol?* Diabetes, hypothyroidism, and certain kidney and liver disorders can raise cholesterol levels. If so, the condition(s) will be treated and your cholesterol reevaluated.

2. *Are you on any medication that is raising your cholesterol?* If you are taking cortisone, anabolic steroids, progestins, or certain high blood pressure drugs, your doctor may advise you to change your medication.

3. *Do you have a genetic disorder affecting cholesterol metabolism?* By testing you and your family members, your physician will better understand how to treat you and them. For example, 1 in 500 people has an inherited condition called *familial hypercholesterolemia*. It usually raises total cholesterol above 300 mg/dL and is associated with premature heart disease. If this is your diagnosis, your doctor will likely start you on a low-fat eating plan immediately. He or she will observe your LDLs, HDLs, and triglycerides often for a few weeks and then consider specific cholesterol-lowering medications. Your doctor may not want to wait several months to assess the effectiveness of lifestyle changes alone before beginning drug therapy.

4. *What other heart disease risks do you have?* Your overall risk of heart disease is the big issue in cholesterol treatment. At a given elevated cholesterol level, a fifty-year-old man may, for example, be treated more aggressively than a twenty-year-old man or a thirty-five-year-old woman. If you have heart disease or diabetes, your physician may want to use lifestyle changes plus medical treatment to get your LDL levels as low as possible. The recommended goal for the LDL level if you have heart disease is lower than 100 mg/dL.

5. *Do you have angina or have you had a heart attack?* A large study in Scandinavia has conclusively demonstrated that cholesterol-lowering medication (in this case, simvastatin) can help people with coronary heart disease live longer and have fewer repeat heart attacks. In a study involving more than 4,000 patients, it cut the risk of death—from all causes—by 30 percent. Furthermore, it cut the risk of coronary death by 42 percent. The researchers calculated that six years of simvastatin treatment would provide the following preventive benefits in 100 heart attack and angina patients similar to the patients who participated in the study:

+ Four of nine patients would be spared from coronary heart disease death.
+ Seven of twenty-one patients would escape a nonfatal heart attack.
+ Six of nineteen patients would avoid having coronary bypass surgery or angioplasty.

Depending on other risk factors, most men under age thirty-five and most premenopausal women will have plenty of time to try to lower their cholesterol levels through lifestyle changes. Medication can be started later on, if needed.

Dietary therapy—reducing how much total fat, saturated fat, and cholesterol you eat—is the major strategy for lowering cholesterol and LDLs. At the same time you are eating healthfully, you should minimize your other heart disease risks by exercising, keeping your blood pressure under control, and not smoking.

The dietary pattern your physician suggests is likely to be very similar to the one described in chapter 3. Depending on your lipid levels and how your body responds to changes in what you eat, an eating plan even lower in fat is occasionally suggested.

If you need them, medications are available to help lower cholesterol. Some work mainly on LDL cholesterol; others have a positive effect on LDLs, HDLs, and triglycerides. Your physician will look at which of your lipids are abnormal and what other risk factors you have before suggesting a medication. For most people, the major focus usually is on reducing LDLs.

Bile acid resins (such as cholestyramine and colestipol) attach to bile acids in your intestines and increase their loss in your stool. Normally, most bile acids are reabsorbed and return to the liver. When more are lost, the liver must replace them. Since they are constructed from cholesterol, making new bile acids uses up the liver's cholesterol. The result is an increase in the liver's ability to extract LDL from the blood. This lowers the LDL cholesterol level.

HMG CoA reductase inhibitors limit the production of an *enzyme* that is essential in the body's synthesis of cholesterol. These medications lower LDL levels, the major target of cholesterol-lowering therapy for many patients. They are also called statins (such as lovastatin, pravastatin, and simvastatin).

Niacin, or nicotinic acid, is an acid of the B vitamin complex that can be used to lower total blood cholesterol, LDLs, and triglycerides and to raise HDLs. When you first start taking niacin, it can cause distressing side effects, such as a headache and a bright-red flushing of the face. In recent years, physicians have learned ways to minimize the side effects.

Fibric acid derivatives, which include gemfibrozil and clofibrate, lower triglycerides. To a lesser extent, they increase HDL cholesterol. In some people, they also lower LDLs.

Cholesterol-lowering medication may cause various side effects. Ask your physician for detailed written instructions on how to take the medication. Speak up if you find the side effects tough to handle. The goal is to use the best medicine possible to keep your LDLs in the safe range for the rest of your life. Sometimes a combination of medications provides the best control with the fewest side effects.

Even if you take medication to lower your lipids, continue to eat a low-fat diet and watch your weight. Then if your cholesterol level or LDL level falls beneath the goal you and your doctor have set, the two of you may be able to reduce your medication. Drug therapy doesn't always have to last a lifetime.

Low HDLs

If you have low HDLs, you should exercise regularly, control your weight, and not smoke. If you have diabetes or high blood pressure, follow medical advice to keep your blood sugar and blood pressure under control. However, lipid experts advise that HDL levels are usually very responsive to weight loss and physical activity. The main reason to be aware of your HDL level is to help gauge how imperative it is to keep your LDLs low.

If you have low HDLs and high LDLs, the major focus of your care will be to lower your LDLs. Your physician may set a lower target for your LDLs than if your HDLs were higher. If you need medication to lower your LDLs, niacin is likely to be considered as a first choice. It simultaneously raises HDLs and lowers LDLs.

High Triglycerides

If your triglycerides are high, your doctor will want to find out more about your health and your family history. Taking steps to lower triglycerides is particularly important if you are obese, have diabetes, or come from a family that tends to have premature heart disease. (The high triglycerides may be a family trait as well.)

If you are on estrogen therapy, you may be taken off the medication to see whether your triglyceride levels go down. Some women develop alarmingly high triglyceride levels while taking estrogen. This can occur very quickly after starting on the drug. Besides promoting heart disease, this condition can cause a life-threatening inflammation of the pancreas. If your triglyceride levels are sensitive to estrogen, you and your physician may decide to withdraw the estrogen or to substitute an estrogen patch.

If you drink alcohol, your doctor may suggest restricting or stopping its use on a trial basis. Triglyceride levels in some people are very sensitive to alcohol.

Making changes in lifestyle, especially the ones that bring about weight loss, is the major therapy for high triglycerides. Your doctor should discuss strategies to help you reach and keep a healthy body weight, eat foods low in saturated fat and cholesterol, exercise regularly, and stop smoking. All these things are valuable for any health-conscious person to do.

Childhood Health Checks

CHILDHOOD CANCER CHECKS

Fortunately, it is rare for children to develop cancer. Still, cancers kill more children between the ages of one and fourteen than any other disease does.

To help ensure that childhood cancers are diagnosed as early as possible, take your children for regular medical checkups.

Because the symptoms are sometimes vague and can be difficult to recognize, parents play a big role in helping ensure a timely diagnosis. You know best how your child usually looks and acts. Kids are always getting bumped and bruised, and they can get very sick with an ear infection or other common illness. But if you notice that any of the symptoms listed below occurs and lingers, tell your child's physician.

♦ An unusual mass or swelling;
♦ Unexplained paleness and loss of energy;
♦ Prolonged, unexplained fever or illness;
♦ Frequent headaches, often with vomiting;
♦ Sudden eye or vision changes;
♦ Excessive, rapid weight loss.

> *"When he looks and acts perfectly fine, you hate to think that your precious little baby needs an operation. But later we were very glad that we didn't put it off."*

Some children are born with conditions that, while not posing a health hazard immediately, should be corrected because cancerous changes can occur later on. Two examples are moles and undescended testicles.

Let the doctor know if your child was born with a mole. Moles present from birth are more likely to become cancerous than those appearing later. Usually, they should be removed during childhood.

A boy's testes are formed in the abdomen, but by about the eighth month of gestation they have usually descended into the scrotum. If your son is born with an undescended or partially descended testicle, it can be moved by simple surgery. It should be fixed before his sixth birthday. Testicles that remain undescended are much more likely to become cancerous.

If your child has cancer, a combination of treatments may be suggested. The success of treatment depends on the type of cancer. Since 1950, treatments have improved enough overall to boost survival rates by 60 percent.

CHILDHOOD HEART CHECKS

The road to heart disease is a long one, and it often starts in childhood. As a parent, you already know you can do a lot to help children be physically active, enjoy low-fat foods, stay at a healthy weight, and never pick up the smoking habit. Still, whether because of inheritance or the habits of their young lives, many children develop heart disease risk factors before they get to high school. The earlier these are identified and dealt with, the healthier the future your child can look forward to.

> *"The kids have had their blood pressure checked, but I don't know what was found. My pediatrician has never suggested getting the boys' cholesterol checked, even though my father had bypass surgery and my father-in-law died of a heart attack in his forties.*
>
> *"When I ask, the doctor says it might be a good idea. He's very low-key about it, however, and there's always something else to do at a visit. I'm going to have to insist."*

Blood Pressure

The American Heart Association recommends that all children—even babies—have yearly blood pressure measurements. Physicians routinely measure blood pressure whenever examining a child.

Why do kids get high blood pressure? In some children, another disease is the culprit. When that other disease is successfully treated, pressure usually returns to normal. Some children develop high blood pressure as a side effect of medications taken for other health problems. When the medication is discontinued or changed, the blood pressure should become normal.

In newborns, high blood pressure is most often a complication of severe respiratory distress or of various birth defects involving the kidneys or heart. In children younger than six, kidney disease and kidney or heart defects are the most likely culprits. In children six and older, kidney disease is still a frequent reason for high blood pressure—but it also becomes common that no medical condition can be found to underlie a child's high blood pressure.

Children who have high blood pressure for no known reason may be alerting us that they are at risk for heart disease later in life. In general, children who tend to have high blood pressure for their age are more likely to grow into adults with high blood pressure. Overweight kids generally have higher blood pressure than slimmer kids the same age. The tendency toward high blood pressure can be inherited from one or both parents. A familial tendency toward high blood pressure tends to occur more frequently—and to be more severe—in families of African-Americans than in families of whites.

How Do You Get the Best Test?
For the most accurate reading, the ideal situation is to have your child's blood pressure checked under certain conditions. Those are when he or she is not ill; is not taking medication; is not crying; is in a calm, quiet room; and has not been running around in the last few minutes. Obviously, the ideal often is not possible! Therefore, it's important to repeat the measurement twice under ideal conditions if blood pressure seems high. Make certain that the blood pressure cuff and the technique are appropriate for a child.

Normal blood pressure for a child is lower than that for an adult. Is your child heavier, taller, or more physically mature than other children the same age? If so, the doctor may decide it is normal for his or her blood pressure to be higher than in a smaller child of that age.

Only one child in twenty has blood pressure as high as or higher than the levels listed in the chart on the next page. If your child is in one of these categories, talk to the doctor.

If blood pressure is consistently high, your child's doctor may suggest a urinalysis or other tests to see whether a heart or kidney problem needs treatment. Remember, depending on your child's height and weight, the blood pressure your child's physician considers worrisome may differ from the chart on the next page. An underlying medical problem is more likely when a younger or thinner child has high blood

| HIGH BLOOD PRESSURE IN CHILDREN ||
Years of Age	Upper 5 Percentile of Blood Pressure
3–5	116/76 or higher
6–9	122/78 or higher
10–12	126/82 or higher
13–15	136/86 or higher
16–18	142/92 or higher

pressure. Careful control of blood pressure in children with diabetes or certain kidney diseases can help prevent kidney damage.

If someone who isn't your child's regular doctor takes the blood pressure, be sure to mention your child's health problems and medications. If your child was sick as a newborn and needed an umbilical (belly button) catheter, mention this also. In some children, this *catheterization* results in interference with blood flow to the kidneys later in childhood. Because alcohol, cocaine, or steroids can cause elevated blood pressure, adolescents should be asked about the use of these substances. Birth control pills can also raise blood pressure.

The child most likely to have high blood pressure is at least twelve and is overweight or comes from a family with high blood pressure or heart disease. He or she has already started on the path toward heart disease risk.

Changes in the child's diet and exercise may be recommended to help control weight and to lower blood pressure. Unless he or she is having symptoms, a child with high blood pressure can—and should—participate in physical activity. Occasionally a child will need medications to reduce high blood pressure.

Cholesterol
Elevated cholesterol levels early in life play a role in the development of heart disease in adults. A healthful lifestyle helps prevent high cholesterol in children. If it occurs anyway, detecting it early and taking steps to lower it may prevent future damage and fat buildup in the arteries.

High cholesterol and its damaging effects are not rare in young people. Thirty-seven percent of Americans age nineteen and under are believed to have high cholesterol. Autopsies on young soldiers killed in battle have shown that three out of four already had demonstrable atherosclerosis. If they had lived, these people might not even have known of their heart disease symptoms for decades.

Your family history can help determine whether it is important to have your child's cholesterol level measured. The National Cholesterol Education Program advises testing if a child has a parent or grandparent who had any of the following problems before the age of fifty-five:

- Atherosclerosis seen with angiography;
- Heart attack;
- Angina;
- Diseased blood vessels in the arms and legs;
- Stroke;
- Sudden heart-related death;
- Cholesterol level over 240 ml/dL at any age.

If family members are not in contact or are unable to provide information, a child's cholesterol should be measured.

How Do You Get the Best Test?

Like adults, children don't need to skip a meal or do any special preparation before having their total cholesterol measured. If your child is ill or has an infection, you may want to reschedule the cholesterol check.

Let your child sit quietly for at least five minutes before blood is taken for the cholesterol measurement. Because of all the activity and hubbub, screening at a mall or in a school setting is likely to be less accurate than if done as part of a medical visit.

What Do the Results Mean?

The cutoff points for normal cholesterol levels are the same for children between the ages of two and nineteen. Levels for adults are somewhat higher.

A reading between 170 and 199 mg/dL is in the top 25 percentile for kids. A reading of 200 mg/dL ranks in the top 5 percent.

TOTAL CHOLESTEROL IN CHILDREN	
Less than 170 mg/dL	Acceptable
170–199 mg/dL	Borderline high
200 and above	High

Children with high cholesterol levels are three times more likely to have high cholesterol as adults than are kids with low cholesterol levels. However, high cholesterol by itself does not usually mean that your child is sick or that you need to be overly concerned. You have plenty of time to pay attention to the many factors that influence cholesterol levels and heart disease risk.

What's Next?

If a single cholesterol test is high, your physician may want to order a repeat test or to get a more specific breakdown of LDL and HDL cholesterol and triglycerides.

If a repeat test confirms that cholesterol is high, your physician will want to ensure that no underlying medical condition or medication reaction is causing the problem.

Let the tester know if your child is on any medication. Several drugs, including some that may be used by adolescents without a parent's knowledge, can change the levels of cholesterol and other lipids. The antiacne drug isotretinoin (Accutane) can raise triglyceride levels. Steroids, alcohol, certain anticonvulsants, and certain birth control pills may raise cholesterol levels.

A checkup including blood cholesterol testing and a urinalysis can rule out most underlying medical problems that can raise cholesterol. Of these, the most common is diabetes. A child also may have inherited a genetic tendency toward abnormal lipids. If a genetic problem is suspected, other family members should be screened.

Unless an underlying problem needs treatment, the major concern if your child has high cholesterol will be to reduce the risk of heart disease. You may be asked to reduce how much fat your child eats and to help your child attain and stay at a normal weight if he or she is overweight. You'll also want to encourage regular physical activity and to help your child stop (or, better yet, never start) smoking.

The entire family may need to change eating habits. When cholesterol is elevated in a child, one or both parents will often have elevated cholesterol, too. Many times, they aren't aware of this problem. All the family may also need to become more active and quit smoking.

Cholesterol-lowering medications are rarely used in children, especially under age ten. The National Cholesterol Education Program suggests that doctors should not prescribe such medications unless a child has other heart disease risk factors and keeps having very high LDL cholesterol despite following a low-fat eating plan.

Summary

In terms of prevention, health-care providers have more to offer today than ever before. If you take advantage of screening tests and use the expertise and partnership of health professionals to help you control your risk factors, you will reduce your chance of developing heart disease and cancer. You'll also get the most from your health-care dollar.

CHAPTER 6

Other Ways to
Take Care of Yourself

EATING HEALTHFULLY, KEEPING ACTIVE, STAYING AWAY FROM TOBACCO, and getting prevention-oriented health care can reduce your risk of both heart disease and cancer. In this chapter, we briefly discuss other ways to keep yourself healthy.

The chapter is divided into four sections. First, we recommend prevention strategies you can use right now. Next, we discuss strategies that the American Heart Association and the American Cancer Society haven't recommended for general use but that are currently being used with promising results in large-scale tests. Some health professionals are advocating them for certain patients. Third, we discuss what research currently under way may be able to tell us about the best ways to stay healthy. Finally, we give pointers on how to be a sophisticated reader of medical research news on these topics and others.

Strategies You Can Use *Now*

ENJOY THE SUN SAFELY

"When I was growing up, I wanted nothing more than to be one of the bronzed girls at the lake. Every year I tried, and every year I got more burns and more freckles. Now almost every year I have a skin cancer removed."

When you fantasize about your favorite spots for relaxation, what do you picture? A beach? Ski slope? Boat drifting on a lake? Golf course or tennis court? Your own backyard garden?

In your mind's eye, these spots may call up memories of calming sounds, stress-relieving sports, and soothing sun. But skin specialists see something different: your body bombarded by cancer-causing ultraviolet radiation. Each year, more than half a million cases of skin cancer are detected in the United States. Virtually *all* of them are sun related.

Solar radiation is a mixture of different rays: infrared rays that warm, visible rays that give light, and invisible ultraviolet rays that can damage healthy skin cells. The three types of ultraviolet rays are discussed below.

UVB (ultraviolet B) rays can lead to sunburns and cancer. When specialized skin cells are hit by UVB, they produce melanin, or pigment. That spreads to neighboring cells to help protect against UVB by producing a tan. How easily you burn and how deeply you tan, as well as your skin tone, depend on whether your skin is richly or sparsely supplied with pigment-producing cells. That's an inborn characteristic you can't change.

A sunburn is UVB damage you can see. Redness and swelling will appear four to sixteen hours after the rays have damaged skin cells and blood vessels. Usually the skin repairs the damage in a few days, but sometimes cell damage is permanent. If cancerous changes occur in a melanin-producing cell, a dangerous melanoma can eventually develop. If other skin cells are permanently damaged, less deadly basal cell and squamous cell cancers may occur.

UVA (ultraviolet A) is up to one thousand times more intense than UVB. UVA penetrates into deeper layers of the skin. There it causes wrinkles and helps cause skin cancer. UVA can damage the immune system and the lens of the eye.

UVC (ultraviolet C) rays are considered to be the most carcinogenic. The protective ozone layer in the atmosphere absorbs almost all these rays. However, skin cancers become a very serious concern as the ozone layer thins and develops holes over certain parts of the earth.

Learn about Ultraviolet Rays

The sun's heat and light are most apparent during the summer and at midday. At those times, you can be sure that skin-damaging ultraviolet rays are also intense. But significant ultraviolet radiation can penetrate your skin at times when you may not expect that to happen. Some facts you may not know about ultraviolet radiation follow.

- UVA rays are constant throughout the day.
- UVA rays can go right through glass to reach you in your car or on a glassed-in patio. They get through at such an angle that they lose much of their power, however.
- The higher up in altitude you go, the more intense the ultraviolet radiation.
- When there is a thin cloud cover, 60 to 80 percent of ultraviolet rays still get through.
- After hitting sand, snow, water, or pavement, 25 to 70 percent of ultraviolet rays bounce back up at you. This means that, for example, a beach umbrella may not be as protective as you hope.
- The farther south you travel in the United States, the stronger the ultraviolet intensity.

In 1994, sun-conscious Americans got some new help in assessing the intensity of damaging rays from the sun. The National Weather Service now issues a daily solar warning index that forecasts just how much ultraviolet exposure a city will get on a given day. Check your weather forecast for the ratings. Then use them as you plan your outings. The chart below summarizes ratings on the ten-point system.

SOLAR WARNING INDEX

	Estimated Exposure Time Before Burning	
	Fair Complexions	Darker Complexions
0–2 Minimal Risk	30 minutes	2 hours
3–4 Low Risk	15–20 minutes	1¼–1½ hours
5–6 Moderate Risk	10–12 minutes	1 hour
7–9 High Risk	7–8 minutes	33–40 minutes
10 and above	5 minutes	30 minutes

The American Cancer Society applauds any information that keeps you aware of the risks from sun exposure. Nevertheless, it advises you to avoid midday sun, wear appropriate clothing, and use sunscreen even if your area has a low rating.

Shield Yourself

To guard against sun damage, avoid sun exposure between eleven in the morning and three in the afternoon. Stay away from tanning parlors. Don't use sunlamps or reflecting devices.

When you are in the sun, shield your skin with sunscreens and other protectors, discussed below. This is especially important if you work outdoors and can't avoid the sun.

Dress for the Sun

Follow the fashion advice of people in hot climates. Choose cool, loose-fitting clothing that covers a lot of skin. Wide-brimmed hats, long sleeves, and caftans are wise choices. On the other hand, gauzy, loose weaves can let in more sun than you want. If you can see light through a piece of clothing, ultraviolet rays are also getting through.

Wear Sunglasses

Ultraviolet rays are associated with cataracts and eye cancers, so don't forget your sunglasses. Both clear and tinted glasses can be treated to filter out most ultraviolet rays. If you have an eyeglass prescription filled, ask for this protection. If you buy nonprescription sunglasses, look for a tag that states what percentage of ultraviolet rays is blocked. Or buy sunglasses whose tag rates the lenses according to the following system, approved by the Food and Drug Administration and the American National Standards Institute.

- *Cosmetic.* The lenses absorb 70 percent of UVB and 20 percent of UVA. They are not protective enough for extended wear.
- *General purpose.* The lenses block at least 95 percent of UVB and 60 percent of UVA. They are suitable for most people.
- *Special purpose.* The lenses block at least 99 percent of UVB and 60 percent of UVA. This level of protection is recommended for lifeguards and other people who will spend their days in bright sun enhanced by reflection off snow, sand, or water.

In buying sunglasses, the most dangerous thing you can do is buy darkly tinted lenses without ultraviolet protection. Because the tint is dark, your pupils will open wider. That lets in even more radiation than if you went without the lenses. When wearing sunglasses, be sure to use enough sunscreen on your nose. It gets extra rays reflected off your glasses.

Choose and Use Sunscreen Correctly

A generation ago, kids who didn't tan were either left out of the beach fun or suffered painful, peeling sunburns. Now, sunscreen is tailor-made for each skin type.

Chemical sunscreens include ingredients that absorb up to 80 percent of UVA and more than 90 percent of UVB. For maximum protection, choose a broad-spectrum sunscreen that blocks both UVB and UVA. At least one laboratory study has implied that UVB-only sunscreen, because it prevents burning, may encourage people to stay out longer. That allows UVA to do *more* damage than if they had used no sunscreen at all.

To decide how strong a sunscreen to use, find the right SPF (sun protection factor) for your skin type. SPF values rate protection from the burning rays of UVB. These values compare the amount of time it takes for a person's skin to start reddening without a sunscreen to the amount of time it takes with a sunscreen. For example, if you usually start getting red in about half an hour, a number 2 sunscreen will offer an hour of protection. You can get about seven and a half hours of protection from a number 15 sunscreen.

Use the following chart as an aid when you need to pick the SPF.

CHOOSING THE SUNSCREEN FOR YOUR SKIN TYPE

Skin Type	Complexion	Susceptibility to Burning/Tanning	SPF
1	Very Fair	Always burns easily, never tans	15+
2	Fair	Burns easily, tans minimally	15
3	Light	Burns moderately, tans eventually	10–15
4	Medium	Burns minimally, always tans well	6–10
5	Dark	Rarely burns, tans readily	4–6
6	Black	Never burns, gets deeply pigmented	2–3

If an area of skin burns and peels after sun exposure, it is particularly sensitive. You'll need a higher SPF screen until the area is completely healed. Also, your skin may be temporarily more susceptible to burning if you are using antibiotics, antibacterial soaps or lotions, or tretinoin (Retin-A). The same holds true if you're taking barbiturates or birth control pills.

Which active ingredients do you want in your sunscreen? The choice depends on your skin type and any special sensitivities you may have. Zinc oxide and titanium oxide are thick, opaque sun blockers. They keep out all types of ultraviolet rays. Because they are gloppy and visible, most people use them only on their most sun-sensitive body parts. Those include the bridge of the nose, tops of ears, and shoulders. One of the first chemical sunscreen ingredients to become available was PABA (para-aminobenzoic acid). It works fine, but it can stain clothing. Also, some people break out in a rash and may experience stinging. Many effective PABA-free sunscreens are now on the market.

Are you taking medication? Do you currently have a skin condition? Have you ever had a sunburn reaction to a medication? If you answered yes to any of these, ask your doctor's advice about what sunscreen to use. You may need to avoid certain sunscreen ingredients. Do you develop sun sensitivity when you take thiazide diuretics, furosemide, sulfa drugs, or carbonic anhydrase inhibitors? If so, you shouldn't use sunscreens with PABA, aminobenzoate, menthylanthranilate, or padimate a. Choose an alternative.

The same active sunscreen ingredient may be available in several different preparations. Some are light and alcohol based; others are thicker and creamier. Pick the one that best suits your skin type.

After you've picked the right sunscreen or array of sunscreens for you and your family, make sure you apply them thickly and reapply them often enough. It takes about three tablespoonfuls to cover the average swimsuit-clad adult body. No matter what SPF you choose, reapply water-resistant sunscreen after forty minutes. Reapply waterproof sunscreen after an hour and twenty minutes of swimming, sweating, or heavy exercise. Reapplying a sunscreen does *not* extend the amount of time you are protected. If you use a sunscreen offering five hours of protection, reapplying it after a swim at hour three won't add five more hours. It just ensures that you are protected for the remaining two hours.

If you have fair skin, use sunscreen year-round on exposed parts of your body. Check into sunscreen-containing moisturizers, lip gloss, and foundation.

As you read about protection, you may look back with some regret to the sunning habits of your youth. Cover up now, make it a habit to do a skin self-exam periodically, and ask for a skin check as part of your routine checkups (see page 222). Luckily, most skin cancers develop slowly and can be successfully treated if detected early.

Sunproof Your Children

They may squirm and get impatient when you pull out the sunscreen, but sunproofing your kids can save their lives.

Severe sunburns in childhood have been related to the development of melanomas later in life. Although this usually occurs in older people, it sometimes happens by the teenage years. Some scientists have calculated that people often receive up to half of their total life's exposure to UV light by the age of eighteen. They believe that up to 80 percent of skin damage could be avoided if children used sunscreen.

Parents and teachers can help make sun protection second nature for children. The American Academy of Dermatology and the American Cancer Society bring the message home to kids in kindergarten to third grade with some sun ABC'S:

> *A is for AWAY*—Stay away from the sun in the middle of the day.
> *B is for BLOCK*—Use a number 15 or higher sunblock.
> *C is for COVER UP*—Wear a T-shirt and a hat.
> *S is for SPEAK OUT*—Talk to your family and friends about sun protection.

Protecting kids from too much sun is easier today than ever before. Waterproof sunscreens don't have to be reapplied after every sweaty game or dunk in the pool. Zinc oxide now comes in bright colors that kids love to use on their noses and ears—and you can't find better sun protection. Some sunscreens are even combined with bug repellents. If your children complain about sunscreen, let them help pick the products they are willing to use.

Don't wait until you get to the beach or the ball field to pull out the sunscreen. Sunscreen takes thirty minutes to an hour to penetrate and become fully effective. If you wait, you've already let too many ultraviolet rays get through. Apply sunscreen to your kids at home when they're getting dressed, before they're wearing a layer of scratchy sand. Another benefit of at-home application is that other kids won't tease your children for being fussed over.

AVOID UNNECESSARY X RAYS

> *"I remember being five years old and putting my feet in a special box at the shoe store. There was a greenish light, and I could see my bones right through my shoes and socks. It was magic!"*

Even to adults, X rays are magical. Doctors being able to see inside the body with the help of X-ray vision revolutionized the diagnosis of broken bones, tuberculosis, hidden tooth decay, and breast cancer.

Unfortunately, in the early zeal to use the invisible rays, doctors and others used high doses of radiation on many people. X rays were made en masse to screen for tuberculosis and too-tight shoes. They were also used as therapy for everything from eczema to enlarged tonsils. Later, some of the people who had been X-rayed developed cancer induced by radiation damage to the genetic material in their cells.

Today, most medical and dental X rays are adjusted to deliver the lowest dose possible without sacrificing the quality of the picture obtained. Don't be afraid to take advantage of the information X rays can provide. Do, however, reduce unneeded radiation exposure by asking a few questions whenever your doctor suggests an X ray.

- *Ask what the test will tell and why it will be helpful.* Some X rays became standard procedure as part of presurgical or preemployment physicals, but they are not always warranted. For example, routine chest X ray is no longer considered of medical value. No major health agencies still recommend it. Ask what your doctor is looking for. If you have already had that part of your body X-rayed, be sure to let him or her know. Your old records may have all the necessary information.

  Make sure the X ray isn't being taken just for your peace of mind. Sometimes a physical examination can provide all the information that is needed to treat you properly.
- *Check on the equipment.* How old is it? Has it been inspected recently?
- *Ask for lead shielding, even for a low-dose dental X ray.* You should be offered lead shielding to place over radiation-sensitive areas, such as your thyroid gland and your ovaries or testes.
- *Inform your physician or X-ray technician if you may be pregnant.* A fetus is particularly vulnerable to the adverse effects of radiation.

GET A RADON CHECK

"Our radon test was borderline high. We plugged up the holes from the basement into the crawl space, and that was all it took to make it fine. If it was a finished basement that we spent lots of time in, I'd probably put in a radon pump."

You can't see it, smell it, or taste it, but a radioactive gas may be present in your home. And it can put you and your family at increased risk of lung cancer.

Radon is a radioactive gas created by the natural breakdown of uranium or radium in the soil. Mixed with outdoor air, radon is nothing to worry about. However, you should learn whether the soil in your area contains a high concentration of either of these radioactive elements. Radon gas can seep into your home through drains, cracks, and other openings in the foundation. Once inside, it becomes trapped. Then the radioactive levels can become many times higher than those found outdoors.

Most of our information about radon risk comes from uranium miners who have been exposed to extremely high levels of radioactive gas. The exact risk of lower radon levels is not known. Breathing radon is considered to be the number-one cause of lung cancer in nonsmokers. In smokers, radon greatly enhances the cancer risk.

Your state health department or the state and local offices of the Environmental Protection Agency (EPA) can tell you whether radon is known to be a problem in your area. The EPA can give you information about reliable ways to test your home. It can also tell you how to lower the radon level if it is too high.

What kinds of things are tested for radon? In some areas, radon testing is a routine part of the home inspection before purchase. If you drink well water, it can be tested for the presence of radon. Radon testing is particularly important if you have a child's bedroom in the basement. Generally, radon is more likely to accumulate in the lowest level, either the basement or the first floor.

Sometimes, sealing cracks and blocking off crawl spaces can solve the radon problem. However, you may need to install a special radon pump to ventilate air from the basement to the outside of your home. This is especially necessary if you use the basement as living quarters.

As happens with other carcinogens, the longer the exposure, the greater the risk.

PROTECT AGAINST SEXUALLY TRANSMITTED VIRUSES

"I got divorced when I was fifty. I can hardly believe that if I start dating, I'll have to think about condoms. I can't even get pregnant!"

"I came of age in the sexual revolution, and I want my kids to feel good about their sexuality. But when it comes to condoms, you have to be a hard-nose. Make it clear they have no choice about protecting themselves."

What do AIDS, hepatitis, and genital warts have in common? The three correct answers are all important in protecting your health:

1. Viruses cause all of them.
2. Those affected can pass on the viruses through sexual contact.
3. They all increase your risk of cancer.

Human immunodeficiency virus (HIV) attacks the immune system and can result in AIDS. If you have AIDS, you are at increased risk to develop Kaposi's sarcoma. That type of cancer is rare in people whose immune systems are working properly. If you have AIDS, you are also more likely to develop non-Hodgkin's lymphomas. That's a group of cancers that strike the lymph glands.

Hepatitis B infects the liver. After an initial infection, some people become chronic carriers of the virus. Over many years, it can result in liver damage. That damage can include cirrhosis of the liver and, occasionally, liver cancer. Hepatitis C may produce similar long-term problems in some people. Before the hepatitis C virus was identified, this infection was often diagnosed as non-A, non-B hepatitis. It still hasn't been detectable long enough to have generated good studies lasting many years.

A vaccine is available against hepatitis B. Currently, the Centers for Disease Control and Prevention (CDC) recommends vaccinating all infants. Unless the parents definitely are not infected, the CDC suggests vaccination for children whose parents were born where hepatitis B is common. These areas are southeast Asia, Africa, the Amazon basin, the Pacific Islands, and the Middle East. Adolescents should be vaccinated if they are sexually active or inject drugs. Adults should be vaccinated if they work in health care or any other job that exposes them to human blood. Other adults who may need the vaccine have hemophilia, live with someone who has had a lifelong hepatitis B infection, have more than one sexual partner, or have a sexual partner who has hepatitis B. Adults who inject drugs or plan to travel to areas with a high prevalence of hepatitis B also may need to be vaccinated.

Human papillomavirus (HPV) causes warts. More than seventy types of HPV exist. Some cause warts on the feet. Others are associated with warts on the penis, vulva, or cervix. Researchers have identified a few types of HPV as a principal cause of cervical cancer. (Most women infected with HPV will not develop cervical cancer.) Some research is under way to develop a vaccine to combat HPV. Other research hopes to better understand how HPV encourages formerly normal cells to become cancerous, so the process can be thwarted.

If you have genital warts, they can be removed. A Pap smear can detect whether the virus damaged the cells of your cervix (see page 233). If so, the problem can be treated. The virus itself cannot be eliminated from the body, but it is less likely to cause cell damage if you are well nourished and don't smoke.

It makes sense to protect yourself against all infections that can be sexually transmitted. Having one sexually transmitted disease, such as syphillis, can make you more vulnerable to getting others. Latex condoms can help prevent the transmission of the virus during sexual intercourse. The maturing cells of the cervix of a teenage girl are particularly vulnerable to HPV infection. Therefore, it is particularly important for teens to abstain from sex or to use latex condoms.

Intercourse isn't the only means for passing on these worrisome viruses. HIV and hepatitis viruses can also be passed from mother to child during pregnancy and delivery. Or they can be transmitted through blood transfusions, by sharing contaminated needles, and through breast-feeding. Passing on HPV does not always require the exchange of body fluids. You can have the virus since birth or have it passed to you on an infected towel or piece of clothing.

LOWER THE RISK OF CONGENITAL HEART DEFECTS

In 1 of every 100 births, the infant's heart or the blood vessels near the heart have not developed normally. These infants have what is known as *congenital heart defects*. Thirty-five types of this complex problem have been detected. In many cases, scientists don't know why heart development goes wrong. However, the risk of a congenital heart defect does go up when the fetus is exposed to certain viruses or chemicals.

If you are pregnant or planning to become pregnant soon, follow these suggestions to reduce the risk:

◆ Avoid being exposed to viral infections (especially rubella, also called German measles).

- Don't drink alcohol.
- Don't use recreational drugs, particularly cocaine.
- Don't use any medications not prescribed by a physician who knows you are pregnant or planning to become pregnant.

Heart experts believe that if all pregnant women followed these strategies, a great number of heart defects could be prevented.

Strategies under Study

TRANSLATING GENETIC INFORMATION INTO BETTER PREVENTION

When people study the twentieth century, they may designate it the beginning of the genetic era. Within a few decades, scientists have gone from not understanding even the basic structure of DNA to a mammoth systematic effort to map all the genetic material in humans.

Genetic information is being used to help prevent deaths from heart disease and cancer. If you have a strong family history of breast cancer or colon cancer, your physician is likely to recommend more frequent or more extensive screening tests. If you have high cholesterol, your children can be tested at a young age. That gains for them the advantage of early attention to cholesterol-lowering strategies if they have inherited the same tendency.

Recent research is making it possible to develop specific genetic tests to supplement family history information. These tests look directly for a gene *mutation* that increases the susceptibility to a disease. If you are someday found to have a genetic predisposition to heart disease or cancer, you don't need to have a fatalistic attitude. The information is a signal that you need to take extra precautions with lifestyle factors and to take full advantage of early diagnostic tests.

One of the great appeals of genetic testing is its potential for more precise preventive care. For example, if you are from a family with an inherited form of cancer, finding out you inherited the gene may mean you will seek more frequent cancer checkups. On the other hand, finding out you did *not* inherit the gene may mean a need for *less* rigorous health scrutiny in the future. Knowing that you have a specific genetic tendency toward high cholesterol or high blood pressure may help your doctor select the best medication for the problem.

Various genetic tests are at different stages of development. When you hear that a gene for a specific disease has been identified, that is only the beginning. A test to detect it in an individual may or may not follow. Extensive research is needed before it is determined that a genetic test is feasible, accurate, and helpful, and under what circumstances.

As you hear about genetic tests or consider using them, keep these general principles in mind:

+ *"Genetic" does not mean "untreatable."* Diseases or risk factors—even if they were genetically determined—often can be treated or addressed through lifestyle.
+ *No matter what your genetic legacy, you can benefit from developing a healthful lifestyle and getting good health care.* Heart disease and cancer are complex, common diseases. To a different extent in different people, they are influenced by a variety of genes and environmental factors, including lifestyle.
+ *Genetic tests are not inherently more foolproof than other medical tests.* Ask the same questions about accuracy and usefulness that you would for any other new medical test.
+ *Take advantage of genetic counseling.* If you are concerned about disease risk in your family, a genetic counselor can help you gather information and make the most of existing health-care options.

TAKING AN ASPIRIN A DAY TO KEEP DISEASES AWAY

Aspirin has been around for a century. You probably use it to ease headaches and lower fevers. Recently, aspirin has gained recognition as a potential preventive for heart attacks, stroke, and possibly some cancers.

In 1985 the Food and Drug Administration approved aspirin to help prevent heart attacks in patients who have had one. Despite its low price and over-the-counter availability, aspirin is a very powerful anticlotting substance. A heart attack often involves the formation of a blood clot inside one of the arteries feeding the heart (see page 7). Therefore, giving an anticlotting medication helps prevent a heart attack from happening again. The vast majority of people should be treated with aspirin after a heart attack, heart experts believe. In fact, if you think you may be having a heart attack, one of the best things you can do (along with getting prompt medical attention, of course) is to take an aspirin.

Would it also make sense to give aspirin to healthy people to lower their risk of ever having a heart attack? The question is getting serious research attention, but the answer is not yet in. Balancing what we know and don't know about aspirin, the AHA urges you *not* to start long-term aspirin use on your own to try to prevent heart disease.

In a major test of aspirin's preventive potential, researchers gave a pill every other day to the thousands of doctors participating in the Physicians' Health Study. Half got aspirin; the other half a look-alike placebo. At the end of five years, the group who took aspirin suffered only half as many first heart attacks as the group taking placebos. In that sense, the study was a rousing success.

However, aspirin is not for everyone, and it is not free of side effects. If you have had coronary bypass surgery or angioplasty to open a clogged artery, aspirin may reduce the chance that vessels will clog again. However, in the Physicians' Health Study, aspirin-takers did not have a clean bill of health. Although aspirin lowered the risk from clots, it increased the risk of intestinal bleeding. To a much lesser degree, it also increased the risk of bleeding in the brain. Overall, the aspirin-takers' risk of death from all cardiovascular causes—and from all causes of death combined—was no lower than that of participants who didn't take aspirin.

If, based on your medical history and heart disease risk factors, your physician suggests low-dose aspirin, remember to do the following three things:

1. *Let him or her know if you have liver or kidney disease, an ulcer, high blood pressure, asthma, or any bleeding problems, including bleeding in your gastrointestinal tract.* Some people with these conditions should not take aspirin. Of course, be sure to tell your doctor if you are allergic to aspirin.

As you discuss starting a program of regular aspirin usage, make sure your doctor knows about any other medicines and vitamins you take, including over-the-counter products. Some products can affect your need for aspirin and influence how well the aspirin will work.

2. *Stick with your healthful lifestyle.*

3. *If you need dental work or even the smallest surgical procedure, tell the dentist or physician your aspirin dose.* Aspirin affects clotting and prolongs bleeding. The tendency to bleed will persist for up to ten days after you stop taking aspirin. That's why you need to mention it even if you plan to forgo aspirin on the day of the procedure.

On the cancer side, several intriguing reports have suggested that aspirin may help prevent or inhibit cancers of the digestive tract. Besides restraining blood clotting, aspirin and related antiinflammatory medications inhibit prostaglandins. These hormonelike chemicals are involved in many body processes and are produced in increased amounts in tumors of the colon, lung, and breast.

Small-scale research reports suggested that antiprostaglandin medications might suppress the growth of polyps in people with an inherited tendency to form polyps and get colon cancer. The reports also suggest that people who took aspirin regularly had lower rates of colorectal cancer. The American Cancer Society then conducted a much larger study on aspirin prevention. ACS researchers used a huge database from the Cancer Prevention Study II. It includes lifestyle information collected in 1982 on more than a million Americans, as well as follow-up medical information on them.

Going back into the database for facts about more than 600,000 men and women, ACS researchers found that people who used aspirin more than fifteen times a month were only half as likely to die of colon cancer as those who didn't. Less frequent use of aspirin offered some protection. Taking painkillers that don't work by inhibiting prostaglandins (such as acetaminophen) did not protect, however.

It is still an open question whether aspirin interferes with tumor growth (perhaps by blocking the synthesis of prostaglandins). In the ACS study, aspirin didn't show protection against prostaglandin-related breast or lung tumors. Aspirin may not prevent colon cancer at all. It may, however, make the cancer more likely to be diagnosed—and hence less fatal because it is identified and treated earlier. Such diagnosis is possible because aspirin enhances bleeding from the tumor (see information on colon cancer screening tests on page 219).

Several more studies have now been conducted in different countries. Some but not all of them indicate a protective effect from aspirin. Studies analyzing giving aspirin to people at increased risk of colon cancer are under way. Again, aspirin is not a benign medication. As of now, the American Cancer Society does not believe the evidence is conclusive enough to recommend aspirin for most healthy people. As new research emerges, the organization is looking for answers to three important questions:

1. Do antiprostaglandin medications, such as aspirin, actually inhibit the growth of tumors?
2. If these medications do work, which antiprostaglandin would be the best to take, and what dose should be used?
3. Who should not take antiprostaglandins because of the potential for gastrointestinal bleeding or bleeding into the brain?

WEIGHING THE RISKS AND REWARDS OF HORMONE USE FOR WOMEN

If you are a woman, your body goes through predictable cycles of hormonal changes. These occur from the time you enter puberty until the time you reach menopause. Usually, only pregnancy or hormone treatment can interrupt these cycles. Month after month, your body produces the hormones estrogen and progesterone in a carefully timed sequence. The sequence spurs the release of an egg from the ovaries and thickens the lining of the uterus (the endometrium). That allows the uterus to be prepared if you become pregnant. If you do not, the lining is shed in your menstrual flow. Then the cycle starts again.

When evaluating your risk of breast cancer, your doctor will be interested in the pattern of your menstrual cycles. Studies have suggested that if you had more than forty years of hormonal cycling between your first period and when you entered menopause, you may be at increased risk compared with women who had fewer years of menstrual cycles. If you never go through pregnancy and childbirth, your risk is higher. If you have a child before your late twenties, you have a lower risk than a woman who had a child later or not at all. If you breast-feed, your risk may be lower.

Exactly how your menstrual and pregnancy history translates into cancer risk is not clear. One possibility is that breast tissue is more vulnerable to assault by cancer-causing agents before it fully matures. This process takes place only as your body prepares for breast-feeding during pregnancy. Another possibility is that menstrual history is an indication of how much estrogen is present in your body and that higher estrogen levels encourage cancer growth.

Cancer experts look at the course of women's hormonal life and see a risk in too much estrogen. On the other hand, heart disease experts look at the same lifespan picture and believe that estrogen plays a role in heart disease protection. After women enter menopause, they lose the protective factor (many believe it is estrogen) that keeps their heart disease rates so much lower than men's. Within ten years after your body stops pumping out regular, hefty doses of estrogen, your heart disease risk rivals that of a man.

The answers on hormones and pregnancy remain incomplete. Questions about cancer and heart disease risk and protection are, however, very much on the minds of physicians as they consider prescribing medications to alter the balance of hormones in women's bodies.

Birth Control Pills

When people mention the birth control pill, is danger or safety the first thing that pops into your mind? After an initial euphoria when it was introduced more than a quarter century ago, the Pill's image has vacillated between fashionable and frightening.

Now, with medical information gleaned by tracking women over decades, more information exists than ever before. Put together with an eye toward cancer and heart disease prevention, it tells us several things:

* The Pill is safer today than it used to be.
* Some women should not take the Pill.
* The Pill may help prevent certain cancers.

Effectiveness has never been a problem with the Pill. Composed of various combinations of two female hormones, estrogen and progesterone, the Pill is more than 99 percent effective in preventing pregnancy.

By providing low levels of hormones that mimic pregnancy, the Pill signals the body's hormonal system that the ovaries don't need to release an egg. Furthermore, it tells the hormones they don't need to thicken the lining of the uterus to prepare for a possible new pregnancy that month.

Cancer Concerns

Over the short term, breaking the ovulation cycle prevents unplanned pregnancy. Over the long term, interrupting the relentless cycle of ovulation and growth of the endometrium seems to have a cancer-prevention payoff. In large research studies, five years of using birth control pills cuts a woman's lifetime risk of developing ovarian or endometrial cancer by more than 50 percent. In 1994 a National Institutes of Health consensus panel concluded that the use of oral contraceptives reduces the risk of ovarian cancer.

Nevertheless, concerns remain about the relationship between use of the Pill and breast cancer risk. Overall, the risk does not seem to be increased. However, this is still a very active area of research, and the results to date have not been consistent. Some studies, but not all, have detected an increased risk for premenopausal breast cancer. Some studies noted a higher breast cancer risk in women who took the Pill over a long period of time than in women who didn't. Other studies point to increased risk in women who started the Pill at an early age.

Lower-dose Pills and Pills using progesterone may not have the same risk for cancer as higher-dose Pills and Pills using estrogen. Information on Pill risk over the longest term involves older, higher-dose Pills.

Heart Concerns

When the Pill was introduced, it contained much higher levels of estrogen than today's Pill. Women who used those early Pills were found to have an increased risk of heart disease. That was true especially if they were heavy smokers. High-dose Pills often had an unwelcome effect on women's lipids, raising low-density lipoproteins while lowering high-density lipoproteins. This resulted from the high-dose progesterone component. Women taking high-dose Pills were more likely than those not on the pill to develop high blood pressure and blood clots. These problems are related to the high doses of estrogens. Research also links oral contraceptives with an increased risk of stroke, primarily among women who have high blood pressure and smoke.

Recent studies show that the newer, lower-dose birth control pills are less risky. Physicians today can predict which women are most likely to have side effects and suggest that they choose another contraceptive. Some Pills available today actually lower LDLs and raise HDLs, welcome changes for many women.

To help determine whether birth control pills are the right contraceptive for you, your physician will want to discuss the issues that follow.

♦ *Do you smoke?* If you do, it is very important that you stop smoking or stay off the Pill to avoid a dangerously elevated health risk. In some studies, Pill users who smoke are up to thirty-nine times more likely to have a heart attack than are women who neither smoke nor take the Pill. In the same comparison, the Pill users who smoke also are up to twenty-two times more likely to have a stroke.

♦ *How old are you?* High-dose Pills caused the most heart-related problems in women over age thirty-five. The effect of low-dose Pills on heart disease risk is not clear for women in this age group. Many physicians believe that the Pill is a fine choice if you are under thirty-five, particularly if you don't smoke and don't have high cholesterol or high blood pressure.

The American Fertility Society advises its members that oral contraceptives can be safely used in women over thirty-five unless they smoke, have diabetes, are obese, or have high cholesterol.

♦ *Do you have a family history of ovarian cancer?* If so, that may tilt the balance in favor of the Pill as you choose a contraceptive. Even if no contraceptive is needed, some physicians have begun to prescribe the Pill to help lower the risk for patients whose family history shows a strong tendency toward ovarian cancer.

♦ *What are your risk factors for heart disease?* If you have high blood pressure or high cholesterol or have ever had a problem with blood clots, that may influence the type of Pill your physician recommends. It may also affect whether he or she suggests the Pill at all. You are more likely to develop high blood pressure while taking the Pill if you are overweight. The same is true if you developed high blood pressure during any pregnancies, have kidney problems, or have a family history of high blood pressure.

♦ *Have you had breast cancer?* A personal history of breast cancer is an indication to avoid all hormonal methods of birth control.

If you decide to use oral contraceptives, be sure to get the recommended checkups and blood tests. Some side effects cannot be predicted and would make it dangerous to continue the Pill. An on-the-Pill checkup should include a breast exam, Pap smear, blood pressure check, lipid test that includes triglyceride measurements, and blood test to assess liver function. The latter two tests are needed because taking estrogen raises some women's triglycerides and the Pill can increase the chance of noncancerous liver tumors. Estrogens are particularly dangerous in women with an inherited tendency to have high triglycerides (over 300 mg/dL).

Hormone Replacement Therapy

When you go through menopause, your ovaries gradually stop putting out estrogen. That doesn't leave you entirely without the hormone (your adrenal glands and fat tissues produce a little), but it definitely changes the hormonal picture and the health concerns that emerge.

After menopause, your risk of heart attack begins to rise. In older women, heart disease is the major cause of death. If menopause occurs suddenly because the ovaries and uterus were removed surgically, the rise in risk of heart disease occurs quickly. If menopause happens gradually, that risk goes up more slowly. Other health concerns include the troublesome menopausal symptoms (such as hot flashes and vaginal dryness) that many women experience. A gradual loss of calcium from the bones, leading to an increased risk of bone fractures and osteoporosis in many women, is another concern.

In the 1960s doctors began to prescribe estrogen to counter menopausal symptoms. However, a sometimes-serious side effect emerged from the high doses of estrogen used then. Estrogen stimulates growth of the lining of the uterus, and some women having *hormone replacement therapy* developed endometrial cancer (see page 235). The rate was two to eight times higher than in women not taking the hormones. Women taking high doses of estrogen also seemed to have a higher risk of stroke, heart attack, and angina. Estrogen replacement quickly fell out of favor with women.

Today's estrogen replacement is quite different. As happened with birth control pills, the amount of estrogen has been dramatically reduced. Unless a woman has had a hysterectomy (removal of the uterus), progestin (a synthetic form of the female hormone progesterone) is usually prescribed along with the estrogen. This causes the uterine lining to shed periodically, much as it did before menopause. It also decreases (but does not eliminate) the risk of endometrial cancer.

From a number of studies using low-dose estrogen alone, there is strong evidence that women on hormone replacement therapy gain some important health benefits. Compared with postmenopausal women not on hormones, they were only half as likely to develop heart disease. Also, they had only half as many strokes and a third to a half as many heart attacks. In addition, women on hormones sustained 25 percent fewer bone fractures caused by osteoporosis.

Whether an estrogen-progestin combination is just as beneficial to the heart is still being studied. Several progestins are available, and their effects may vary. The three-year-long PEPI (Postmenopausal Estrogen/Progestin Interventions) trial, sponsored by the National Institutes of Health, tested the influence of different hormone combinations on various heart disease risk factors among 875 women. The results, summarized below, provided some safety reassurance and were very promising in regard to heart disease protection.

1. *Compared with taking a placebo, taking estrogen alone significantly increased the risk of endometrial hyperplasia.* That's a potentially harmful condition that sometimes develops into uterine cancer (see page 235).

However, when either a synthetic or a natural progestin was taken along with the estrogen, the risk of hyperplasia did *not* increase.

2. *Estrogen alone, and all the estrogen/progestin combinations tested, increased levels of HDL cholesterol and decreased levels of LDL cholesterol.* However, estrogen taken alone resulted in the most positive changes.

3. *None of the hormone replacement therapy combinations raised blood pressure.*

Despite the encouraging short-term findings, long-term studies are needed to determine whether the changes in cholesterol levels have a payoff in terms of fewer heart attacks and heart disease deaths. The National Institutes of Health is funding the Women's Health Initiative, under way at forty centers across the country, to track the health of 100,000 postmenopausal women for fifteen years. Meanwhile, another 63,000 women will participate in tests of various preventive strategies: Can a low-fat eating plan prevent breast cancer, colon cancer, and heart disease? Can hormone replacement therapy prevent heart disease and bone fractures due to osteoporosis? Can supplements of calcium and vitamin D prevent osteoporosis and colon cancer? Do these preventive treatments have any long-term side effects?

In the meantime, what's a woman to do? The AHA believes that hormone replacement therapy is quite promising as a long-term protector against heart attack and that it works well to help prevent osteoporosis. Without a clear delineation of the therapy's risks and benefits, however, it is up to you and your physician to discuss your medical history and decide whether hormone replacement therapy is right for you.

The factors below may make you a particularly good candidate for hormone replacement therapy:

♦ If you are at increased risk of heart disease because of high cholesterol, high blood pressure, or other factors;
♦ If you are at increased risk of osteoporosis;
♦ If you are troubled by hot flashes, mood swings, and dryness of the vaginal tissues;
♦ If endometrial cancer is not a concern because your uterus has been removed.

Other factors may make you a poor candidate for hormone replacement therapy. They include whether:

+ You have unexplained vaginal bleeding;
+ You have recently had blood clots form in your blood vessels;
+ You have had breast cancer or uterine cancer;
+ You have active liver disease or impaired liver function.

If you go on hormone replacement therapy, be sure to perform breast self-exams. You'll also need regular cancer-related checkups, including mammograms as recommended. Your doctor may suggest that your checkup should include an endometrial biopsy to test for uterine cancer. That's because Pap smears usually don't find that disease (see page 235 on uterine cancer).

If you are on hormone replacement therapy, your checkup should include a blood pressure check. You'll also need a lipid test with triglyceride measurements, since taking estrogen might boost your triglycerides to dangerous levels. A blood test will assess your liver function (the hormones can increase the chance of noncancerous liver tumors).

Tamoxifen

Tamoxifen is an estrogen look-alike substance with some intriguing properties. In some ways, it acts just like estrogen; in other ways, it doesn't. These properties have proved valuable in cancer treatment and may also aid in prevention.

For example, estrogen promotes the growth of breast cancer cells, but tamoxifen slows or stops the growth of cancer cells in the body. Tamoxifen has been used for many years to treat patients with advanced breast cancer. More recently, it is also being used as an adjuvant, or additional, therapy following surgery for some women with early-stage breast cancer. In these patients, tamoxifen helps prevent the original breast cancer from returning. It also prevents the development of new cancers in the other breast. In addition, researchers are studying whether tamoxifen is useful in treating melanoma and certain other cancers.

Although tamoxifen acts against the effects of estrogen in breast tissue, it mimics estrogen in other body systems—in both positive and negative ways. If you take tamoxifen, you may gain some of the benefits of hormone replacement therapy after menopause, lower blood cholesterol, and slower loss of bone density. However, tamoxifen seems to mimic several of the worrisome properties of estrogen as well. It raises the risk of endometrial cancer by stimulating growth of the uterine lining. It also increases the chance of developing blood clots or liver cancer.

Large studies are under way to test the ability of tamoxifen to prevent breast cancer in women who have an increased risk for developing the disease. Even if it can do so, the studies will need to determine whether there are few enough side effects to warrant confidently recommending its use in healthy women. Studies are also assessing the drug's ability to protect against heart disease and osteoporosis.

HORMONE TREATMENTS FOR MEN

Of all the areas of the body, the prostate gland is where men are most likely to develop cancer. The prostate gland is the walnut-sized male sex gland that wraps around the urethra. That's the tube that empties urine from the bladder. Already the most common cancer in men, prostate cancer is on the rise. About 13 percent of American men will be diagnosed with prostate cancer during their lifetime. About 3 percent will die of the disease.

Prostate cancer is usually very slow growing and is most often detected in older men. It is rare for men to be diagnosed with prostate cancer before the age of forty-five. Most are at least in their seventies. Prostate cancer is more common in African-American men and in men with a family history of the disease.

Efforts to prevent prostate cancer from occurring, or from advancing to a serious stage, have focused on male hormones. Testosterone, the primary male hormone produced by the testes, is converted to a related hormone called dihydrotestosterone (DHT). DHT promotes the growth of the prostate gland—normal growth as well as prostate cancer and a noncancerous enlargement, called *benign prostatic hyperplasia (BPH)*. That condition is common in men over fifty.

When studies have compared prostate cancer rates in large groups of men, those who convert less testosterone to DHT are the ones who have lower rates of prostate cancer.

Since 1992, a medication has been available that keeps testosterone from being transformed into DHT. Called *finasteride* (and sold under the brand name Proscar), the drug is FDA approved for use in men with urinary problems or other symptoms of BPH. More than half a million men have used the drug, which shrinks the prostate.

BPH is not cancer and does not cause cancer. However, because the same hormones influence BPH and prostate cancer, researchers are asking whether giving finasteride to healthy men might prevent cancer.

In the ongoing Prostate Cancer Prevention Trial from the National Cancer Institute, men at centers across the United States are taking a daily dose of either finasteride or a placebo. Over several years, researchers will determine whether men taking the hormone blocker develop prostate cancer at a lower rate than men not receiving the drug. Since finasteride has not been on the market very long, the trial may also help identify any long-term side effects of the medication. That's certainly a big question to answer before considering prescribing something for healthy people to take for many years.

If you have an enlarged prostate, ask your physician whether finasteride might be a good treatment for you. Other approaches include surgery, other medications, or stretching the urethra so urine can flow more easily. Watchful waiting—seeing your doctor regularly but not taking any special action unless symptoms become more troublesome—is another possibility.

As of now, finasteride has not been shown to protect against cancer and is not recommended for use in healthy men.

BOLSTERING PREVENTION WITH VITAMINS

We know for certain that it's healthful to eat plenty of fruits and vegetables. Exactly why is another matter. Nature packages thousands of compounds in the plant leaves, fruits, and roots that we eat. Scientists are actively trying to find which parts might be the key protectants and how they might work.

One focus of interest is a group of vitamins called *antioxidants*. These include vitamin C, vitamin E, the vegetable form of vitamin A (beta-carotene), and selenium, a mineral.

Antioxidants counter oxidation, a chemical process that you can see at work every day. Oxidation turns steel into rust and can turn a pleasant-smelling vegetable oil into something rancid that you can't wait to throw out. In the body, unstable forms of oxygen, called free radicals, can also cause oxidation. Among other things, oxidation can induce unwelcome changes in the DNA that carries genetic information. It can also turn LDL cholesterol into a form that is more damaging to the arteries.

The creation of free radicals is part of living. Our bodies are constantly creating them and then mopping them up. Pollution, aging, eating rancid foods, and smoking boost the amount of free radicals in our bodies. Antioxidants can deactivate free radicals, and diets rich in fruits and vegetables reduce free radicals by providing substantial amounts of antioxidant vitamins. In comparing eating habits from around the world, those with lots of antioxidants have been shown to be beneficial in the prevention of certain cancers, including breast, colon, and lung. In an ongoing study of women nurses in the United States, those with a high intake of beta-carotene or vitamin E have a lower risk of heart disease. Vitamins C and E may help prevent cataracts.

Research is ongoing to detail the benefits of antioxidants. Researchers also are trying to better understand the balance of risks and benefits in taking supplementary antioxidants. To date, the ACS and the AHA believe that the evidence is not definitive that supplements can help prevent cancer and heart disease. The two organizations aren't even sure that supplements are safe to give to healthy people over the long term. In one study, beta-carotene taken in pill form by longtime smokers didn't reduce their risk of getting lung cancer. Most antioxidants are considered nontoxic. However, selenium, though essential, can also be quite dangerous when people eat food with high levels of it. Pregnant women who consume excessive amounts of vitamin A can have babies with serious birth defects.

As scientists do more antioxidant research, the two organizations may offer more-specific suggestions regarding antioxidant vitamins. In the meantime, make sure you are eating foods rich in these and other vitamins. You'll get high levels of beta-carotene in orange and dark green fruits and vegetables, such as broccoli, cantaloupes, carrots, sweet potatoes, pumpkin, and spinach. Citrus fruits, broccoli, peppers, tomatoes, and dark, leafy greens contain high levels of vitamin C. Nuts, some vegetable oils and oil-based margarines, olives, wheat germ, and asparagus supply vitamin E, which is dissolved in fat. Good sources of selenium are fish, meat, shellfish, whole grain cereals, and Brazil nuts.

Vitamin A in another form, retinol, is also the focus of specific research related to cancers involving epithelial cells. These cells line the lungs and make up the surface of the skin and mucous membranes. In laboratory studies, mice and rats fed synthetic retinoids (substances like vitamin A) develop fewer cancers than animals that eat a normal diet. One form of vitamin A has been effective in preventing new tumors in patients who have had cancer of the head and neck. It did not, however, prevent recurrences of the original tumors. Studies are under way to see whether retinoids can help prevent skin, colon, and lung cancers in people at high risk. Workers who were exposed to asbestos for many years would be in this group.

As a treatment for acne or for premature aging of the skin, many people already apply one retinoid, tretinoin, to their skin. Scientists are studying cream and salve forms of tretinoin and other retinoids to see whether they can prevent skin cancer or reverse precancerous changes of the cervix. Although these agents seem to be a promising approach to cancer prevention, much study is needed before scientists can conclude that the agents help prevent cancer in humans.

In some people, retinoids given for acne can markedly elevate triglycerides or reduce HDL cholesterol. Taken for prolonged periods, these regimens may increase heart disease risk.

Prevention Clues under Investigation

WILL HOMOCYSTEINE BE THE NEXT HEART DISEASE PREDICTOR?

When doctors diagnose what is wrong with you, they can hunt for a possible "zebra" or first restrict their search among the "horses." Zebras are one of the rare but fascinating illnesses that might cause your symptoms. Horses are the less flashy but common conditions that are more likely to be the root of your symptoms.

In medical research, sometimes paying close attention to the zebras can provide the best clues about health factors affecting all creatures. Homocysteinuria, an inherited zebra-status condition that affects 1 in every 200,000 people, interferes with the way the body breaks down protein. Children with the disorder are mentally retarded and have serious problems with their eyes and bones. They also have a very high rate of heart disease at a very young age.

When children with this genetic condition eat protein, most of it is broken down perfectly well. The exception is one of protein's amino acids, methionine. That gets stuck once it breaks down into the chemical homocysteine. Because it can't be metabolized any further, homocysteine rises to sky-high levels in the children's blood and urine. Not counting these unusual children, researchers have found that people differ greatly in the levels of homocysteine in their blood. Could moderately high levels also put people at greater risk for heart disease? That's the question researchers are trying to answer, and, tentatively, there seems to be something to it.

In the ongoing Physicians' Health Study, researchers looked at men with homocysteine levels in the top 5 percent of all participants. Compared with men with lower levels, their risk of heart attack was tripled. That's a boost roughly on par with having a cholesterol level in the high 200s.

Several studies have now linked increased homocysteine in the blood with a greater chance of developing heart disease before the age of fifty-five. Preliminary laboratory research suggests a possible reason why. When the inside lining of arteries is damaged, homocysteine seems to misdirect repair efforts toward methods that encourage further blockage (see page 7).

Lifestyle intervention may both lower high homocysteine and lessen the damage that it does to the arteries. Here again, we can thank research on zebras for providing some horse sense for all of us. Treatment for some children with homocysteinuria may include giving them extra B vitamins and restricting the amount of methionine-rich proteins they eat. That means large vitamin doses and pretty unpleasant diet restrictions.

In research on elderly people, those with lower vitamin B in their blood tend to have higher levels of homocysteine. Taking extra B vitamins seems to bring down the homocysteine. Whether it will guard against heart disease remains to be seen.

We are a long way from homocysteine testing or trying to prevent heart disease through the use of B vitamins. In the meantime, the intriguing theory is further incentive to stick with the nutrition recommendations in this book. In case a lower homocysteine level turns out to be better for heart health, you can get to such a level if you eat foods with plenty of B vitamins and eat less meat. (Meat is the largest source of methionine.) Good choices include orange juice, green vegetables, beans, bananas, peas, fish, potatoes, and fortified cereals.

IS IT DANGEROUS FOR CHOLESTEROL TO BE *TOO* LOW?

The link between high cholesterol and heart disease is clear, and so is its lifestyle lesson. The body can make all the cholesterol it needs, and that is a tiny amount. Eating cholesterol- and fat-rich foods isn't necessary or desirable. In general, lowering blood cholesterol reduces the risk of heart attack and death from coronary heart disease. Several studies measuring cholesterol in young people found that the lower the cholesterol, the longer the life span.

However, at least one large study on cholesterol noted that people with the very lowest cholesterol levels, below 160 mg/dL, did not seem to live longer than people with high levels.

This raised an important scientific question that is the subject of ongoing study. However, at this point most heart specialists aren't concerned about the risks of low cholesterol. One reason is that in many countries, a major portion of the population has cholesterol levels in this low range throughout life—and without serious health problems. (In the United States, fewer than 6 percent of the population have cholesterol levels below 160 mg/dL). Also, it isn't necessary to reduce cholesterol below 160 mg/dL with medication or lifestyle changes to lower the risk of heart disease.

As in almost everything else, extremes in cholesterol levels aren't desirable, however. Most health factors show the same pattern of greater risk at both very high and very low levels. If your blood pressure is high, you are at risk for stroke, heart attack, and kidney damage. In general, the lower your blood pressure, the better. Extremely low blood pressure, however, is often caused by illness. The same is true for weight. In general, the heavier you are, the greater your risk for heart disease. However, the thinnest people tend to have a variety of medical problems, including cancer and thyroid disease. The illnesses often caused the weight loss, not the other way around. Blood cholesterol, like blood pressure and weight, is best at a low, but not exceptionally low, level. Very sick people have lower cholesterol.

Cancer, a hyperactive thyroid, some lung diseases, and liver disease can all lower cholesterol levels. The relationship of low cholesterol and mortality that some research studies have found may primarily reflect the presence of these serious diseases in a small segment of the population. It may be that the disease, not the low cholesterol, came first. However, it will take further study to find whether a true hazard to cholesterol lowering exists.

CAN TOO MUCH IRON HARM YOUR HEART?

When most scientists examine the gender gap in heart disease between men and premenopausal women, they think about the protective effects of estrogen. However, another theory has been around since the early 1980s. This theory holds that women are protected because iron is lost during each menstrual flow, and men are at greater risk, not because of their gender or their hormones, but because they have excess iron.

So far, ongoing research on the iron-excess theory has been contradictory. There can be no definite answer until more research has been done.

Iron is an important nutrient, especially for children and others who engage in intense physical activity, women who experience heavy menstrual bleeding, and anyone with a medical condition that results in excessive bleeding. The American Heart Association believes that more research is needed on the relationship between iron status and heart disease. Based on the studies available now, the organization does *not* recommend that you specifically set out to reduce your iron intake. However, if you have cut back on the amount of red meat you eat, you have already reduced one source of iron that is easily absorbed and stored by the body. If you take iron supplements for any reason, you may wish to discuss their health risks and benefits with your physician, particularly if you have high levels of LDL cholesterol.

CAN STRESS MAKE YOU SICK?

If you are angry, tense, or fearful, you feel it in your body. The classic fight-or-flight response is one well-understood example. When you are faced with an immediate danger, such as an approaching guard dog or the sight of your child nearing a busy street, your body reacts in a predictable way. You breathe faster and your heart pumps harder. Also, your blood vessels widen so that more blood goes to the large arm and leg muscles you need to use right now. Blood is shunted away from the organs that perform functions that can wait until later, such as digestion. After the danger is past, your hormones and body functions usually return to normal.

But what if the dangers and stresses of your life *don't* go away? You live uneasily from paycheck to paycheck. You juggle responsibilities for children and relatives in ill health. You are angry at the way your boss treats you but don't feel free to speak up or leave your job. Driving on busy roads makes you tense and frightened.

The effects of these types of ongoing stress on your body and mind are less well understood and less predictable. The complex links between stress, our emotions, our life situations, and our physical health are a source of great interest to both cancer and heart disease researchers.

An exciting and ongoing area of cancer research focuses on the impact of stress on hormones and on the immune and endocrine systems. *No* proof currently exists that shows that personality traits will cause cancer or that people under stress are more likely to develop cancer. Overstating possible links between personality and cancer has increased both the stress and the distress of many cancer patients who feel they are being blamed for their illness.

Research continues in this area, however. Just a few years ago, discussion of stress and heart disease focused on the so-called Type A personality, an intense, stressed-out (or stress-seeking) workaholic. This hypothesis has now been refined to focus on a measurable pattern of hostility and anger. In ongoing research, this pattern shows important links with the risk of coronary heart disease and with various heart disease risk factors (smoking, high blood pressure, and high cholesterol levels). It has not been proved that your personality or reaction to stress is a heart disease risk factor in and of itself. However, stress becomes problematic if you cope with it by taking up unhealthful habits.

If you are concerned about the relationship between stress and your health, try to find healthful ways to relieve stress. Don't overeat, don't smoke, and don't stop exercising. Instead, take the time to prepare and eat healthful foods, talk to friends, do a combination of vigorous and calming exercises, and breathe deeply to take in clean air instead of smoke.

And don't add the fear of stress to the stresses in your life. A lack of challenge and stimulation in your life isn't healthful. Stress isn't necessarily a bad thing—it's more in how you handle it. Stress includes physical effort or preparation—your body primed before a race or before throwing a baseball—and the welcome heightened attention and clarity you feel when you focus on an important test or project. It's often helpful to learn techniques to keep your attention focused, rather than being pulled in many directions.

DO EARLY CANCERS LEAVE TELLTALE SIGNS IN THE BLOOD?

For years, hints that our blood may carry the secret of whether cancer is growing in our bodies have tantalized us. A general screening test for cancer would help prevent serious illness and death, since the earlier cancer is detected, the better the chance for successful treatment.

So far, the one-test cancer test has been elusive. Some tests are not *specific* enough. They are positive when people have cancer but are also positive when some other medical conditions exist. Sometimes they're positive even in healthy people. This kind of mistake is called a false positive. Other tests are not *sensitive* enough. These tests can be negative even when a person is known to have cancer. This kind of mistake is called a false negative.

As an example, both these problems have limited researchers' enthusiasm regarding one widely publicized blood test, the *CEA test*. It measures a substance called *carcinoembryonic antigen,* which is present in the blood of some patients with cancer. In general, a higher CEA level suggests a higher amount of tumor activity. CEA, along with other tests, can be very helpful as an indication that a previously treated cancer has recurred. However, it is not currently a good test for healthy people.

Some people known to have cancer have normal results on the CEA test. On the other hand, some people without cancer have abnormal CEA tests. The latter group includes smokers; people with ulcerative colitis, liver disease, chronic lung disease, or benign tumors; and even some people in perfect health.

Likewise, other early detection tests for cancer have not proved specific and sensitive enough to be helpful. A lack of specificity is the problem with the CA 125 test for ovarian cancer (see page 228). The test is positive in women who are pregnant or who have pelvic inflammatory disease, endometriosis, or hepatitis, as well as in those with ovarian cancer. The *TPA test* measures *tissue polypeptide antigen,* a substance secreted into the blood and urine when cells are dividing rapidly. A majority of patients with certain tumors have elevated TPA. However, the test misses more than one in four patients and is falsely positive in about 10 percent of healthy people. The *GT-II test* looks for an enzyme that seems to be shed into the blood from the surface of tumor cells. It is rarely detected in the blood of healthy people but fails to detect more than one in four persons with cancer. GT-II is being studied to see whether it can be used with other tests to provide early detection of pancreatic cancer.

Are the Air You Breathe and the Water You Drink Dangerous?

This book has been written because the American Heart Association and the American Cancer Society believe that you can personally take control over many of the risk factors for heart disease and cancer. But what about possible hazards that you, as an individual, can't easily assess or influence? What might be lurking in the environment?

Evaluating the possible health hazards posed by environmental factors is a continuing focus of cancer and heart disease research. Two indoor pollutants, radon and environmental tobacco smoke, have already been related to cancer and/or heart disease risk (see pages 265 and 41). Research has led to warnings about workplace hazards and how to avoid them.

When experts look at studies trying to assess environmental risks and propose safety precautions, they seek two types of information. The first, *hazard identification*, evaluates the toxicity of a chemical or other hazard. This includes laboratory testing using animals or cell cultures, under precise conditions and with measured amounts of the substance in question. It also includes observing what has happened to people known to be exposed (epidemiology studies). Special emphasis is given to evidence suggesting that the cancer risk goes up with the amount of a substance a person or animal is exposed to. This is called a dose-response relationship.

If a potential hazard is identified, the second step is to *measure exposure*. This determines how much of the substance is present in air, water, workplaces, food, medications, and other sources where people are likely to be exposed. The true carcinogenic dose depends on how the body interacts with the substance. Is it absorbed into the body? Does it reach the organs that may be the most vulnerable to damage? Is it metabolized, or chemically changed, in the body in a way that makes it more or less powerful? Can the body get rid of it, or is it stored in body tissues so that the true levels build up with time? For example, if a dandruff treatment included an ingredient that caused cancer when fed to laboratory animals, that would ring enough alarm bells to warrant further study. If it was then found that the ingredient cannot penetrate the skin of the scalp, scientists would be less concerned.

Answers to these questions will determine how scientists assess the risk to humans and what they suggest should be done. At stages in the process, when no direct evidence exists, scientists make their best guess based on the information at hand. To be on the safe side in evaluating incomplete information, it is common to assume that if a substance is toxic to animals, it will also be toxic to humans. Another safe assumption is that the damage a substance causes at high doses is an indication of the damage that might be expected at low doses in susceptible individuals. Occasionally, a scientific opinion or cautionary statement based on these assumptions will be altered later on, when more-specific evidence is available.

Evaluating What You Read

When you hear about the latest diet of the week or danger of the week, how do you know whether to worry? Should you alter your lifestyle because of the information? Here's some advice from doctors about how they evaluate new research:

- *Don't make too much of a single study.* The statistical standard for calling a finding "significant" is a probability of less than 1 in 20 that an association could have happened strictly by accident. In other words, there's a small chance in any study—no matter how well designed— that the results were simply a fluke and no real association exists. A single study should almost always be thought of as preliminary.
- *Look for a consistent pattern of results.* Do studies by different researchers show the same association? Has the research been done in both men and women, in people of different races, and in people of various ages? If so, it's time to start paying attention. Medical experts look for a growing body of evidence pointing in the same direction.
- *Does a study make biological sense?* With what we know about carcinogens, information about tobacco smoke makes sense. With what we know about the development of atherosclerosis, information about fat consumption makes sense. Cancer development is a slow process. That's why a study suggesting that you are more likely to be diagnosed with cancer today because of something you ate or did just last weekend wouldn't seem to make biological sense. Or if a study came out linking something totally off-the-wall with heart disease or cancer, such as having a hangnail causing heart attack or wearing purple gloves causing skin cancer, the scientists need to offer you a plausible explanation why. There may be one: Wait for it.
- *Could the real factor be hidden?* Sometimes we look at the factor we're interested in and ignore the bigger picture. Let's say a study showed that people taking a prescription medication for acne were less likely to die of skin cancer. One conclusion is that something in the medication is a cancer protector. That's worth looking into further. But it might also be that these patients developed fewer fatal cancers

because they were regularly examined by a dermatologist, so any cancers that developed were detected and treated early.

The possibility of hidden factors is one reason for the American Cancer Society and the American Heart Association being so cautious about research on nutrition. Foods are complex, containing some factors that are well understood and others that may be just as important but are not as well studied. If a study said that people who eat plenty of oranges are protected from a certain illness, you might therefore wonder whether vitamin C was the crucial factor. It might be, and it might not. Another nutrient or a particular combination of nutrients might be just as important. Vitamin or nutrient supplements may not deliver the same benefits as eating the "whole" food they were derived from.

◆ *Is a new test both* sensitive *and* specific? (See page 287.) When you read about research on new cancer or heart disease tests, look for a full disclosure of the percentage of false positives and false negatives. Be especially sure to do this if you are offered an early-detection blood test.

Finally, please take advantage of the resources of the AHA and the ACS. The lifestyle information presented in this book is solid. We have recommended the basic eating plan and lifestyle advice for years, and new research continues to make a stronger and stronger case for its preventive value. Because both organizations take a cautious approach to research findings, you won't need to worry that they'll give you advice today only to reverse their recommendations tomorrow.

Do you have questions about cancer or heart disease research or a particular prevention strategy? If you do, feel free to call the American Heart Association at 1-800-AHA-USA1 (1-800-242-8721) or the American Cancer Society at 1-800-ACS-2345 (1-800-227-2345).

Afterword

YOU CAN PUT THIS BOOK INTO ACTION IN THOUSANDS OF WAYS.

Use the combination of approaches and tools that is personally right for you. If you have medical questions or restrictions, ask your health-care provider for advice about how to adapt the information in this book to your needs.

As you weave healthful changes into your lifestyle, you will make the exhilarating discovery that each change makes the others easier. Stopping smoking makes exercise easier. Exercise makes it easier to maintain a healthful weight. Eating healthfully and not being over-weight give you more energy.

Living a healthful lifestyle does not demand drastic changes. You don't have to deprive yourself of good food or devote all your leisure time and attention to making yourself healthier. Moderate changes may alter your health outlook significantly. After you have integrated them into your life, you can take your focus off tomorrow's health and just appreciate how good they make you feel today.

Savor your newfound energy, your freedom from tobacco, your appreciation for wholesome foods, and your greater understanding of the workings and care of your body.

Congratulations! *You* made it happen.

Glossary

Angina pectoris Medical term for chest pain due to coronary heart disease. A condition in which the heart muscle doesn't receive enough blood, resulting in pain in the chest. Also called angina.

Angioplasty A procedure sometimes used to dilate (widen) narrowed arteries. A catheter with a deflated balloon on its tip is passed into the narrowed artery segment, the balloon inflated, and the narrowed segment widened.

Antigen A protein or foreign agent that stimulates the formation of antibodies in the body. Some cancer cells have unique antigens that the body recognizes as foreign.

Antioxidants Compounds that inhibit oxidation and are thought to reduce the risk of some cancers and heart disease. Examples are beta-carotene and vitamins C and E.

Arrhythmia (or **dysrhythmia**) An abnormal rhythm of the heart.

Artery Any one of a series of blood vessels that carry blood from the heart to the various parts of the body. Arteries have thick, elastic walls that can expand as blood flows through them.

Atherosclerosis A condition in which the inner layers of artery walls become thick and irregular due to deposits of fat, cholesterol, and other substances. This buildup is sometimes called plaque. As the interior walls of arteries become lined with layers of these deposits, the arteries become narrowed, and the flow of blood through them is reduced.

293

Basal cell cancer   A common form of skin cancer. Basal cell carcinoma grows slowly, seldom spreads to other areas of the body, and is easily detected and cured when treated promptly.

Benign tumor   An abnormal growth that is not cancer and does not spread to other areas of the body.

Beta-carotene   A precursor of vitamin A that is found mainly in yellow and orange vegetables and fruits; it functions as an antioxidant and may be important in cancer prevention. Beta-carotene is a member of a larger family of vitamin A-like compounds, the retinoids.

Biopsy   The removal of a small piece of tissue for microscopic examination to determine whether cancer cells are present. Biopsies can be done with a needle or through an open incision.

Blood clot   A jellylike mass of blood tissue formed by clotting factors in the blood. This clot can then stop the flow of blood from an injury. Blood clots also can form inside an artery whose walls are damaged by atherosclerotic buildup and can cause a heart attack or stroke.

Blood pressure   The force or pressure exerted by the heart in pumping blood; the pressure of blood in the arteries.

Cancer   A general term for more than a hundred diseases, all characterized by uncontrolled growth and spread of abnormal cells. Cancer cells invade and destroy surrounding tissue; they eventually spread via the lymph system or bloodstream to distant areas of the body (see **malignant tumor; metastasis**).

Cancer cell   A cell that divides and reproduces abnormally.

Carcinogen   Any agent—chemical, physical, or viral—that causes cancer. For example, tobacco smoke is a carcinogen.

Cardiac   Pertaining to the heart.

Cardiac arrest   The stopping of the heartbeat, usually because of interference with the electrical signal (often associated with coronary heart disease).

Cardiovascular   Pertaining to the heart and blood vessels. (*Cardio* means heart; *vascular* means blood vessels.) The circulatory system of the heart and blood vessels is the cardiovascular system.

Carotid artery   A major artery in the neck.

Catheterization   The process of examining the heart by introducing a thin tube (catheter) into a vein or artery and passing it into the heart.

Cholesterol   A fatlike substance found in animal tissue and present only in foods from animal sources, such as whole-milk dairy products, meat, fish, poultry, animal fats, and egg yolks.

Clinical trial   Scientific studies in humans to determine the usefulness or toxicity of medicines or procedures for the prevention, diagnosis, or treatment of disease. Clinical trials are usually conducted after those experiments and preliminary studies in animals that suggest usefulness and safety.

Colonoscopy   A technique used to examine the entire colon visually by means of a flexible instrument with a light. This procedure may also obtain biopsy specimens of suspicious tissue, such as colon polyps.

Congenital   Refers to conditions existing at birth.

Congenital heart defects   Malformation of the heart or of its major blood vessels present at birth.

Congestive heart failure   The inability of the heart to pump out all the blood that returns to it. This results in blood backing up in the veins that lead to the heart and sometimes in fluid accumulating in various parts of the body.

Coronary arteries   Two arteries arising from the aorta that arch down over the top of the heart, branch, and provide blood to the heart muscle.

Coronary bypass surgery   Surgery to improve blood supply to the heart muscle. This surgery is most often performed when narrowed coronary arteries reduce the flow of oxygen-containing blood to the heart itself.

Coronary heart disease   Disease of the heart caused by atherosclerotic narrowing of the coronary arteries likely to produce angina pectoris or heart attack; a general term.

Diabetes   A disease in which the body doesn't produce or properly use insulin. Insulin is needed to convert sugar and starch into the energy needed in daily life. The full name for this condition is diabetes mellitus.

Diastolic blood pressure   The lowest blood pressure measured in the arteries, it occurs when the heart muscle is relaxed between beats.

Diuretic   A drug that increases the rate at which urine forms by promoting the excretion of water and salts.

DNA   Deoxyribonucleic acid, the self-reproducing component of chromosomes and many viruses. DNA consists of a sugar-phosphate backbone and four chemicals called purine/pyrimidine bases. The sequence of the bases makes up a code that determines the hereditary characteristics of the organism. The average gene is about 1,500 bases long.

Electrocardiogram (**ECG** or **EKG**)   A graphic record of electrical impulses produced by the heart.

Endocarditis   An infection of the heart lining or valves. People with abnormal heart valves or congenital heart defects are at increased risk of developing this disease.

Enzyme   Proteins that are capable of speeding up the rate of specific chemical reactions in living cells.

Fibrin   A protein in the blood that enmeshes blood cells and other substances during blood clotting.

Finasteride   A drug that interferes with testosterone metabolism, used to treat enlarged prostate glands. A clinical trial is under way to evaluate finasteride in preventing prostate cancer.

Gene   A unit of heredity. Individuals have about 100,000 genes, each of which determines the sequence of amino acids needed to form a specific protein or enzyme.

Heart attack   Death of, or damage to, part of the heart muscle due to an insufficient blood supply.

Heredity   The genetic transmission of a particular quality or trait from parent to offspring.

High blood pressure   A chronic increase in blood pressure above its normal range.

High-density lipoprotein (HDL)   A carrier of cholesterol believed to transport cholesterol away from the tissues and to the liver, where it can be removed from the bloodstream.

Hormone   Substance produced and released by one tissue that affects another tissue's growth, metabolism, and reproduction. Manipulating the concentrations of hormones is one method of treatment for hormone-dependent cancers, such as breast and prostate.

Hormone replacement therapy (HRT)   Usually refers to the hormones taken by women to relieve menopausal symptoms and prevent osteoporosis (bone thinning). However, it can apply to any hormones taken to replace those that are lost due to surgery or other causes.

Hypertension   Same as high blood pressure.

Initiator   A substance that can lead to cancer by causing a mutation, or irreversible genetic damage, in a cell (as opposed to "promoter").

In situ   In place; localized and confined to one area. A very early stage of cancer.

Lipid   A fatty substance insoluble in blood.

Lipoprotein The combination of lipid surrounded by a protein; the protein makes it soluble in blood.

Low-density lipoprotein (LDL) The main carrier of "harmful" cholesterol in the blood.

Lymph A fluid circulating throughout the body (in the lymphatic system) that contains white blood cells and antibodies. It is important in fighting foreign materials and infections.

Lymph nodes Collections of lymphocytes that produce lymph. They normally act as filters of impurities in the body. (Sometimes called lymph glands.)

Malignant tumor A mass of cancer cells. A malignant tumor invades surrounding tissues and has the potential to spread to distant areas of the body (see **metastasis**).

Mammography X-ray examination of the breast to detect breast cancer at an early stage.

Melanoma A type of skin cancer originating from the cells that produce skin pigmentation. Although most skin cancers rarely spread to other areas of the body and are easily treated and cured, melanoma can be more dangerous if not detected early.

Metastasis The spread of cancer cells to distant areas of the body by way of the lymph system or bloodstream. The term *metastases* refers to these new cancer sites.

Monounsaturated fat A type of fat found in many foods but predominantly in canola, olive, and peanut oils and avocados.

Mutation An alteration, or permanent change, in a sequence of DNA. Mutations can be caused by environmental carcinogens or can occur as the result of random mistakes made during cell division.

Myocardial infarction The damaging or death of an area of the heart muscle (myocardium) resulting from a blocked blood supply to that area. A heart attack.

Myocarditis An infection of the muscular wall of the heart. The wall contracts to pump blood out of the heart and then relaxes as the heart refills with returning blood.

Neoplasia The formation of any new abnormal growth. May be benign or malignant.

Obesity The condition of being significantly overweight. It's usually applied to a condition of 20 percent or more over ideal body weight. Obesity puts a strain on the heart and can increase the chance of developing high blood pressure and diabetes.

Oncogene   One of the sixty or more genes necessary for normal cell growth, division, or differentiation that has been altered by mutation so that it is expressed in a different form or amount. Usually only one gene of the normal pair has to be mutated to have a cancer-causing effect.

Pap test (Pap smear)   A simple, widely used method of taking a sample of cells from a woman's cervix to check for early signs of cancer.

Pericarditis   Inflammation of the outer membrane surrounding the heart.

Plaque   A deposit of fatty (and other) substances in the inner lining of the artery wall characteristic of atherosclerosis.

Platelet   A cellular component of the blood that is necessary for blood clotting.

Polyps   An abnormal growth of tissue that lines a cavity, such as the colon, nose, or vocal cords. Polyps can be benign or malignant; in the colon, benign polyps can be the precursors of colon cancer.

Polyunsaturated fats   Oils of vegetable origin, such as corn, safflower, sunflower, and soybean, that are liquid at room temperature.

Precancerous   Abnormal cellular changes that are potentially capable of becoming cancer. These early lesions are very treatable.

Promoter   A substance that increases the chance that cancer will develop, either by causing increased division of a cell that has already undergone mutation or by increasing the chances that a cancer-causing mutation will occur. Promoters are not in themselves carcinogenic; estrogen is believed to be a promoter of breast cancer.

Prostate-specific antigen (PSA)   A protein present on dividing prostate cells that is found in the bloodstream in especially high levels in prostate cancer patients, often before any other symptoms are present.

Radon   A radioactive gas that is emitted from soil and sometimes accumulates inside houses.

Retinoids   Vitamin A and synthetic compounds similar to vitamin A.

Saturated fats   Types of fat found in foods of animal origin and a few of vegetable origin; they are typically solid at room temperature.

Sigmoidoscopy   The visual inspection of the rectum and lower colon by a tubular instrument called a sigmoidoscope that is passed through the rectum. The instrument may be either rigid or flexible.

Sodium   An element essential to life found in nearly all plant and animal tissue. Table salt (sodium chloride) is nearly half sodium.

Sphygmomanometer   An instrument for measuring blood pressure.

Squamous cell cancer   A form of skin cancer that usually appears as red, scaly patches or modules, typically on lips, face, or tips of ears. It can spread to other parts of the body if left untreated.

Stress   Bodily or mental tension within a person resulting from his or her response to physical, chemical, or emotional factors. Stress can refer to physical exertion as well as mental anxiety.

Stroke (also called apoplexy, cerebrovascular accident, or cerebral vascular accident)   Loss of muscle function, vision, sensation, or speech resulting from brain cell damage caused by an insufficient supply of blood to part of the brain.

Systolic blood pressure   The highest blood pressure measured in the arteries. It occurs when the heart contracts with each heartbeat.

Tamoxifen   An antiestrogen drug used in treating breast cancer. Tamoxifen binds to estrogen receptors in cells and prevents the stimulation of growth by estrogen. Tamoxifen is now undergoing testing as a breast cancer preventive in high-risk women.

Thrombus   A blood clot that forms inside a blood vessel or cavity of the heart.

Tissue   A collection of cells of similar type. Four basic types of tissue exist in the body: epithelial (skin, lining of organs, glands), connective (bone, cartilage), muscle, and nerve.

Transient ischemic attack (TIA)   A temporary strokelike event that lasts for only a short time and is caused by a temporarily blocked blood vessel.

Tumor   An abnormal tissue swelling or mass; can be either benign or malignant.

Ultrasound   High-frequency sound vibrations, not audible to the human ear, used in medical diagnosis.

Vascular   Pertaining to blood vessels.

Vein   Any one of a series of blood vessels of the vascular system that carries blood from various parts of the body back to the heart.

Virus   Tiny organisms that invade cells, alter the cells' chemistry, and cause them to produce more viruses. Viruses are the cause of many diseases and are associated with liver cancer, cervical cancer, Burkett's lymphoma, and a form of T-cell leukemia.

X ray   Radiant energy used to diagnose and treat disease, such as cancer. High doses of X rays can kill cancer cells.

FOR FURTHER INFORMATION ABOUT AMERICAN HEART ASSOCIATION
PROGRAMS AND SERVICES, CALL **1-800-AHA-USA1** OR CONTACT
US ONLINE AT **http://www.amhrt.org.**

American Heart Association
National Center
7272 Greenville Avenue
Dallas, TX 75231-4596
214-373-6300

Affiliates

AHA, Alabama Affiliate, Inc.
1449 Medical Park Drive
Birmingham, AL 35213
205-592-7100

AHA, Alaska Affiliate, Inc.
2330 East 42nd Avenue
Anchorage, AK 99508
907-563-3111

AHA, Arizona Affiliate, Inc.
2929 S. 48th Street
Tempe, AZ 85282
602-414-5353

AHA, Arkansas Affiliate, Inc.
909 West 2nd Street
Little Rock, AR 72201
501-375-9148

AHA, California Affiliate, Inc.
1710 Gilbreth Road
Burlingame, CA 94010
415-259-6700

**AHA of Metropolitan
Chicago, Inc.**
208 South LaSalle Street,
Suite 900
Chicago, IL 60604-1197
312-346-4675

**AHA of Colorado/Wyoming,
Inc.**
1280 S. Parker Road
Denver, CO 80231
303-369-5433

**AHA, Connecticut Affiliate,
Inc.**
5 Brookside Drive
Wallingford, CT 06492
203-294-0088

AHA, Dakota Affiliate, Inc.
1005 Twelfth Avenue, S.E.
Jamestown, ND 58401
701-252-5122

AHA, Delaware Affiliate, Inc.
1096 Old Churchmans Road
Newark, DE 19713
302-633-0200

AHA, Florida Affiliate, Inc.
1213 16th Street North
St. Petersburg, FL 33705-1092
813-894-7400

AHA, Georgia Affiliate, Inc.
1685 Terrell Mill Road
Marietta, GA 30067
770-952-1316

AHA, Hawaii Affiliate, Inc.
245 North Kukui Street, Suite
204
Honolulu, HI 96817
808-538-7021

AHA of Idaho/Montana
270 South Orchard, Suite B
Boise, ID 83705
208-384-5066

AHA, Illinois Affiliate, Inc.
1181 North Dirksen Parkway
Springfield, IL 62708
217-525-1350

AHA, Indiana Affiliate, Inc.
8645 Guion Road, Suite H
Indianapolis, IN 46268
317-876-4850

AHA, Iowa Affiliate, Inc.
1111 Ninth Street, Suite 280
Des Moines, IA 50314
515-244-3278

AHA, Kansas Affiliate, Inc.
5375 S.W. 7th Street
Topeka, KS 66606
913-272-7056

AHA, Kentucky Affiliate, Inc.
333 Guthrie Street, Suite 207
Louisville, KY 40202-1899
502-587-8641

**AHA, Greater Los Angeles
Affiliate, Inc.**
1055 Wilshire Blvd., Ninth
Floor
Los Angeles, CA 90017
213-580-1408

AHA, Louisiana Affiliate, Inc.
105 Campus Drive East
Destrehan, LA 70047
504-764-8711

AHA, Maine Affiliate, Inc.
20 Winter Street
Augusta, ME 04330
207-623-8432

AHA, Maryland Affiliate, Inc.
415 N. Charles Street
Baltimore, MD 21201-4441
410-685-7074

**AHA, Massachusetts Affiliate,
Inc.**
20 Speen Street
Framingham, MA 01701
508-620-1700

AHA, Michigan Affiliate, Inc.
16310 West Twelve Mile Road
Lathrup Village, MI 48076
810-557-9500

AHA, Minnesota Affiliate, Inc.
4701 West 77th Street
Minneapolis, MN 55435
612-835-3300

**AHA, Mississippi Affiliate,
Inc.**
4830 McWillie Circle
Jackson, MS 39206
601-981-4721

AHA, Missouri Affiliate, Inc.
4643 Lindell Boulevard
St. Louis, MO 63108
314-367-3383

AHA, Nation's Capital Affiliate, Inc.
5335 Wisconsin Avenue, N.W., Suite 940
Washington, DC 20015
202-686-6888

AHA, Nebraska Affiliate, Inc.
3624 Farnam
Omaha, NE 68131
402-346-0771

AHA, Nevada Affiliate, Inc.
6370 West Flamingo, Suite 1
Las Vegas, NV 89103
702-367-1366

AHA, New Hampshire/ Vermont Affiliate, Inc.
20 Merrimack Street, Suite 1
Manchester, NH 03101-2244
603-669-5833

AHA, New Jersey Affiliate, Inc.
2550 Route 1
North Brunswick, NJ 08902
908-821-2610

AHA, New Mexico Affiliate, Inc.
1330 San Pedro N.E., Suite 105
Albuquerque, NM 87110
505-268-3711

AHA, New York City Affiliate, Inc.
122 East 42nd Street, 18th Floor
New York, NY 10168
212-661-5335

AHA, New York State Affiliate, Inc.
100 Northern Concourse
North Syracuse, NY 13212
315-454-8166

AHA, North Carolina Affiliate, Inc.
300 Silver Cedar Court
Chapel Hill, NC 27515
919-968-4453

AHA, Northeast Ohio Affiliate, Inc.
1689 East 115th Street
Cleveland, OH 44106
216-791-7500

AHA, Ohio Affiliate, Inc.
5455 North High Street
Columbus, OH 43214
614-848-6676

AHA, Oklahoma Affiliate, Inc.
3545 N.W. 58th Street, Suite 400C
Oklahoma City, OK 73112
405-942-2444

AHA, Oregon Affiliate, Inc.
1425 N.E. Irving #100
Portland, OR 97232-4201
503-233-0100

AHA, Pennsylvania Affiliate, Inc.
Pennsboro Center, 1019 Mumma Road
Wormleysburg, PA 17043
717-975-4800

Puerto Rico Heart Association, Inc.
Cabo Alverio 554
Hato Rey, Puerto Rico 00918
809-751-6595

AHA, Rhode Island Affiliate, Inc.
40 Broad Street
Pawtucket, RI 02860
401-728-5300

AHA, South Carolina Affiliate, Inc.
400 Percival Road

Columbia, SC 29206
803-738-9540

AHA, Southeastern Pennsylvania Affiliate, Inc.
625 West Ridge Pike, Building A, Suite 100
Conshohocken, PA 19428
610-940-9540

AHA, Tennessee Affiliate, Inc.
1200 Division Street, Suite 201
Nashville, TN 37203-4012
615-726-0108

AHA, Texas Affiliate, Inc.
1700 Rutherford Lane
Austin, TX 78754
512-433-7220

AHA, Utah Affiliate, Inc.
645E-400S
Salt Lake City, UT 84102
801-322-5601

AHA, Virginia Affiliate, Inc.
4217 Park Place Court
Glen Allen, VA 23060
804-747-8334

AHA, Washington Affiliate, Inc.
4414 Woodland Park Avenue North
Seattle, WA 98103
206-632-6881

AHA, West Virginia Affiliate, Inc.
211 35th Street, S.E.
Charleston, WV 25304
304-346-5381

AHA, Wisconsin Affiliate, Inc.
795 North Van Buren Street
Milwaukee, WI 53202
414-271-9999

For FURTHER INFORMATION ABOUT AMERICAN CANCER SOCIETY
PROGRAMS AND SERVICES, CALL **1-800-ACS-2345** OR CONTACT US
ONLINE AT http://www.cancer.org.

American Cancer Society
National Home Office
1599 Clifton Road, NE
Atlanta, GA 30329-4251
404-320-3333

Chartered Divisions

Alabama Division, Inc.
504 Brookwood Boulevard
Homewood, AL 35209
205-879-2242

Alaska Division, Inc.
1057 West Fireweed Lane
Suite 204
Anchorage, AK 99503
907-277-8696

Arizona Division, Inc.
2929 East Thomas Road
Phoenix, AZ 85016
602-224-0524

Arkansas Division, Inc.
901 North University
Little Rock, AR 72207
501-664-3480

California Division, Inc.
1710 Webster Street
Oakland, CA 94604
510-893-7900

Colorado Division, Inc.
2255 South Oneida
Denver, CO 80224
303-758-2030

Connecticut Division, Inc.
Barnes Park South
14 Village Lane
Wallingford, CT 06492
203-265-7161

Delaware Division, Inc.
92 Read's Way
Suite 205
New Castle, DE 19720
302-324-4227

**District of Columbia
Division, Inc.**
1875 Connecticut Avenue,
NW
Suite 730
Washington, DC 20009
292-483-2600

Florida Division, Inc.
3709 West Jetton Avenue
Tampa, FL 33629-5146
813-253-0541

Georgia Division, Inc.
2200 Lake Boulevard
Atlanta, GA 30319
404-816-7800

Hawaii Pacific Division, Inc.
Community Services Center
Bldg.
200 North Vineyard
Boulevard
Suite 100-A
Honolulu, HI 96817
808-531-1662

Idaho Division, Inc.
2676 Vista Avenue
Boise, ID 83705-0386
208-343-4609

Illinois Division, Inc.
77 East Monroe
Chicago, IL 60603-5795
312-641-6150

Indiana Division, Inc.
8730 Commerce Park Place
Indianapolis, IN 46268
317-872-4432

Iowa Division, Inc.
8364 Hickman Road
Suite D
Des Moines, IA 50325
515-253-0147

Kansas Division, Inc.
1315 SW Arrowhead Road
Topeka, KS 66604
913-273-4114

Kentucky Division, Inc.
701 West Muhammad Ali
Boulevard
Louisville, KY 40201-1807
502-584-6782

Louisiana Division, Inc.
2200 Veterans' Memorial
Boulevard
Suite 214
Kenner, LA 70062
504-469-0021

Maine Division, Inc.
52 Federal Street
Brunswick, ME 04011
207-729-3339

Maryland Division, Inc.
8219 Town Center Drive
Baltimore, MD 21236-0026
410-931-6850

Massachusetts Division, Inc.
30 Speen Street
Framingham, MA 01701
508-270-4600

Michigan Division, Inc.
1205 East Saginaw Street
Lansing, MI 48906
517-371-2920

Minnesota Division, Inc.
3316 West 66th Street
Minneapolis, MN 55435
612-925-2772

Mississippi Division, Inc.
1380 Livingston Lane
Lakeover Office Park
Jackson, MS 39213
601-362-8874

Missouri Division, Inc.
3322 American Avenue
Jefferson City, MO 65102
314-893-4800

Montana Division, Inc.
17 North 26th Street
Billings, MT 59101
406-252-7111

Nebraska Division, Inc.
8502 West Center Road
Omaha, NE 68124-5255
402-393-5800

Nevada Division, Inc.
1325 East Harmon
Las Vegas, NV 89119
702-798-6857

New Hampshire Division, Inc.
Gail Singer Memorial
    Building
360 Route 101, Unit 501
Bedford, NH 03110-5032
603-472-8899

New Jersey Division, Inc.
2600 US Highway 1
North Brunswick, NJ 08902
908-297-8000

New Mexico Division, Inc.
5800 Lomas Boulevard, NE
Albuquerque, NM 87110
505-260-2105

New York State Division, Inc.
6725 Lyons Street
East Syracuse, NY 13057
315-437-7025

Long Island Division, Inc.
75 Davids Drive
Hauppauge, NY 11788
516-436-7070

New York City Division, Inc.
19 West 56th Street
New York, NY 10019
212-586-8700

Queens Division, Inc.
112-25 Queens Boulevard
Forest Hills, NY 11375
718-263-2224

Westchester Division, Inc.
30 Glenn Street
White Plains, NY 10603
914-949-4800

North Carolina Division, Inc.
11 South Boylan Avenue
Suite 221
Raleigh, NC 27603
919-834-8463

North Dakota Division, Inc.
123 Roberts Street
Fargo, ND 58102
701-232-1385

Ohio Division, Inc.
5555 Frantz Road
Dublin, OH 43017
614-889-9565

Oklahoma Division, Inc.
4323 NW 63rd, Suite 110
Oklahoma City, OK 73116
405-843-9888

Oregon Division, Inc.
0330 SW Curry
Portland, OR 97201
503-295-6422

Pennsylvania Division, Inc.
Route 422 & Sipe Avenue
Hershey, PA 17033-0897
717-533-6144

Philadelphia Division, Inc.
1626 Locust Street
Philadelphia, PA 19103
215-985-5400

Puerto Rico Division, Inc.
Calle Alverio #577
Esquina Sargento Medina
Hato Rey, PR 00918
809-764-2295

Rhode Island Division, Inc.
400 Main Street
Pawtucket, RI 02860
401-722-8480

South Carolina Division, Inc.
128 Stonemark Lane
Westpark Plaza
Columbia, SC 29210-3855
803-750-1693

South Dakota Division, Inc.
4101 Carnegie Place
Sioux Falls, SD 57106-2322
605-361-8277

Tennessee Division, Inc.
1315 Eighth Avenue, South
Nashville, TN 37203
615-255-1227

Texas Division, Inc.
2433 Ridgepoint Drive
Austin, TX 78754
512-928-2262

Utah Division, Inc.
941 East 3300 S
Salt Lake City, UT 84106
801-483-1500

Vermont Division, Inc.
13 Loomis Street
Montpelier, VT 05602
802-223-2348

Virginia Division, Inc.
4240 Park Place Court
Glen Allen, VA 23060
804-527-3700

Washington Division, Inc.
2120 First Avenue North
Seattle, WA 98109-1140
206-283-1152

West Virginia Division, Inc.
2428 Kanawha Boulevard
    East
Charleston, WV 25311
304-344-3611

Wisconsin Division, Inc.
N19 W24350 Riverwood
    Drive
Waukesha, WI 53188
414-523-5500

Wyoming Division, Inc.
4202 Ridge Road
Cheyenne, WY 82001
307-638-3331

Index

beta-carotene, 77, 78, 281, 282
biking, 182–83
  stationary, 183
birth control pills
  breast cancer risk, 274–75
  cancer prevention role, 274–75, 276
  decision to use, 275–76
  effect on cholesterol, 275, 276
  high blood pressure risk, 238–39
  high-dose, 275
  risks, 262, 274–75
  side effects, 276
  smoking and, 238–39, 275
  sunburn risk, 262
bladder cancer, 33, 36, 78
blood pressure
  low, 285
  measurements, 239–40
  normal, 240
  See also high blood pressure
body weight
  benefits of losing, 83
  calories needed, 130–31
  cancer and, 85
  commercial diets, 156–57
  desirable, 99–103
  distribution of, 84, 104
  exercise and, 164–65
  healthful, 99–100, 129–32
  heart disease and, 10, 83–84
  reducing, 129–32
  when quitting smoking, 63–64
  See also obesity
bones
  effects of smoking on, 34
  osteoporosis, 34
BPH (benign prostatic hyperplasia), 280
brain, effects of smoking on, 32
breast cancer
  alcohol and, 82
  clinical breast exams, 214–16
  mammography, 216–18
  research, 279–80
  risk factors, 12, 74, 75–76, 82, 85, 167, 273, 274–75
  screening tests, 212–18
  self-examination, 212–14, 215
  tamoxifen and, 279
breast milk, 149
  effects of smoking on, 33

C

CA 125 blood test, 228–29, 288
calcium
  recommended amounts, 118
  sources, 118
calcium channel blockers, 242
calories
  in alcohol, 129
  daily needs, 130–31
  in fat, 89
  used in exercise, 198–99
cancer
  aspirin research, 270, 271–72
  biology of, 10–11
  birth control pills and, 274–75
  bladder, 33, 36, 78
  breast (*see* breast cancer)
  causes, 11
  cervical (*see* cervical cancer)
  in children, 251–52
  colon (*see* colorectal cancer)
  detection (*see* screening tests)
  diet and, 69, 70, 74–76, 77, 80
  esophageal, 12, 33, 36, 78, 80, 81
  eye, 261
  gallbladder, 12, 85, 167
  GI tract, 75, 77, 271–72
  Kaposi's sarcoma, 267
  kidney, 33, 36, 167
  larynx, 36, 78, 81
  lifestyle influences, 12–13
  liver, 12, 81
  lung (*see* lung cancer)
  lymph, 267
  metastasis, 10–11
  mouth (*see* oral cancer)
  occupational hazards, 13
  ovarian (*see* ovarian cancer)
  pancreatic 36, 288
  penis, 34, 36
  personality and, 287
  promoters, 11
  prostate (*see* prostate cancer)
  radiation as cause, 13
  research, 271–72, 279–81, 282–83, 287–88
  risk factors, 12–13, 70, 74–76, 77, 80, 85, 167–68
  skin (*see* skin cancer)